8088 Assembler Language Programming:
The IBM PC

David C. Willen earned his BS and MS in Electrical Engineering at the Polytechnic Institute of New York. He has worked for IBM as a senior associate engineer in advanced processor development. Mr. Willen is now president of Computer Applications Unlimited, a company specializing in the design and development of microcomputer software. A member of IEEE and ACM, he also teaches computer science at the Polytechnic Institute of New York.

Jeffrey I. Krantz is now vice president of Computer Applications Unlimited, where he is responsible for the development of custom microcomputer applications. Previously, he investigated future MVS design and performance issues for IBM. Mr. Krantz obtained his BS in Electrical Engineering and MS in Computer Science from the Polytechnic Institute of New York. He has authored many microcomputer software development tools and is currently working on entertainment-related products for the IBM PC.

8088 Assembler Language Programming:
The IBM PC

By

David C. Willen

and

Jeffrey I. Krantz

Computer Applications Unlimited

Howard W. Sams & Co., Inc.

4300 WEST 62ND ST. INDIANAPOLIS, INDIANA 46268 USA

Preface

Today the microcomputer can be found in ever-increasing numbers in both the home and the office. The current technology allows powerful computing capabilities to be placed into a desktop-sized unit for less than the cost of a new car. Software for these machines is available to perform a wide variety of tasks. Many microcomputer users, however, eventually wish to write their own software. Homebrew software has the advantage of being uniquely tailored to its author's needs. By writing your own software, you will gain a deeper understanding and respect for your microcomputer.

This book is about writing machine-language software for the IBM Personal Computer, one of the newest and most powerful microcomputers available today. It is also about the Intel 8088 microprocessor, a state-of-the-art chip that serves as the heart of the Personal Computer.

Programmers familiar with high-level languages such as BASIC and Pascal will find this an excellent introduction to the more intricate art of assembler-language programming. Experienced assembler-language programmers can benefit by the addition of the 8088 to their repertoire. The book also contains detailed information about the internal structure of the Personal Computer; this information will be invaluable to anyone writing programs for this machine.

We would like to thank the Intel Corporation and Howard W. Sams & Co., Inc. for their assistance in the preparation of this book.

DAVID C. WILLEN
JEFFREY I. KRANTZ

Contents

CHAPTER 1

Introduction

In August of 1981, IBM introduced its Personal Computer, nicknamed the "IBM PC." The PC incorporated several significant advances. The most important of these was the use of the Intel 8088 microprocessor as the central processing element.

Although technically an 8-bit chip, the 8088 supports the same architecture as its big brother, the 16-bit 8086. This gives the PC the ability to make use of large amounts of memory; while most microcomputers can handle at most 64K of memory, the PC can handle up to 1024K, or 1 *megabyte*. Taking advantage of this feature, IBM provided a large and powerful BASIC language interpreter in the ROM (read only memory) of the machine. It is therefore not surprising that most people who write programs for the PC do so in BASIC.

THE PROBLEM WITH BASIC

While the BASIC language is easy to learn and use, it does have certain disadvantages. The BASIC programmer views the PC as a computer that is capable of executing BASIC statements and functions. In reality, however, the PC is capable of executing only those functions provided by its central processor, the 8088. These *machine instructions* are a great deal more primitive than the familiar BASIC statements. The BASIC statement PRINT, for example, is implemented by hundreds of 8088 machine instructions. When a BASIC program is executed, each statement must be decoded as it is reached. The appropriate series of machine instructions is then employed to effect the execution of the statement. This process, illustrated in Fig. 1-1, is called *interpretive execution* and is inherently slow.

If we write a program that is composed only of machine instructions, then it can be executed directly by the 8088 central processor. Such a program will execute many times faster than its BASIC counterpart because

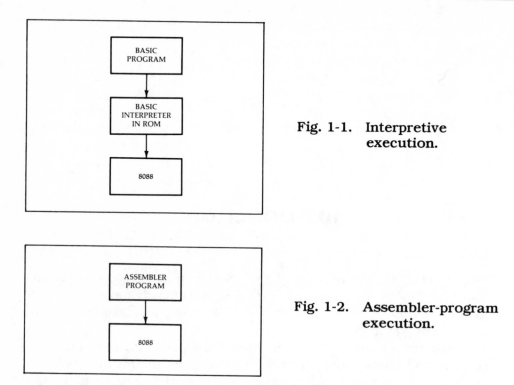

Fig. 1-1. Interpretive execution.

Fig. 1-2. Assembler-program execution.

we have eliminated the overhead of having to decode each program statement. This is illustrated in Fig. 1-2. Programs that consist of machine instructions are written in *assembler language*. The assembler language used to generate 8088 machine-instruction programs is called *8088 Assembler Language*.

Speed of execution is not the only advantage to be gained by using assembler language. As mentioned earlier, the BASIC programmer views the computer as a BASIC computer. This limits him or her to using only those features and facilities provided by the BASIC language. The assembler-language programmer, however, views the computer at its lowest level and can take advantage of every hardware feature that it contains. It is an extremely gratifying experience to see your own assembler-language creation run on the PC. You know that you are in control of the very circuits that make the machine work.

WITH POWER COMES RESPONSIBILITY

The power of assembler language is formidable, but there is a cost associated with using it (nothing ever comes free). To be able to program well in assembler language, you must be intimately familiar with the internal components of the computer. The most important of these is the 8088 microprocessor. We will study its internal structure and learn about the many instructions that it can execute.

There are other components in the PC system that we must study as well. For example, there is a chip that can be used to time events accurately. It is programmable and can be used to perform various timing functions under control of our program. To be able to do so, however, we must first understand its internal structure, as well as how it is integrated into the rest of the PC system. Similarly, there are special chips and/or circuits to control the speaker, handle interrupts, maintain the video display, etc. Each of them must be understood in detail if we are to take control of these systems.

In addition, we must be aware of the system support programs. These programs come with the PC—some are stored permanently in the ROM of the machine, and others are provided on the DOS diskette. They establish the software environment that allows us to write and run our own assembler-language programs. Any program we write must run under this environment, and so we must understand it.

A LOOK AHEAD

In the chapters that follow, we will cover all of the subjects mentioned above. No previous assembler-language experience is necessary to use this book. However, the reader should be familiar with the concepts involved in writing computer programs as well as at least one programming language such as BASIC.

Chapter 2 discusses the binary and hexadecimal number systems and introduces the structure of assembler language. If you are familiar with other assembler languages, you can probably skip this chapter (one note of warning: many common assembler-language conventions do not apply to the 8088).

The architecture of the 8088 is described in Chapter 3. Here we will cover the registers, memory addressing scheme, and instruction set of this very powerful microprocessor. In Chapter 4, we will learn how to use the IBM Macro Assembler. We will also take a close look at IBM DOS, from the assembler-language programmer's point of view. This chapter contains the first of many sample programs. These programs can be actually entered and run on your PC. To do so, you will need at least 64K of memory, one disk drive, the monochrome adapter and display, and the IBM DOS and IBM Macro Assembler programs. The reader should be familiar with standard DOS operations such as creating and maintaining disk files. An understanding of the EDLIN program, which is used to enter and alter program text, is assumed.

Chapter 5 describes the PC system board, which is the heart of the Personal Computer. We will learn how to control the interrupt structure of the machine, as well as the keyboard and timer mechanisms, in this chapter. Chapter 6 covers the monochrome and color display adapters, as well as the printer adapter. To run the sample programs associated with the color adapter, you will, of course, need the adapter as well as a color display.

Chapter 7 explains the main concepts behind serial communications and describes how to use the asynchronous communications adapter. The ability to communicate with other computers at remote locations opens up an entire world of possibilities. A sample program that converts the PC into a data terminal is presented. The asynchronous communications adapter is needed to run this program.

Finally, Chapter 8 covers disk input and output. Disk operations at two different levels will be described. The higher level allows us to manipulate standard DOS disk files, and the lower level allows us to access the tracks and sectors of a disk directly.

CHAPTER 2

Fundamental Concepts

As we have seen, an assembler-language programmer must have an intimate understanding of the internal components of his computer. In this chapter, we will study the basic building blocks of all modern microcomputers and gain a deeper understanding of what makes these machines tick.

Today's microcomputer can be broken down logically into four fundamental parts, as shown in Fig. 2-1. The heart of the system is the *central processor*, which is capable of fetching and executing the instructions that make up the programming of the computer. The *system support hardware* provides pathways for data flowing into and out of the central processor, and it also performs such miscellaneous tasks as keeping track of interrupts and supplying a "heartbeat" used to maintain the time of day within the computer. The *main memory* is used to store information for immediate access by the central processor. The *i/o devices* provide an interface between the system and the outside world. The keyboard and video display are the most common i/o devices, but mass data storage devices such as disk and tape drives also fall into this category.

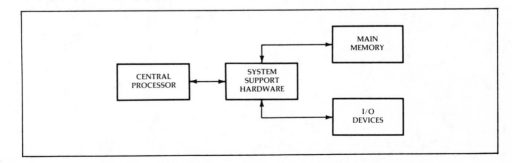

Fig. 2-1. Fundamental parts of a microcomputer.

REPRESENTING INFORMATION ELECTRONICALLY

The microcomputer system depicted in Fig. 2-1 is capable of storing and manipulating information very rapidly and very accurately. To be able to program this system, we must understand how information can be represented within it.

We are all used to representing numeric information with the decimal number system. The fundamental unit of information in this system is the *decimal digit*, of which there are ten. These digits are, of course, the numbers 0, 1, 2, 3, 4, 5, 6, 7, 8, and 9. In a computer, information is stored as either the presence or absence of an electronic signal; therefore, there can be only two, not ten, different digits. We call these digits 0 and 1. All information within a computer is stored as combinations of these two different digits.

Because there are *two* digits, we say that the computer number system is a *binary* number system, and we use the term *bit* (an acronym for binary digit) to refer to the fundamental unit of information storage, which can of course take on either the value 0 or the value 1.

Now we are obviously going to have to use more than one of these information storage units, or bits, if we wish to represent numbers that range in value beyond the numbers 0 and 1. If we put two of these bits together, they can take on any one of four different combinations: both bits 0, both bits 1, the first bit 0 and the second bit 1, and the first bit 1 and the second bit 0. We can use these different combinations to represent the numbers 0 through 3. If we added a third bit, we would have eight different possible combinations and could thus represent the numbers 0 through 7. It becomes evident quickly that each time we add a bit we double the range

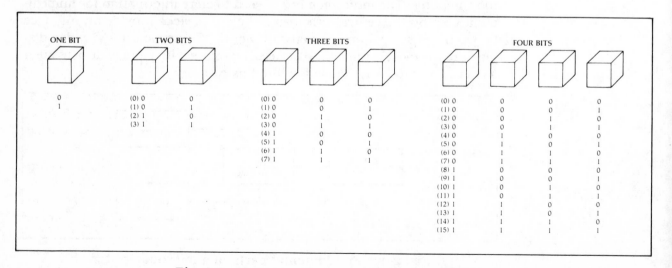

Fig. 2-2   Representing numeric data with bits.

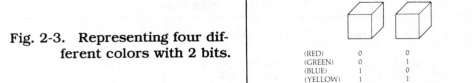

Fig. 2-3. Representing four different colors with 2 bits.

(RED)	0	0
(GREEN)	0	1
(BLUE)	1	0
(YELLOW)	1	1

of values that we can represent; thus with four bits we could represent sixteen different values (Fig. 2-2).

By defining the number of bits that we wish to use to represent some item of information, we automatically define how many different possible values that item can take on. These different values can represent numbers ranging from zero to some upper limit, as we have already seen. It is important to realize, however, that we are in no way limited to representing only numbers with this scheme. For example, if we want to store the color of an object as one of the four possible values red, green, blue, or yellow, then we could use two bits as shown in Fig. 2-3. Here, each of the four possible values that can be produced by using two bits has been assigned to a specific color.

Some time ago, it was wisely decided that if computers were going to be really useful, we would have to be able to communicate with them by using conventional words and symbols, and not just endless streams of numbers. To do this requires a means of representing each letter of the alphabet as well as all of the numeric digits and the punctuation symbols. Taken together, there are close to a hundred different characters that we will want to represent. By using seven bits, we can represent 128 different values and, as shown in Table 2-1, easily handle both upper-case and lower-case alphabetic characters, numeric and punctuation symbols, and a variety of "control" codes. These character representations have been standardized and are used throughout the computer industry. They are known as the American Standard Code for Information Interchange, or ASCII for short. It is really very nice to have such a standard, because we know that we can walk up to practically any computer and it will recognize the binary code 1000001 as the upper-case letter A.

By adding one more bit to these seven-bit ASCII groups, we create what is known as a _byte_, the most commonly referenced unit of information storage within a computer. The eight-bit byte can take on 256 different values, the first 128 of which can be interpreted as being part of the ASCII character set. The byte can also be used to represent numeric values from 0 to 255. When we need to represent larger numbers, we often pair up two bytes to create what is called a _word_. The word, con-

Table 2-1.   The American Standard Code for Information Interchange (ASCII)

Binary	Hex	Char	Binary	Hex	Char	Binary	Hex	Char
0000000	00H		0110000	30H	0	1100000	60H	`
0000001	01H		0110001	31H	1	1100001	61H	a
0000010	02H		0110010	32H	2	1100010	62H	b
0000011	03H		0110011	33H	3	1100011	63H	c
0000100	04H		0110100	34H	4	1100100	64H	d
0000101	05H		0110101	35H	5	1100101	65H	e
0000110	06H		0110110	36H	6	1100110	66H	f
0000111	07H	<BELL>	0110111	37H	7	1100111	67H	g
0001000	08H	<BKSP>	0111000	38H	8	1101000	68H	h
0001001	09H	<TAB>	0111001	39H	9	1101001	69H	i
0001010	0AH	<LF>	0111010	3AH	:	1101010	6AH	j
0001011	0BH		0111011	3BH	;	1101011	6BH	k
0001100	0CH		0111100	3CH	<	1101100	6CH	l
0001101	0DH	<CR>	0111101	3DH	=	1101101	6DH	m
0001110	0EH		0111110	3EH	>	1101110	6EH	n
0001111	0FH		0111111	3FH	?	1101111	6FH	o
0010000	10H		1000000	40H	@	1110000	70H	p
0010001	11H		1000001	41H	A	1110001	71H	q
0010010	12H		1000010	42H	B	1110010	72H	r
0010011	13H		1000011	43H	C	1110011	73H	s
0010100	14H		1000100	44H	D	1110100	74H	t
0010101	15H		1000101	45H	E	1110101	75H	u
0010110	16H		1000110	46H	F	1110110	76H	v
0010111	17H		1000111	47H	G	1110111	77H	w
0011000	18H		1001000	48H	H	1111000	78H	x
0011001	19H		1001001	49H	I	1111001	79H	y
0011010	1AH		1001010	4AH	J	1111010	7AH	z
0011011	1BH		1001011	4BH	K	1111011	7BH	{
0011100	1CH		1001100	4CH	L	1111100	7CH		
0011101	1DH		1001101	4DH	M	1111101	7DH	}
0011110	1EH		1001110	4EH	N	1111110	7EH	~
0011111	1FH		1001111	4FH	O	1111111	7FH	Δ
0100000	20H	space	1010000	50H	P			
0100001	21H	!	1010001	51H	Q			
0100010	22H	"	1010010	52H	R			
0100011	23H	#	1010011	53H	S			
0100100	24H	$	1010100	54H	T			
0100101	25H	%	1010101	55H	U			
0100110	26H	&	1010110	56H	V			
0100111	27H	'	1010111	57H	W			
0101000	28H	(	1011000	58H	X			
0101001	29H	)	1011001	59H	Y			
0101010	2AH	*	1011010	5AH	Z			
0101011	2BH	+	1011011	5BH	[			
0101100	2CH	,	1011100	5CH	\			
0101101	2DH	-	1011101	5DH	]			
0101110	2EH	.	1011110	5EH	∧			
0101111	2FH	/	1011111	5FH	—			

Note: Control codes denoted by < > (BKSP = backspace, TAB = tabulate, LF = line feed, CR = carriage return.

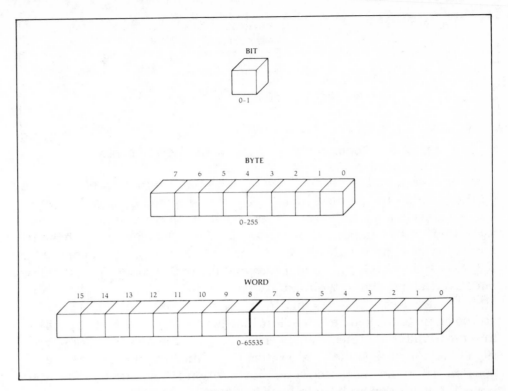

Fig. 2-4. Units of information storage.

sisting of 16 bits, can take on 65,536 different values and is often used to represent numbers in the range from 0 to 65,535. These different sized units of information storage are shown in Fig. 2-4. Note that the bits are numbered from right to left, starting with the number 0. When we need to reference a specific bit within a byte or word, this is the numbering convention we will use.

The *binary number system* is used to define the numeric value of each bit combination shown in Fig. 2-4. You are probably familiar with our own *decimal number system*, in which there are ten different digits and each digit position represents another power of ten. Thus the decimal number 916 is composed of a 9 digit in the hundreds position (10 to the 2nd power), plus a 1 digit in the tens position (10 to the 1st power), plus a 6 digit in the ones position (10 to the 0th power). In the binary number system, there are only two different digits, and so each digit position represents a successive power of 2. The binary number 101 is therefore composed of a 1 digit in the fours position (2 to the 2nd power), plus a 0 digit in the twos position (2 to the 1st power), plus a 1 digit in the ones position (2 to the 0th power). The equivalent decimal value for the binary number 101 is 5, as shown in Fig. 2-5.

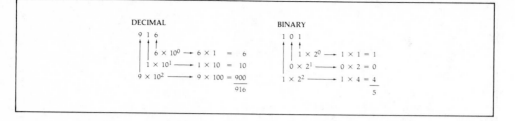

Fig. 2-5. Decimal versus binary numbering systems.

We have seen that as our numbers get larger, the number of bits that we need to express them grows rapidly. To avoid becoming bogged down in long streams of ones and zeros, we use the *hexadecimal number system* as a kind of shorthand. Hexadecimal (or "hex" for short) is a base-16 number system, and so there are 16 fundamental digits, as shown in Fig. 2-6. Note that we use the familiar decimal digits 0 through 9 for the first ten hexadecimal digits. We need six more, so the first six letters of our alphabet are used; thus, hex digit A is worth 10, hex digit B is worth 11, and so on up to the last hex digit, F, which is worth 15. Each digit position in a hex number represents a power of 16. Thus the digit positions, from right to left, are called the ones position (16 to the 0th power), the sixteens position (16 to the 1st power), the 256s position (16 squared), and so on. We will always denote hexadecimal numbers by suffixing the letter H to them. Therefore, when we write the number 2FH we are representing the value equal to 2 times sixteen plus F (15) times one, which is equivalent to 47 decimal. If a hexadecimal number starts with any of the digits A through F, we will always prefix it with a zero digit (i.e., 0A2H, 0FFH, etc.). This is done to avoid confusing the number with a label, since the latter always starts with a letter.

HEXADECIMAL DIGIT	EQUIVALENT SET OF 4 BINARY DIGITS	EQUIVALENT DECIMAL VALUE
0	0 0 0 0	0
1	0 0 0 1	1
2	0 0 1 0	2
3	0 0 1 1	3
4	0 1 0 0	4
5	0 1 0 1	5
6	0 1 1 0	6
7	0 1 1 1	7
8	1 0 0 0	8
9	1 0 0 1	9
A	1 0 1 0	10
B	1 0 1 1	11
C	1 1 0 0	12
D	1 1 0 1	13
E	1 1 1 0	14
F	1 1 1 1	15

Fig. 2-6. The hexadecimal number system.

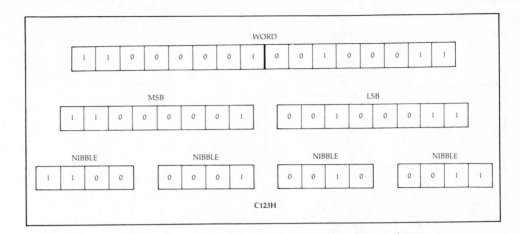

Fig. 2-7. Most-significant and least-significant components.

We can now divide our eight-bit byte into a four-bit upper half and a four-bit lower half and represent each half with a hex digit. Bytes will often be written this way, as a pair of hex digits with the H suffix. The hex digit, being half a byte, is often referred to as a _nibble_. Thus each _byte_ consists of a leftmost, or _most significant_, nibble and a rightmost, or _least significant_, nibble. Similarly, each _word_ consists of a leftmost, or _most significant, byte as well_ as a rightmost, or _least significant_, byte. These last two terms are often referred to as MSB and LSB, respectively. These terms are defined graphically in Fig. 2-7.

BINARY AND HEXADECIMAL ARITHMETIC

Because we will be working with the binary and hexadecimal number systems, we must understand how to perform arithmetic in them. The processes are similar to those used in the decimal system with which we are all familiar. When we add two decimal numbers, we work from right to left, adding each pair of digits in each column. When the sum of a pair exceeds 9, the largest decimal digit, we carry over a 1 to the next digit position and place the remainder after subtracting 10 in the current column. In binary, whenever such a sum exceeds 1, the largest binary digit, we must carry over a 1 to the next digit position and place the remainder after subtracting 2 in the current column. Similarly, in hexadecimal, whenever a sum exceeds FH (15), we must carry over a 1 to the next digit position and place the remainder after subtracting 16 in the current column. Examples of these operations are shown in Fig. 2-8.

Up to now we have been working solely with absolute, that is, positive numbers. To represent negative numbers in binary requires using a scheme called _twos complement_. In a twos-complement number, the

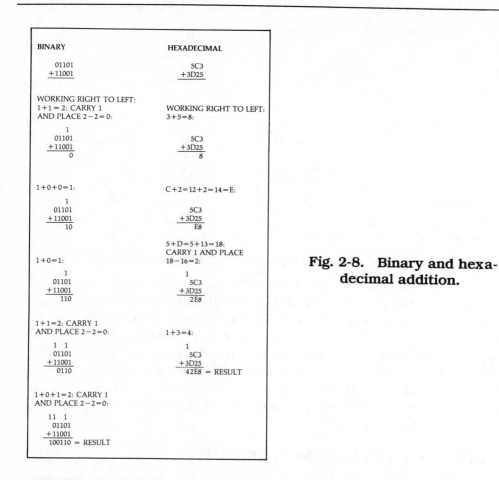

Fig. 2-8. Binary and hexadecimal addition.

leftmost (most significant) bit is used to represent the sign of the number. If this *sign bit* is 0, then the number is considered positive. If the sign bit is 1, then the number is considered negative. To obtain the negation of any twos-complement number, we simply flip all of the bits (zeros become ones and ones become zeros) and then add 1. This is illustrated in Fig. 2-9.

Using this scheme, the largest positive and negative numbers that we can express depend on how many bits we have. With an eight-bit byte, the largest positive number that can be expressed is 01111111, or 7FH, or +127. The largest negative number is 10000000, or 80H, or −128. (The smallest negative number will be 11111111, or FFH, or −1). With a 16-bit word, the largest positive number will be 0111111111111111, or 7FFFH, or +32,767. The largest negative number will be 1000000000000000, or 8000H, or −32,768. The smallest negative number will be 1111111111111111, or FFFFH, or −1. The important aspect of twos-complement representation, however, is that we can add any combination of positive and negative numbers together by using standard binary arithmetic and get the correct result.

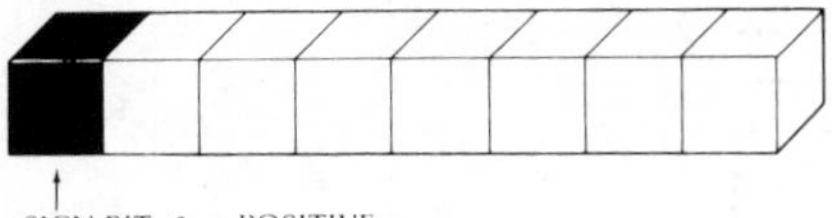

SIGN BIT: 0 = POSITIVE
         1 = NEGATIVE

EXAMPLES:

```
0 0 0 0 0 0 1 1
↑
SIGN BIT = 0: POSITIVE NUMBER + 3


1 1 1 1 1 1 0 0
↑
SIGN BIT = 1: NEGATIVE NUMBER

   TO OBTAIN EQUIVALENT POSITIVE VALUE:
   STEP 1. FLIP ALL BITS:

   0 0 0 0 0 0 1 1

   STEP 2. ADD ONE:

   0 0 0 0 0 0 1 1
 +           1
   ─────────────
   0 0 0 0 0 1 0 0  = 4

   THEREFORE 1 1 1 1 1 1 0 0 = −4
```

Fig. 2-9.   Twos-complement numbers.

STORING INFORMATION IN MAIN MEMORY

We have seen how various different kinds of information can be represented by strings of bits. During the time that our computer is working with this information, it stores these bits in the *main memory*. Main memory is made up of a large number of cells, each of which can hold one byte of information, which you will recall is equivalent to eight bits. Each of these cells is assigned a unique *address*, starting with the number 0 and going up by 1 for each successive cell. The central processor accesses the information contained in any one of these cells by specifying its address (Fig. 2-10). Memory addresses are often manipulated by the central processor just like the data that they contain, and so they are often represented in hexadecimal form.

The number of memory cells that our computer has is referred to as its *memory size*. This number is often expressed as a multiple of "K," such as "32K." The "K" represents a value of 1024, or 400H. Thus a 32K computer has 32 × 1024, or 32,768 (8000H) memory cells.

In Fig. 2-10, we saw how a byte of data stored in memory might be referenced by the appropriate address. To store a *word* in memory, we use two consecutive memory locations (see Fig. 2-11). The word is then referenced by using the *lower* of the two memory addresses. In addition, the two bytes that make up the word are stored in *reverse order* from what we might

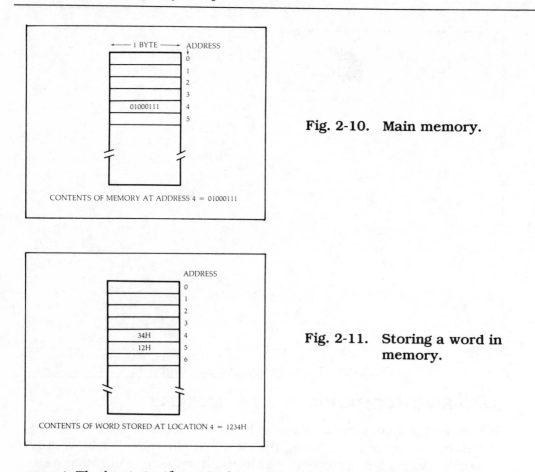

Fig. 2-10. Main memory.

Fig. 2-11. Storing a word in memory.

expect. The least significant (rightmost) byte is stored at the lower address, and the most significant (leftmost) byte is stored at the higher address.

THE ROLE OF THE CENTRAL PROCESSOR

The job of the central processor is to execute a sequence of instructions that are placed into the main memory of the computer. It is given a *starting address* and begins fetching data bytes from the location in memory. Each byte of data is interpreted by the central processor as representing some function that the processor can perform. Additional bytes following this *opcode* byte may contain specific data to be used in performing the function. These additional bytes are known as *operands*.

Once the processor has performed the appropriate function, it goes on to the next successive opcode byte in memory and executes the function specified therein. Thus we can see that programming the computer consists of preparing a sequence of bytes that represent the desired functions (in the desired order of operation), placing these data bytes into memory, and instructing the processor to start executing at the appropriate address.

The repertoire of functions that the central processor can execute is known as its *instruction set*. Each instruction within the instruction set is represented by a different data-byte value. Very often more than one data byte is required to define the instruction fully. In these cases, one or more operand bytes will be used.

The kinds of functions that the central processor can execute usually involve moving data from one point to another within the system, or manipulating data within the processor itself. Within the processor is a set of *registers*. These registers are used to hold data while it is being manipulated by the processor. A typical instruction, therefore, would be to fetch a byte of data from a specific memory address and place it in a specific register within the processor. The next instruction might be to add the contents of this register to the contents of another register. In this fashion, instruction by instruction, a large and complex calculation can be programmed.

WHY WE NEED AN ASSEMBLER LANGUAGE

Nowadays, the central processor of a microcomputer is usually contained entirely on one chip and is called a *microprocessor*. In spite of its tiny size, the microprocessor is capable of recognizing and executing hundreds of different instructions. As we have seen, each instruction is represented within the computer as a different bit pattern. When we program sequences of these instructions, we do not want to be bothered with having to remember the proper bit pattern for each instruction. Instead, what we will do is use a symbolic name, or *mnemonic*, to represent each of the various functions that the processor can perform. We can now program our machine by writing sequences of commands in this symbolic language. The *assembler* will translate our symbolic program into the actual bit patterns that the processor recognizes so that we may load the program into our computer and execute it.

Let us look at a simple example of an assembler-language program. The purpose of the program will be to calculate the sum of two numbers that have been placed in memory, subtract a third number, and place the result back into memory somewhere else. Here is the program:

```
1 DATA    SEGMENT
2 INPUT1 DW 10
3 INPUT2 DW 25
4 INPUT3 DW 8
5 RESULT DW ?
6 DATA    ENDS
7 CODE    SEGMENT
8         MOV AX,INPUT1    ;GET FIRST NUMBER
9         MOV BX,INPUT2    ;GET SECOND NUMBER
10        ADD AX,BX        ;ADD TOGETHER
```

```
11        MOV BX,INPUT3    ;GET THIRD NUMBER
12        SUB AX,BX  ;SUBTRACT FROM FIRST RESULT
13        MOV RESULT,AX    ;STORE FINAL ANSWER
14 CODE   ENDS
```

Statement 1 in this program tells the assembler that we are about to define the information to be placed in a *segment* of memory and that the segment will be called DATA. The concept of memory segments will be explained later and is not important at this moment. The DW command in statements 2, 3, 4, and 5 tells the assembler to *define a word* in memory containing the value which follows. In statement 5 the value is specified as a question mark, which tells the assembler that there is no initial value for this word in memory. The names INPUT1, INPUT2, INPUT3, and RESULT which appear as *labels* on each of these statements can be used later in the program to refer symbolically to the memory addresses just defined. The ENDS command in statement 6 stands for "end segment" and tells the assembler that we are now finished defining the DATA segment. In statement 7 we start defining the CODE segment, which will contain the actual instructions of our program. The MOV command in statement 8 stands for "move" and tells the assembler that we want to move the contents of memory defined by label INPUT1 into the register named AX. Similarly, statement 9 requests that the data at label INPUT2 be moved into register BX. The ADD command in statement 10 will add the contents of the AX register to the contents of the BX register and place the results back into the AX register. Continuing in this fashion, we see that statement 11 gets the data at INPUT3 into the BX register and then statement 12 subtracts the BX register contents from the AX register contents. Statement 13 specifies a move of the contents of the AX register to the memory location labeled RESULT. Finally, statement 14 instructs the assembler that it has reached the end of the CODE segment.

From this simple example, we can learn a lot about the structure of assembly language. We can see, for instance, how each statement in an assembly-language program may be divided into as many as four separate fields. The *label* field always comes first if it is present. It is used to assign a symbolic name to the statement, as in statements 1–7 and 14 above.

The *opcode* field follows the label field. If a label is not used, then one or more blanks must precede the opcode. The opcode specifies the function that we wish the assembler to perform. In statement 2, for example, the opcode "DW" tells the assembler that we wish to "define a word." The opcode "MOV" in statement 8 instructs the assembler to generate a "move" instruction.

The *operand* field follows the opcode if it is needed. This field is used to qualify further the function to be performed. For example, the operand

"10" in statement 2 tells the assembler what value to place into the word it has just defined. Often, more than one operand is required by an instruction. In this case, the operands are separated from each other by commas. For many of the instructions that require two operands, it is possible to identify one of them as the *source* and the other as the *destination* of the operation. A standard assembler-language convention is always to place the destination operand before the source operand.

The *comment* field can optionally follow the operand field. It always begins with the semicolon character (;). In any assembler-language program, it is very important to use lots of good, descriptive comments. If this is not done, you may find yourself reading a program you wrote a month ago and asking, "How does this work?"

To get to that point, however, we must first learn a great deal more about the 8088 microprocessor.

CHAPTER 3

The 8088 Architecture

In this chapter, we will look at the internal components of the 8088 chip and the way in which it addresses memory. We will study the 8088 instruction set and learn how to use it. These concepts comprise the *8088 architecture*.

A block diagram of the 8088 CPU appears in Fig. 3-1. Data travels between the CPU and main memory via the *memory interface*. Incoming data destined to be interpreted as instructions is placed on the *instruction stream byte queue*. The *execution unit control system* takes the instructions from this queue and sends them to the *execution unit* to be interpreted and executed. Even as this is happening, the *bus interface unit* is trying to refill the instruction stream byte queue. This design is referred to as *pipelined* and strives to ensure that whenever the CPU has finished executing an instruction, there will be another instruction waiting to be executed. Most microprocessors must wait after executing an instruction until the next instruction has been read from memory. Because it is pipelined, the 8088 can execute instructions more rapidly.

Contained within the execution unit is the *arithmetic/logic unit*, or alu. This component is responsible for performing all arithmetic calculations and comparisons. In addition to producing a numeric result, the alu often sets various *flags* to indicate the status of the result. For example, if a calculation yielded a result of − 5, the *sign flag* (SF) would be set to indicate that the result was negative.

THE 8088 REGISTER SET

The 8088 *register set* is shown in Fig. 3-2. From the programmer's point of view, the registers are the most important component within the microprocessor. We will be constantly using and making reference to the various 8088 registers as we develop our assembler-language programs.

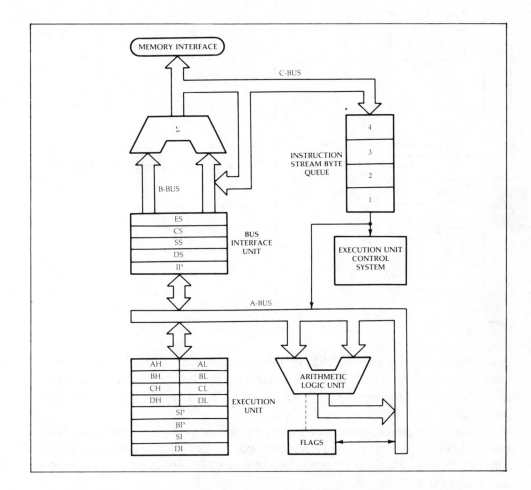

Fig. 3-1. Block diagram of the 8088. (*Courtesy Intel Corp.*)

There are four general-purpose registers, each of which is sixteen bits wide. These are called AX, BX, CX, and DX. Each of these can be optionally referenced as a pair of eight-bit (byte) registers. The lefthand (most significant) byte of the pair is referred to as the "high" byte, and the righthand (least significant) byte is referred to as the "low" byte. Thus register AX can be broken down into registers AH ("A High") and AL ("A Low"); register BX can be broken down into registers BH and BL; etc.

There are two *string index* registers, each of which is sixteen bits wide. These are called SI ("source index") and DI ("destination index") and are often used to point to strings of data in memory. They can also be used as general-purpose 16-bit registers.

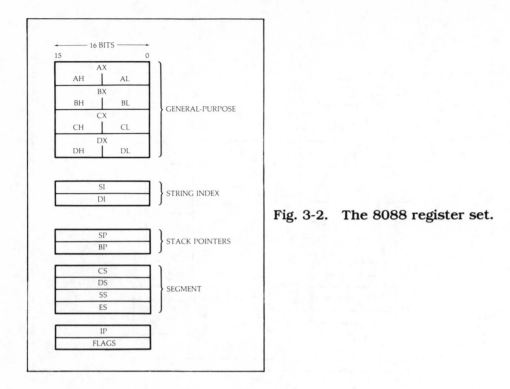

Fig. 3-2.   The 8088 register set.

The *stack pointer* register, SP, is used to implement a hardware stack in memory (use of the stack will be explained shortly). It can be supplemented by the *base pointer* register, BP, which can also be used as a general-purpose 16-bit register.

The four *segment registers* are special-purpose registers. A segment register is used whenever memory is accessed by the 8088. The microprocessor therefore implicitly references one or more of these registers whenever any instruction is executed.

Another special-purpose register is the *instruction pointer* register, IP, which points to the next instruction to be executed. Finally, there is the *flags register*, which contains several one-bit flags that describe the current status of the microprocessor.

MEMORY ADDRESS SEGMENTATION

Traditionally, microprocessors have always referenced data in main memory by using a 16-bit *address word*. Because the address was 16 bits long, the maximum number of unique addresses was 65,536, or 64K. As microcomputers became more sophisticated, their need for memory increased. With the 8088, we still use a 16-bit address word, but total

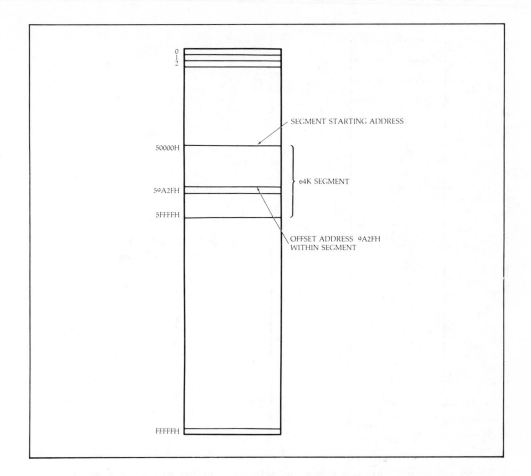

Fig. 3-3.   A 64K segment within the 1M address space.

memory capacity is increased to *one megabyte* (1024K) through a scheme called *memory address segmentation.*

To address a megabyte, we must be able to represent numbers in the range 0–1,048,576, which requires 20 bits. Real memory is addressed by the 8088 using a 20-bit address word. The complete set of 1,048,576 different addresses will often be referred to as a one-megabyte *address space.* From our point of view, however, memory is addressed in blocks that are called *segments.* Each segment can contain up to 64K of data; this allows us to use standard 16-bit addressing within a segment, as shown in the diagram of Fig. 3-3.

A segment may begin at every 16-byte boundary (called a *paragraph*) within the one-megabyte address space. This may be seen in Fig. 3-4. Notice that there are 64K different segment starting addresses; in each one, the low-order four bits are zero. Keep in mind that segments do not have to contain 64K of data; this is only a maximum. A segment may contain one,

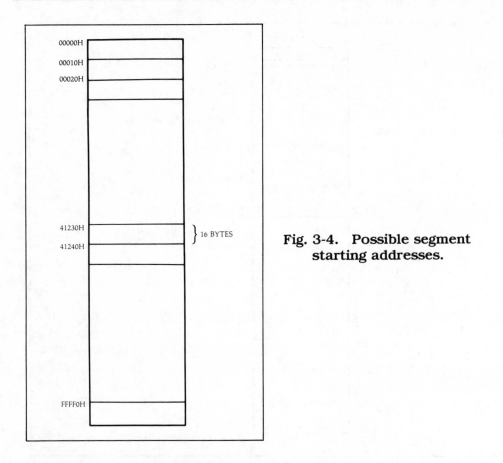

Fig. 3-4. Possible segment starting addresses.

a hundred, or a thousand bytes. In addition, segments may overlap; that is, a given data byte may be accessible from more than one segment starting address.

How does the 8088 use this segmentation scheme? See Fig. 3-5. Whenever the 8088 accesses memory, it selects one of the four *segment registers* to use for the segment starting address. This value is shifted by four bits and added to the *offset address* to form a 20-bit *physical address*. It is the complete physical address that is actually used to access memory.

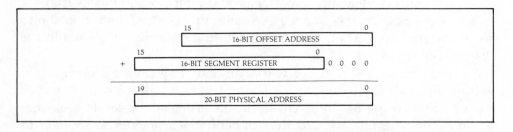

Fig. 3-5. Physical address computation.

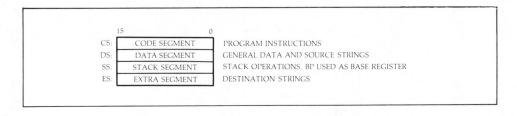

Fig. 3-6. The 8088 segment registers.

Fig. 3-6 shows each of the four segment registers and indicates when each would be selected by the processor for address calculation. The CS register always defines the current *code segment*, which contains the instructions to be executed by the processor. Earlier, we mentioned that the 16-bit IP register points to the instruction to be executed. In fact, when the processor fetches instructions, it does so by combining the *offset address* found in the IP register with the *segment starting address* found in the CS register.

The DS register defines the start of the *data segment*, which will be used for general-purpose data references as well as for the source operands of string manipulation instructions. The SS register defines the start of the *stack segment*, which is used for all stack operations. Finally, the ES register defines the *extra segment*, which can be used as a secondary general-purpose data area. The extra segment is also referenced for the destination operands of string manipulation instructions.

The segment registers allow the 8088 programmer to have simultaneous access to up to four different address spaces, each of which can contain up to 64K bytes of data. Fig. 3-7 gives examples of how the segment registers can be configured. In Fig. 3-7A, the segment registers have been set up to allow access to a maximum amount of memory simultaneously. With this configuration, we can have 64K bytes of instructions, 64K bytes of stack space, and two 64K data spaces. Fig. 3-7B shows a more likely configuration. Here we have an 8K (2000H) program in the code segment, which references 2K (800H) of data in the data segment and makes use of a 256-byte stack. Because the data storage requirements are minimal, an independent extra segment is not needed. The ES register is therefore set so that the extra segment overlaps and is identical to the data segment.

Because the segment registers can be read and written under program control, it is possible to design even more sophisticated configurations in which segment location and size are varied dynamically.

THE 8088 INSTRUCTION SET

As mentioned earlier, the complete set of primitive functions that a microprocessor can perform is known as its *instruction set*. The 8088 instruc-

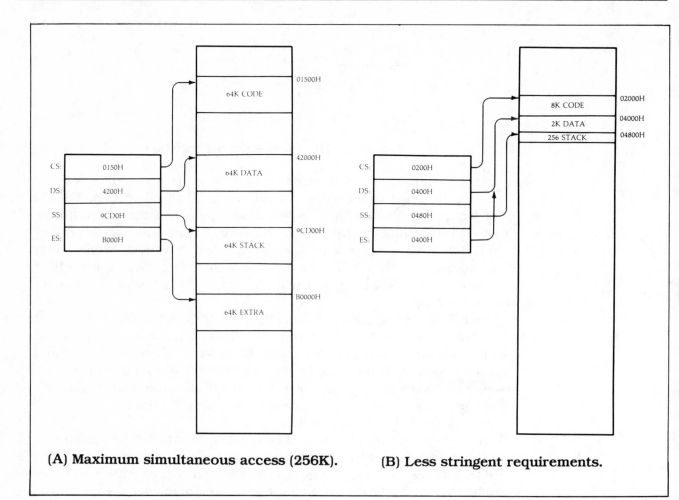

CS:	0150H	
DS:	4200H	
SS:	9CD0H	
ES:	B000H	

(A) Maximum simultaneous access (256K).

01500H
64K CODE

42000H
64K DATA

9CD00H
64K STACK

B0000H
64K EXTRA

CS:	0200H	
DS:	0400H	
SS:	0480H	
ES:	0400H	

(B) Less stringent requirements.

8K CODE   02000H
2K DATA   04000H
256 STACK 04800H

Fig. 3-7.   **Typical segment-register configurations.**

tion set consists of six types of instructions, which are summarized in Fig. 3-8. Successful programming in 8088 assembler language requires an understanding of all of these instruction types, and this will be our next goal. For more detailed information on any specific instruction, refer to Appendix A.

The *data transfer* instructions allow us to move data from one point to another. In general, data may be moved either a byte or a word at a time. Moving data may seem like a simple enough concept, but the situation is complicated because many different *modes* are available for addressing the data to be moved. These different data addressing modes are also used by the *arithmetic* and *logical* instruction types, and so we will gain much ground by studying them now.

Fig. 3-8. The 8088 in-
struction set.

1.	**Data-Transfer Instructions**	
	MOV	Move
	PUSH, POP	Stack operations
	XCHG	Exchange
	IN, OUT	Input/output ports
	XLATB	Translate

2.	**Arithmetic Instructions**	
	ADD	
	INC	Increment
	SUB	Subtract
	DEC	Decrement
	NEG	Negate
	CMP	Compare
	MUL	Multiply
	DIV	Divide

3.	**Logical Instructions**	
	NOT	Complement
	AND, OR	
	XOR	Exclusive OR
	TEST	Test bits
	SHL, SHR	Shift left/right
	ROL, ROR	Rotate left/right

4.	**String-Manipulation Instructions**	
	MOVS	Move string
	CMPS	Compare string
	SCAS	Scan string
	LODS	Load from string
	STOS	Store into string

5.	**Transfer-of-Control Instructions**	
	CALL	Link to subroutine
	RET	Return from sub.
	JMP	Jump
	JZ, JNZ . .	Conditional jumps
	LOOP	Iteration
	LOOPNE, . .	Conditional iteration
	INT	Interrupt
	IRET	Return from INT

6.	**Processor-Control Instructions**	
	CLC, STC . .	Clear/set flags
	HLT	Halt Processor

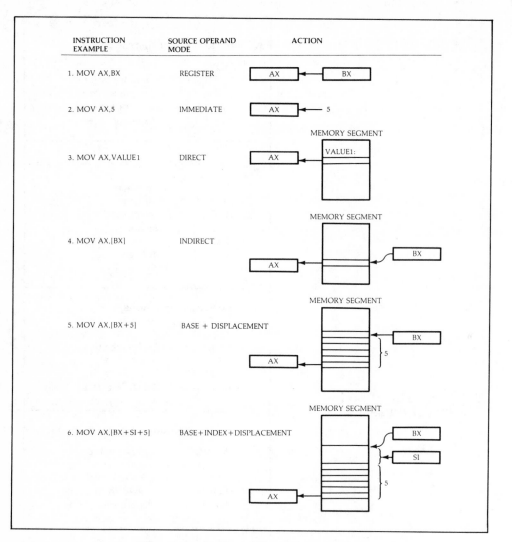

INSTRUCTION EXAMPLE	SOURCE OPERAND MODE	ACTION
1. MOV AX,BX	REGISTER	AX ← BX
2. MOV AX,5	IMMEDIATE	AX ← 5
3. MOV AX,VALUE1	DIRECT	AX ← VALUE1: (MEMORY SEGMENT)
4. MOV AX,[BX]	INDIRECT	AX ← (MEMORY SEGMENT) ← BX
5. MOV AX,[BX+5]	BASE + DISPLACEMENT	AX ← (MEMORY SEGMENT) ← BX, 5
6. MOV AX,[BX+SI+5]	BASE+INDEX+DISPLACEMENT	AX ← (MEMORY SEGMENT) ← BX, SI, 5

Fig. 3-9. Data addressing modes.

DATA-ADDRESSING MODES

Fig. 3-9 shows a number of instructions, each of which selects a word of data and moves it to the AX register. These instructions illustrate the different addressing modes of the 8088. The first example is a simple register-to-register transfer. The contents of the BX register are moved into the AX register. The second example shows *immediate* addressing. In this case, the data to be moved into the AX register, 5, is specified as a constant value *within the instruction itself*. The third example is one of *direct memory addressing:* the contents of the memory address symbolically referred to as "VALUE1" are placed into the AX register.

The remaining modes are even more powerful, as they permit *indirect memory addressing.* In the fourth example, the contents of the BX register are interpreted as a memory address, and the contents of memory at this address are moved into the AX register. The BX register holds a memory address again in the fifth example; in this case, however, a *displacement* value of 5 is added to select the desired memory address. Any of the registers BX, BP, SI, or DI may be used in these *indirect* modes. The last example is the most complex: the contents of BX and the contents of SI and the displacement value 5 are all added together to determine the memory address containing the desired data.

With the exception of the immediate mode, each of these data-addressing modes can be used for the *destination* operand of data-transfer, arithmetic, and logical instruction types. Thus, for example, the instruction

```
ADD [BX],DX
```

will add the contents of the DX register to the contents of memory at the address contained within the BX register, and place the result back into that same memory location.

For almost all of these cases, when the addressing mode specifies an operand in memory, the processor assumes it is in the *data segment* and selects the DS register to calculate the physical address (Fig. 3-5). The only exception is when the BP register is used as a base register; in this case, the *stack segment* is referenced via the SS register. Suppose we need to access data in a different segment? This can be accomplished by prefixing a *segment override* code to the instruction. We can instruct the assembler to use a segment override by specifying the desired segment register, followed by a colon. Thus the instruction

```
MOV AX,ES:[BX]
```

will cause a physical address to be calculated using the ES segment register and the contents of the BX register as an offset address. The word at this memory address, which is of course within the *extra segment*, will be moved into the AX register.

STACK OPERATIONS

The PUSH and POP instructions are special kinds of data-transfer instructions that implement a "last-in, first-out" memory structure known as a *stack*. The operation of these instructions is shown in Fig. 3-10. The stack always resides in the *stack segment*, and so the SS register is always used during stack references; no segment override is possible. The *stack pointer register*, SP, is implicitly used in all stack operations as a memory address. The PUSH instruction decrements the contents of SP by two and then stores its operand into the memory address specified by SP. The POP

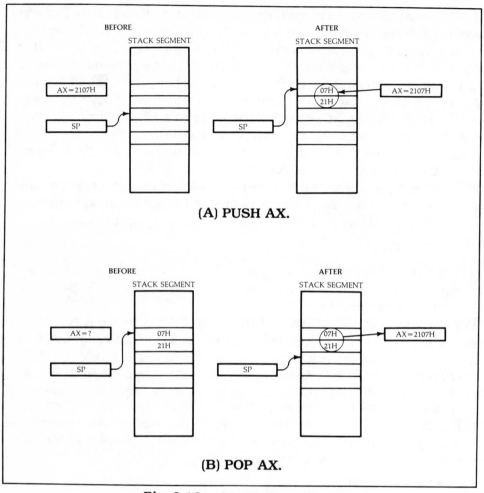

(A) PUSH AX.

(B) POP AX.

Fig. 3-10.   Stack operations.

instruction fetches data at the memory address specified by SP into its operand, and then increments the contents of SP by two. Note that the PUSH and POP instructions always transfer a *word* of data. This is in contrast to the more general MOV instruction, which can move a byte or a word.

The PUSH and POP instructions provide a storage mechanism that can be used to save several different data values and then retrieve them in reverse order from the sequence in which they were saved. The first value available to be POPed off the stack will always be the value that was most recently PUSHed onto the stack. This characteristic makes the stack ideal for temporarily saving a data value when we do not wish to dedicate a specific memory location to the job. For example, suppose we are writing a program, and part of it uses and alters the value in the CX register. If we need to use this value again later in the program, we can save it on the stack as follows:

```
PUSH    CX    ;SAVE VALUE ON STACK
...
...
...
...     section of program that
...     alters the CX register
...
...
...
POP     CX    ;RESTORE ORIGINAL VALUE
```

The operand of PUSH and POP statements may be addressed by using any of the data-addressing modes described in Fig. 3-9. In addition, the contents of the *flags* register may be PUSHed onto and POPed from the stack.

Because of its "last-in, first-out" nature, the stack is used by the subroutine CALL and RETurn instructions, as well as by the 8088 interrupt mechanism. These uses will be explained shortly.

I / O AND OTHER DATA-TRANSFER INSTRUCTIONS

The IN and OUT instructions are used to access the 8088 input/output ports, more often referred to as *i/o ports*. An i/o port is a data pathway between the microprocessor and the outside world. External devices such as terminals, printers, and disk drives communicate with the microprocessor via i/o ports.

The 8088 has 65,536 (64K) i/o ports, and so (you guessed it!) a 16-bit word is needed to address them. When we wish to communicate with an i/o port, we specify a 16-bit *i/o address* to select the port desired. The possible i/o addresses are 0 through FFFFH. An *i/o address* should not be confused with a *memory address*; as its name states, the latter is used to access memory.

Either an 8-bit byte or a 16-bit word may be transferred via an i/o port. Within the 8088, the data must always be sent from (or received into) the *accumulator register*, AX. In cases where only an 8-bit byte is transferred, the lower half of the accumulator, register AL, is used. The i/o address is specified either as the contents of register DX, or as an immediate value within the instruction. In the latter case, only the first 256 i/o ports (i/o addresses 00H through FFH) may be accessed. Examples of i/o instructions follow. (Note that we maintain the convention of placing the destination operand before the source operand. For IN instructions the i/o port is

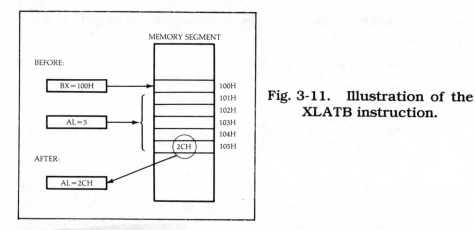

Fig. 3-11.   Illustration of the XLATB instruction.

the *source* and the accumulator is the *destination*; for OUT instructions the reverse is true.)

```
IN  AL,2FH    ;input a byte from port 2FH

OUT 5,AL      ;output a byte to port 5

MOV DX,3FCH
IN  AX,DX     ;input a word from port 3FCH
```

The XCHG instruction *exchanges* the contents of its two operands. The second operand of the XCHG instruction must always be a register. The first operand can be accessed using any of the data-addressing modes described in Fig. 3-9 except the immediate mode. Operation of the XCHG instruction is illustrated below:

```
MOV  AX,5     ;now AX=5
MOV  BX,10    ;now BX=10
XCHG AX,BX    ;now AX=10 and BX=5
```

The XLATB, or *translate*, instruction performs a table lookup operation. This is illustrated in Fig. 3-11. The contents of the AL register are added to the contents of the BX register, and the resulting value is used as a memory address. The byte at this memory address is placed in the AL register. Normally, this instruction is used by initializing the BX register to point to the start of a *translation table*. The XLATB instruction then converts the byte value in AL into its corresponding value from the table.

ARITHMETIC INSTRUCTIONS AND THE FLAGS REGISTER

The arithmetic instructions (see Fig. 3-8) are used to perform mathematical calculations. The ADD, SUB, and CMP instructions all have two operands.

As always, the first operand specified will serve as the destination for the result. Thus the instruction

```
ADD AX,BX
```

will add the contents of the AX register to the contents of the BX register and place the result in the AX register. Similarly, the instruction

```
SUB AX,BX
```

will subtract the contents of the BX register from the contents of the AX register and place the result in the AX register. The *compare* instruction, CMP, performs the same operation as SUB except that neither operand is actually altered. It is used primarily to set the flags, as explained below.

For each of these two-operand functions, there are many combinations of operand types and data-addressing modes. Appendix A lists all available operand combinations for each instruction. To summarize, however, if the first operand (the destination) is a register, then the second operand (the source) may be accessed by using any of the data-addressing modes specified in Fig. 3-9. If the first operand is in a memory location addressed by using methods 3, 4, 5, or 6 of Fig. 3-9, then the second operand may be either a register or an immediate operand.

The INC, DEC, and NEG instructions each take only one operand. It can be addressed by using any of the methods of Fig. 3-9 except the immediate mode. The INC (increment) instruction adds one to its operand, and the DEC (decrement) instruction subtracts one from its operand. The NEG (negate) instruction obtains the twos complement of its operand.

The flexibility of these instructions is increased by our ability to use them with either byte or word operands. In addition, all of the arithmetic instructions set various bits in the flags register to indicate the status of the result. *Conditional transfer* instructions can be used to test these bits and change the flow of a program. Almost all of the decision making that an 8088 does is accomplished through use of the flags. It is time that we took a closer look at some of them.

Fig. 3-12 details the 16-bit flags register. Nine of the bits in this register have special uses and are given names; the rest are unused. The *carry flag*, CF, is kept in bit 0 of the flags register. After an arithmetic instruction has been executed, the carry flag will be *set* (set to 1) if there was a carry out of the high-order bit of the result; it will be *cleared* (set to 0) if there was no carry out. This is illustrated in Fig. 3-13.

In a similar fashion, the *zero flag*, ZF, will be set if the result of the operation is zero; it will be cleared otherwise. The *sign flag*, SF, is set if the result is negative and cleared if the result is positive. (You should realize that SF is simply being set to the high-order bit of the result.) The *overflow flag*, OF, is set if the arithmetic function performed results in a carry into

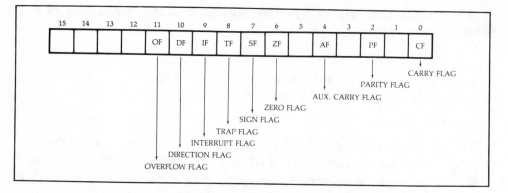

Fig. 3-12.   The 8088 flags register.

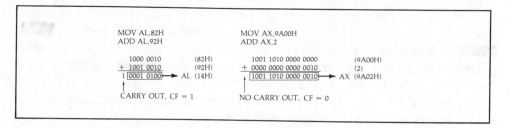

Fig. 3-13.   Operation of the carry flag.

the high-order bit of the result, but not a carry out of the high-order bit, or vice versa; otherwise, OF is cleared. The last was surely very confusing, but just read on, and it will become clear.

The carry and overflow flags indicate that the result of an arithmetic operation is too large to be stored within the destination operand. The need for two such flags stems from the fact that the operands can represent either *unsigned* (i.e., absolute) numbers or *signed* (twos complement) numbers. The carry flag is set if an unsigned result cannot be expressed within the destination operand. For byte operands, this means the result exceeds 255; for word operands, it means the result exceeds 65,535. The overflow flag is set if a signed result cannot be expressed within the destination operand. For byte operands, this means the result is larger than 127 or smaller than −128; for word operands, it means the result is larger than 32,767 or smaller than −32,768.

Multiplication and division are advanced microprocessor functions and are somewhat less flexible to use than the more common arithmetic functions already discussed. The destination operand is always the accumulator register (AX), and so only a source operand is coded with the instruction. It is important to realize that when we multiply a byte by a byte, the result can be as large as a word. Therefore, in a byte multiplication operation, the source operand (a byte) is multiplied by the contents of the AL register, and the result is placed in the entire AX word. In the case of a word multiplication operation, the source operand (a word) is multiplied by the contents of the AX register. The result can be as large as 32 bits; the low-order word is placed in the AX register, and the high-order word is placed in the DX register.

Conversely, in a byte division operation, the numerator, taken as the entire AX register, is divided by the one-byte source operand. The quotient is placed in AL, and the remainder is placed in AH. A word division operation assumes a 32-bit numerator, the high-order word taken from the DX register and the low-order word taken from the AX register. This numerator is divided by the one-word source operand. The quotient is placed in AX, and the remainder is placed in DX.

The MUL and DIV instructions just discussed perform *unsigned* multiplication and division, respectively. *Signed* multiplication and division can be performed by the *integer* versions of these instructions, called IMUL and IDIV.

LOGICAL INSTRUCTIONS

The arithmetic instructions always assumed that their operands represented numeric information. By contrast, the logical instructions (refer to Fig. 3-8) treat their operands as simple strings of bits.

The NOT instruction simply inverts each bit in its single operand, changing all zeros to ones and all ones to zeros. The AND, OR, and XOR instructions each use two operands; the available operand combinations are the same as those that were available for the arithmetic instructions. The result of an AND instruction has bits set only in those positions where *both* of its operands had bits set. It is therefore very useful for *masking*, or forcing to zero, selected bits within its destination operand. The result of an OR instruction has bits set in those positions where *either* of its operands had bits set. It is very useful for forcing selected bits to one within its destination operand. The result of an XOR instruction has bits set only in those positions where *either but not both* of its operands had bits set. It is very useful for inverting selected bits within its destination operand. These instructions are illustrated in Fig. 3-14.

The TEST instruction performs the same function as the AND instruction, except that the destination operand is not altered. It is used primarily to test whether one or more specific bits in a byte or word are set.

The logical instructions just discussed always clear the carry and overflow flags. In addition, they set the zero flag to indicate whether or not the result was all zero.

The *shift* and *rotate* instructions move bits sideways (that is, from left to right, or right to left) within their operands. They are illustrated in Fig. 3-

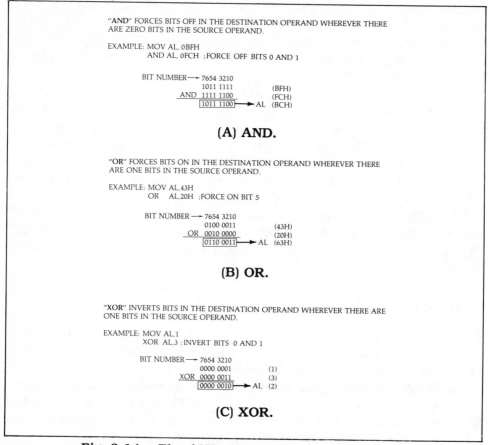

"AND" FORCES BITS OFF IN THE DESTINATION OPERAND WHEREVER THERE
ARE ZERO BITS IN THE SOURCE OPERAND.

EXAMPLE: MOV AL, 0BFH
         AND AL, 0FCH ;FORCE OFF BITS 0 AND 1

    BIT NUMBER ⟶ 7654 3210
                 1011 1111   (BFH)
             AND 1111 1100   (FCH)
                 1011 1100 ⟶ AL (BCH)

(A) AND.

"OR" FORCES BITS ON IN THE DESTINATION OPERAND WHEREVER THERE
ARE ONE BITS IN THE SOURCE OPERAND.

EXAMPLE: MOV AL,43H
         OR   AL,20H ;FORCE ON BIT 5

    BIT NUMBER ⟶ 7654 3210
                 0100 0011   (43H)
             OR 0010 0000   (20H)
                 0110 0011 ⟶ AL (63H)

(B) OR.

"XOR" INVERTS BITS IN THE DESTINATION OPERAND WHEREVER THERE ARE
ONE BITS IN THE SOURCE OPERAND.

EXAMPLE: MOV AL,1
         XOR AL,3 ;INVERT BITS 0 AND 1

    BIT NUMBER ⟶ 7654 3210
                 0000 0001   (1)
             XOR 0000 0011   (3)
                 0000 0010 ⟶ AL (2)

(C) XOR.

Fig. 3-14.   The AND, OR, and XOR instructions.

15. As an example, let us assume that the AL register contains the value 3.
The *shift left logical* instruction, SHL, will cause the following to occur:

AL before = 03H = 0000 0011
execute "SHL AL,1"
AL after = 06H = 0000 0110

Notice how each bit in the destination operand was shifted one position to
the left. A zero bit was shifted in on the right to fill the vacated low-order
bit position. In addition, the high-order bit that was shifted out of the oper-
and is placed into the carry flag, CF. In the example above, the carry flag
would be set to 0.

The *shift right logical* instruction, SHR, functions identically to SHL,
except that the bits are moved in the opposite direction. These instructions
can be used to perform multiplication and division by powers of two. By
shifting the bits of a numeric value to the left, we multiply that value by 2;
this was illustrated by the example above. If we shift the bits of a numeric

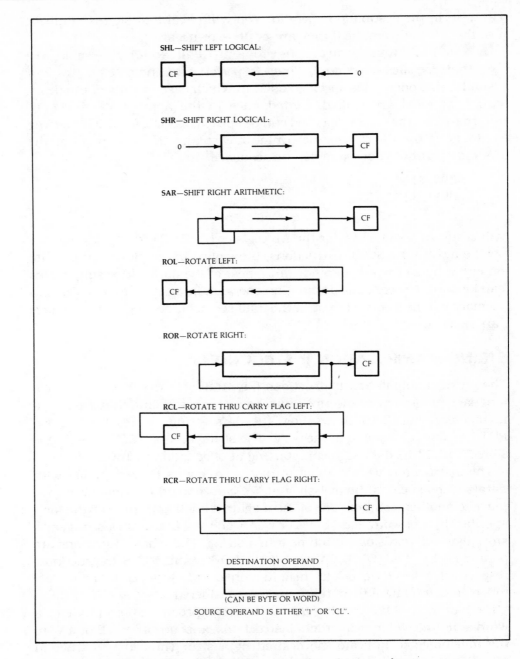

Fig. 3-15.   The shift and rotate instructions.

value to the right, we divide that value by 2. If the numeric value is *signed* (i.e., represented in twos complement format), then division should be accomplished by using the *shift right arithmetic* instruction, SAR. This instruction differs from SHR in that it retains the leftmost, or most significant, bit in the destination operand. You will recall that signed numbers use this bit to determine if they are positive or negative.

The shift and rotate instructions of Fig. 3-15 all require a second operand that specifies *how many times* to perform the indicated operation. Usually, this operand is specified as 1, in which case the bits of the destination operand are shifted/rotated once in the appropriate direction. Alternatively, the second operand can be specified as CL, in which case the contents of the CL register determine how many times to perform the desired operation. For example, the sequence

```
MOV AL,1
MOV CL,3
SHL AL,CL
```

will result in a value of 8 for the AL register ($1 \times 2 \times 2 \times 2$).

Like most other 8088 instructions, the logical instructions can operate on either byte or word operands, and most of the data-addressing modes can be used to specify the destination operand. In most cases, operands in memory will be assumed to be in the data segment, but segment overrides can be used.

STRING-MANIPULATION INSTRUCTIONS

The string-manipulation instructions (Fig. 3-8) give the 8088 assembly-language programmer powerful control over strings of data that are stored in memory. Fig. 3-16 shows how the data string "PERSONAL COMPUTER" might be stored in memory. The string occupies 17 bytes and is stored within the data segment, starting at offset address 1500H.

The instructions we are about to discuss allow us to work easily with data strings such as the one shown. We can *move* the strings from one place to another, *compare* one of them against another, *scan* a string for a specified byte or word, *load* bytes or words one at a time from a string, and *store* bytes or words one at a time into a string. These basic functions are performed by the MOVS, CMPS, SCAS, LODS, and STOS instructions, respectively. Before we look at them in more detail, however, there are factors common to all of them that must be considered.

Each of the five basic string instructions can process either a byte or a word at a time. When using these instructions, append either a B or a W to the mnemonic to indicate the desired data size. Thus, the instruction MOVSB will move a string one byte at a time, but the instruction MOVSW will move a string one word at a time.

The operands of string instructions are always implied, so there is no need to specify them when you write the instruction. Source strings are addressed by the SI register, and destination strings are addressed by the

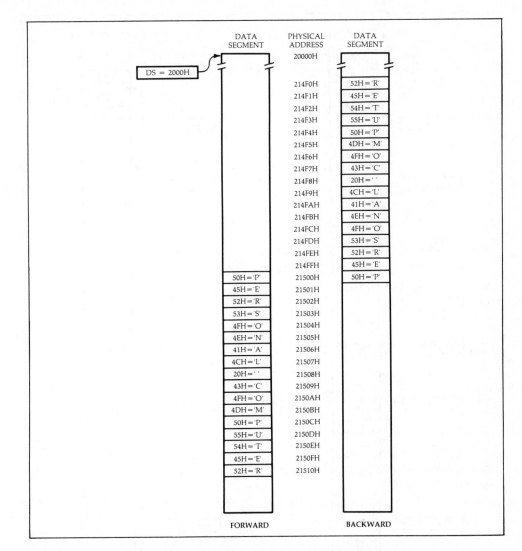

Fig. 3-16. Storing data strings in memory.

DI register. The destination string is always assumed to reside in the *extra segment*. The source string is usually assumed to reside in the *data segment*, although this can be changed by using a segment override. Note that if our two string operands are in the same segment, we must either use a segment override or set the DS and ES registers equal, as in Fig. 3-7B.

This implied addressing scheme is designed so that we can use the SI register as a pointer into our source string while the DI register serves as a pointer into our destination string. The strings can reside in the same segment, or in different segments. Refer to Fig. 3-17A. Here we are preparing

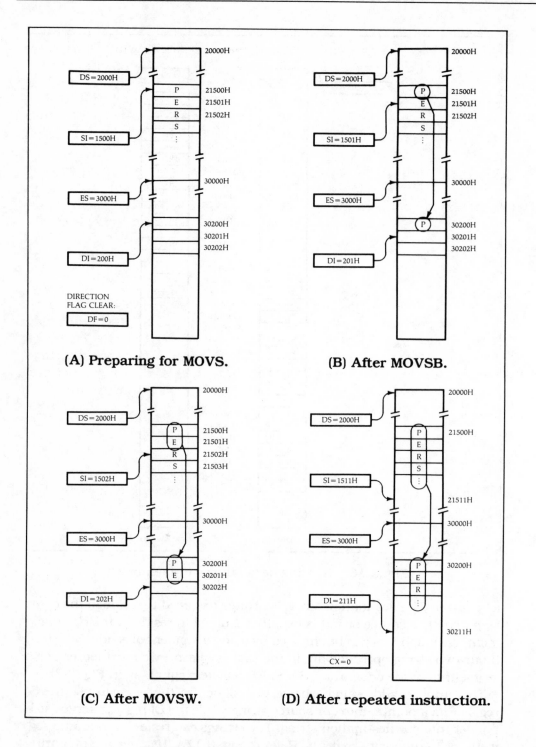

(A) Preparing for MOVS.

(B) After MOVSB.

(C) After MOVSW.

(D) After repeated instruction.

Fig. 3-17.   Move string operations.

to move a string from one segment to another. The DS and SI registers define the starting location of the source string. The ES and DI registers define where the string is to be moved. Execution of the MOVSB instruction will cause the byte at the source location to be moved to the destination location. The SI and DI registers are then automatically updated to point to the next byte in the string (Fig. 3-17B). Note that a MOVSW instruction would have updated SI and DI to point to the next word in the string (Fig. 3-17C).

The automatic updating of the source and destination pointers makes it possible to handle a long data string by simply repeating the basic string operation several times. We can request such a repeated operation by prefixing the basic string instruction with a *repeat code*. An example of this would be:

```
REP MOVSB
```

The repeat code causes the basic string instruction that follows to be repeated for a count specified by the CX register. Each time the basic string instruction is executed, the CX register is decremented by one. When the CX register reaches zero, the processor will proceed to the next instruction. We can thus use the CX register to specify the *length* of strings to be processed by repeated string instructions. Fig. 3-17D shows the result of

```
MOV CX,17
REP MOVSB
```

In the last example, we moved the entire 17-byte "forward" string shown at the left in Fig. 3-16 from one point in memory to another. But suppose this string had been stored backward in memory, as shown at the right in Fig. 3-16. The string operation shown would not work in this case. The 8088 string instructions allow us to work with backward strings through use of the *direction flag*. In all of the examples given until now, we have assumed that the direction flag, DF, was *clear* (i.e., set to 0). When this is the case, the basic string functions assume that strings grow forward in memory and cause the string pointers, SI and DI, to be *incremented* after each operation. To work with strings that grow backward in memory, all we have to do is set the DF flag. This will cause all string operations to *decrement* the SI and DI registers, as shown in Fig. 3-18. Instructions that set and clear the DF flag will be described shortly.

As you can see, there are many different options to be considered when using string instructions. These options are summarized in Fig. 3-19. Keeping them in mind, let us now examine the other basic string functions (Fig. 3-8).

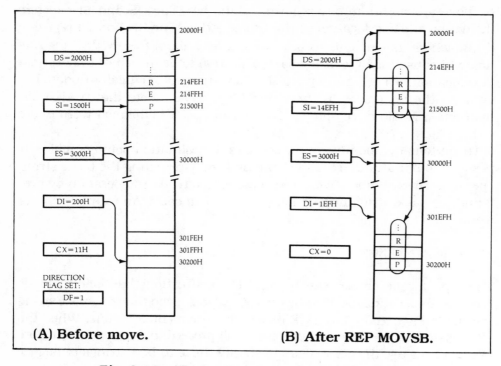

(A) Before move. **(B) After REP MOVSB.**

Fig. 3-18.   Backward move-string operation.

Data Size	Byte	Word
Direction (DF)	Forward	Backward
String Length	Single Operation	REP (CX)
Source String (SI)	Defaults to Data Segment Segment Override May Be Used	
Destination String (DI)	Always in Extra Segment	

Fig. 3-19.   Options common to all string instructions.

The basic *store string* instruction, STOS, stores the contents of the accumulator (AL for byte operations, AX for word operations) into the destination string and then updates the destination string pointer, DI. No reference is made to the source string, so SI is not altered. The instruction REP STOS is extremely useful for initializing blocks of memory to a constant value. An example is given in Fig. 3-20A. Remember that the destination string is always in the extra segment.

The basic *load string* instruction, LODS, is illustrated in Fig. 3-20B. The LODS instruction performs the converse of a STOS instruction. A byte (or

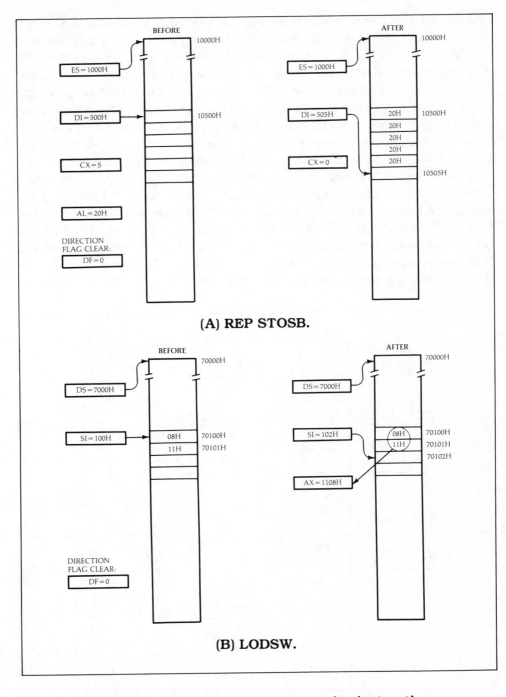

Fig. 3-20. Store string and load string instructions.

word) is fetched from the source string and placed in the AL (or AX) register; the source string pointer, SI, is then updated. No reference is made to the destination string, so DI is not altered. The LODS instruction is useful in language-translation programs (parsers) when one needs to examine each element of a string, one at a time, in the order in which they occur.

The basic ·scan-string instruction, SCAS, subtracts the destination-string byte (or word) from the contents of AL (or AX) and updates the various flags to indicate the result of the comparison. Nothing is altered other than the flags and the destination-string pointer, DI. This instruction can be used to search a string for a specific character. To accomplish this, two additional repeat prefix codes are available. These are *repeat while equal*, REPE, and *repeat while not equal*, REPNE. These prefixes act like the REP prefix in that they cause the specified function to be repeated for the number of times specified in the CX register. In addition, these prefixes will halt the repeating function when the zero flag, ZF, indicates that the desired condition (equal or not equal) has occurred.

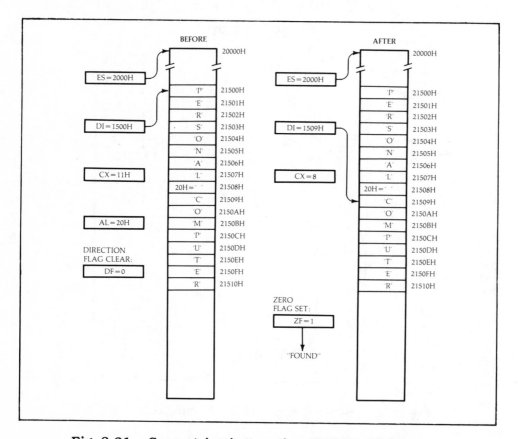

Fig. 3-21. Scan-string instruction (REPNE SCASB).

Fig. 3-21 shows how a repeated SCAS instruction can be used to scan a string for a specific character. In general, we set up the ES and DI registers to point to the string to be searched. The character to search for is placed in the AL register, and the length of the string is placed in the CX register. We then execute REPNE SCASB. If the instruction completes with ZF = 0, then the character was not found in the string. Otherwise, the DI register will point to the position within the string *after* the matched character, and CX will contain the number of characters left in the string (note that these conditions are ideal for resuming the search).

The basic *compare-string* instruction, CMPS, subtracts the destination string byte (or word) from the source string byte (or word) and updates the various flags to indicate the result of the comparison. As with the SCAS instruction, the operands themselves are not altered; only the flags and SI and DI are modified. The CMPS instruction can be used in conjunction with REPE to compare two strings and repeat until a mismatch is found (an example of this is given in Fig. 3-22). Alternatively, it can be used with REPNE to compare two strings until a match is found.

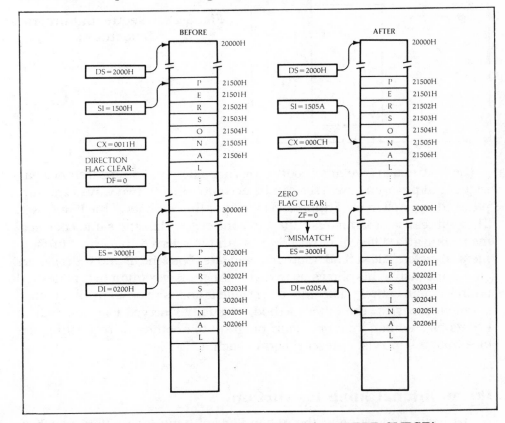

Fig. 3-22. Compare-string instruction (REPE CMPSB).

TRANSFER-OF-CONTROL INSTRUCTIONS

The *transfer-of-control* instructions (see Fig. 3-8) allow us to alter the flow of program execution. As we have already seen, the processor executes instructions by fetching them from memory, one byte at a time. The next instruction to be executed at any time is always in the current *code segment* (defined by the contents of the CS register) at the offset address specified by the *instruction-pointer* register, IP. Under normal conditions, the program flows sequentially from one instruction to the next; this is accomplished by incrementing the IP register as each instruction is executed (Fig. 3-23).

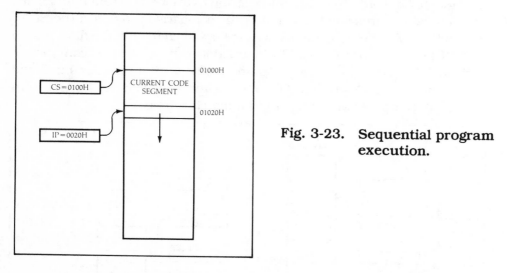

Fig. 3-23.   Sequential program execution.

The instructions we are about to discuss allow us to alter the normal, sequential program flow. This can be accomplished in two ways. The simpler and more often used approach is to alter the contents of the IP register. This will cause program execution to continue within the same code segment, but at a different offset address, and is referred to as an *intrasegment transfer*. The second approach is to alter both the IP and CS registers simultaneously. This allows us to divert program execution to any desired address in an entirely different code segment and is referred to as an *intersegment transfer*. The latter method is usually reserved for such radical events as chaining from one main program to another, or requesting service from a supervisory-level program such as DOS.

Unconditional Jump Instruction

Let us begin by looking at the *unconditional jump* instruction, which is specified by the assembler-language mnemonic JMP. As its name implies,

	TYPE OF ADDRESSING	INSTRUCTION EXAMPLE
INTRASEGMENT		
DIRECT		
16 BIT	DISPLACEMENT	JMP PROG1A
8 BIT("SHORT")	DISPLACEMENT	JMP SHORT QUEST
INDIRECT		
REGISTER	EXACT	JMP BX
MEMORY	EXACT	JMP [BP+JTABLE]
INTERSEGMENT		
DIRECT	EXACT	JMP NEXTROUTINE
INDIRECT		
MEMORY	EXACT	JMP [INTERS+BX]

Fig. 3-24. Jump addressing modes.

this statement will always cause the program flow to be diverted when it is reached. The JMP instruction has one operand, used to specify exactly where the program should continue executing (this value is also referred to as the *jump target*). As always, the situation is made more complex by the various *addressing modes* that are available for defining this operand. Each of these modes is described in Fig. 3-24.

There are two basic kinds of JMP addressing modes, *direct* and *indirect*. The direct modes specify the jump target in the instruction itself. When using the JMP instruction in this manner, we identify the jump target instruction by placing a *label* on it. The label name is then used as the operand of the JMP instruction. The assembler calculates the difference between the address of the JMP instruction itself and the address of the jump target. This *displacement* value is used as the operand of the JMP instruction (see Fig. 3-25A).

The example in Fig. 3-25A was of a SHORT jump. A SHORT jump specifies the displacement operand in one byte. Because we need to be able to jump backward as well as forward in memory, the displacement operand must always be interpreted as a signed, twos-complement number. In this format, one byte can represent values from -128 to $+127$. Thus the SHORT jump only allows us to transfer control within a narrow range of the JMP instruction itself. To transfer control outside this range, the JMP

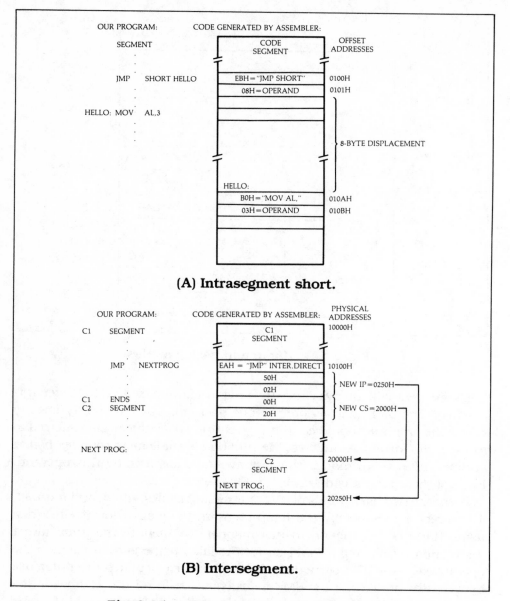

Fig. 3-25. JMP using direct addressing.

instruction with a 16-bit displacement operand is used. This allows us access to any instruction within the 64K (maximal) code segment.

To access directly an instruction outside the current code segment, the assembler can generate an intersegment form of the JMP instruction (Fig. 3-25B). This form includes a four-byte operand that specifies both the new code-segment value (goes into CS) and an offset address within that segment (goes into IP). Exact addresses, not displacements, are used.

The *indirect* modes allow us to calculate dynamically the desired jump target address. For example, we might perform a number of calculations on some input data to determine which part of our program should be executed next. Let us assume that as a result of these calculations the SI register contains the offset address of the selected part of the program. The instruction

```
JMP SI
```

can then be used to transfer control to the selected code.

Intrasegment indirect transfers can be made either through a 16-bit register, as just demonstrated, or through a word in memory. In the latter case, we can use any of data addressing modes 3, 4, 5, and 6 (Fig. 3-9) to specify the memory word. For each of these modes, the memory word selected is assumed to contain an offset address that is loaded into the IP register to effect the jump. Note that all intrasegment indirect transfers use exact addresses, and not displacements, to specify the jump target.

Intersegment indirect transfers may be made only through memory, again using any of data-addressing modes 3 through 6. Once again, the word at the selected memory address is loaded into the IP register. In addition, however, the word following this word is assumed to contain the new code-segment value and is loaded into the CS register, thus completing the intersegment jump.

Conditional Jump Instructions

The *conditional jump* instructions allow us to test for a specified condition. These instructions transfer control to the jump target only if the condition is met; otherwise, program execution continues sequentially.

The conditions that we can test involve the various flag-register bits (Fig. 3-12). As you will recall, these flags are usually set to indicate the result of an arithmetic or logical instruction. By following such instructions with a conditional jump, we enable the processor to make decisions based upon the outcome of its calculations.

For example, suppose we wish to add two 8-bit numbers together (let us say they are in the BL and DH registers) and then go to a special routine if the result is zero. This could be accomplished as follows:

```
ADD   BL,DH
JZ    SPECIAL   ;JUMP IF ZERO TO SPECIAL
...   ...
```

In this example, we are using the *jump if zero* instruction, JZ. This instruction will transfer control to the jump target only if the zero flag, ZF, is set. Since the preceding ADD instruction will set or clear ZF to indicate its result, the action taken will depend upon the contents of BL and DH at the time this code is executed.

The complete 8088 repertoire of conditional jump instructions is listed in Table 3-1. Each instruction can be specified by one or more assembler-language mnemonics. The mnemonics describe the various arithmetic conditions that are being tested (i.e., *jump if less than or equal*, JLE). Note that we can test the zero, sign, carry, overflow, and parity flags directly (i.e., *jump if carry*, JC; *jump if not carry*, JNC; etc.).

Table 3-1. Conditional Jump Instructions

Instruction Mnemonic(s)	Condition Required for Jump	Interpretation ("Jump if ...")
JE or JZ	ZF = 1	"equal" or "zero"
JL or JNGE	(SF XOR OF) = 1	"less" or "not greater or equal"
JLE or JNG	((SF XOR OF) OR ZF) = 1	"less or equal" or "not greater"
JB or JNAE or JC	CF = 1	"below" or "not above or equal" or "carry"
JBE or JNA	(CF OR ZF) = 1	"below or equal" or "not above"
JP or JPE	PF = 1	"parity" or "parity even"
JO	OF = 1	"overflow"
JS	SF = 1	"sign"
JNE or JNZ	ZF = 0	"not equal" or "not zero"
JNL or JGE	(SF XOR OF) = 0	"not less" or "greater or equal"
JNLE or JG	((SF XOR OF) OR ZF) = 0	"not less or equal" or "greater"
JNB or JAE or JNC	CF = 0	"not below" or "above or equal" or "not carry"
JNBE or JA	(CF OR ZF) = 0	"not below or equal" or "above"
JNP or JPO	PF = 0	"not parity" or "parity odd"
JNO	OF = 0	"not overflow"
JNS	SF = 0	"not sign"
JCXZ	CX = 0	"CX register is zero"

There is one conditional jump instruction that does not test the state of the flags. This instruction is *jump if CX is zero*, JCXZ. It will transfer control to the jump target only if the CX register contains zero. You might ask, "Why the CX register? What's so special about it? After all,

```
CMP CX,0    ;COMPARE CX TO ZERO
JE  ...     ;JUMP IF EQUAL TO ...
```

will certainly accomplish the same thing." In fact, the above sequence is probably what you would use if you had to test any other register for zero. But the CX register *is* special. We have already examined several instructions that make special use of it. The REP prefixes allowed us to execute string instructions with a length (or repeat factor) specified by the CX register. The shift and rotate instructions also allowed a repeat factor, in this case specified by the CL register which is, of course, the lower half of CX. Because we will be using CX so often as a count or length value, it is useful to be able to test it for zero in such a convenient way.

One final detail about conditional jump instructions: They must be used with the *intrasegment direct short* addressing mode. This means that conditional jumps can only be made to target addresses within a narrow range of the originating instruction (as in Fig. 3-25A).

Iteration-Control Instructions

In practically every programming application, the need arises to execute a sequence of instructions several times repeatedly. This is usually handled by writing a *program loop*. Just as BASIC has FOR . . . NEXT statements to handle such loops, 8088 assembler language has *iteration-control* instructions.

The iteration-control instructions are defined in Table 3-2. Like the conditional jump instructions, they require a single operand that specifies a jump target address (*intrasegment direct short* addressing mode only).

Table 3-2. Iteration-Control Instructions

Instruction Mnemonic(s)	Action Taken
LOOP	CX = CX − 1, if CX not = 0 then jump, else continue.
LOOPE ("loop while equal") LOOPZ ("loop while zero")	CX = CX − 1, if CX not = 0 and ZF = 1 then jump, else continue.
LOOPNE ("loop while not equal") LOOPNZ ("loop while not zero")	CX = CX − 1, if CX not = 0 and ZF = 0 then jump, else continue.

Let us examine the LOOP instruction. Once again the CX register is assumed to contain a count value. The contents of CX are decremented by one and, if the result is not zero, control is transferred to the jump target. If the result is zero, the program proceeds sequentially.

This instruction comes in handy when you wish to repeat a sequence of instructions several times. Simply load the CX register with the number of times to repeat, and then execute the desired sequence. At the end of the sequence, place a LOOP statement specifying the beginning of the sequence as its jump target.

For example, suppose we had two arrays, each containing 10 one-byte entries. We wish to add each entry in the first array to its corresponding entry in the second array. We will use the SI register as a pointer into the arrays. The main body of our loop will fetch the first-array entry, add it to the second-array entry, and update the array pointer, SI. We will perform this operation 10 times by initializing CX to 10 and using a LOOP instruction:

```
        MOV  SI,0              ;INITIALIZE ARRAY POINTER
        MOV  CX,10             ;INITIALIZE REPEAT COUNT
AGAIN:  MOV  AL,[SI+ARRAY1]    ;GET ARRAY-1 ENTRY
        ADD  [SI+ARRAY2],AL    ;ADD TO ARRAY-2 ENTRY
        INC  SI               ;UPDATE ARRAY POINTER
        LOOP AGAIN            ;DO IT 10 TIMES
```

The *loop while equal* instruction, LOOPE, functions exactly like LOOP, except that it allows us to terminate the loop before the count (CX) has been exhausted if the zero flag (ZF) is clear. Similarly, the *loop while not equal* instruction, LOOPNE, allows the loop to terminate early if the zero flag is set. These instructions can be coded by using the alternative mnemonics LOOPZ and LOOPNZ, respectively.

Subroutines

Very often when writing a program, we find that a particular sequence of instructions is needed at several different points. Since it would be redundant to insert these instructions at each point in the program where they are needed, they are made into a *subroutine*. This subroutine is then *called* from each point in the program where it is needed. Control is transferred to the subroutine when it is called, and the instructions within it are executed. When it has completed, the subroutine *returns* by transferring control back to the point from which it was called. This process is illustrated in Fig. 3-26.

The 8088 implements this subroutine mechanism with the CALL and RET instructions. Both CALLs and RETurns can be made either intrasegment or intersegment. See Fig. 3-27. While the subroutine executes, the location to which control is to be returned is stored in the *stack*. When a CALL is made, the return location is PUSHed onto the stack. This information is POPed off the stack to effect the RETurn.

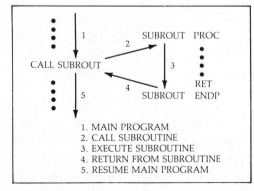

Fig. 3-26. Subroutine mechanism.

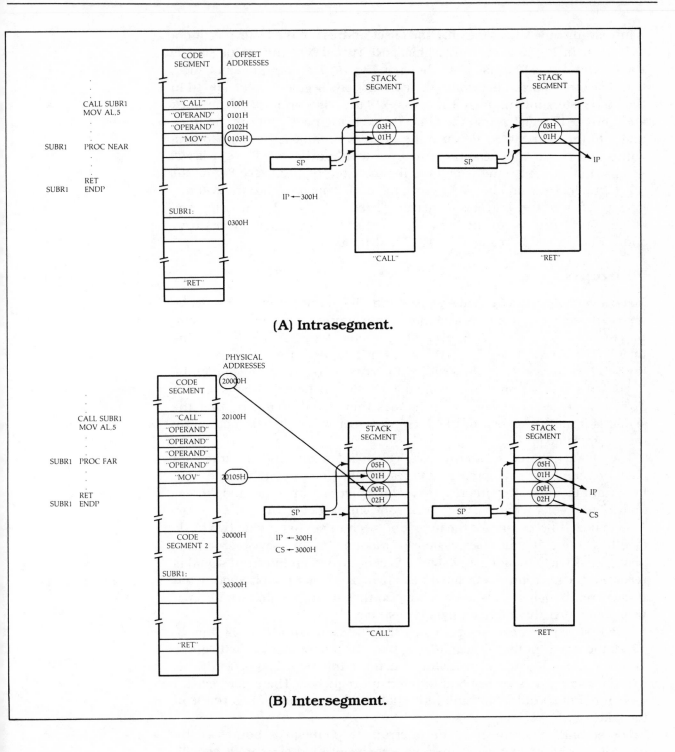

(A) Intrasegment.

(B) Intersegment.

Fig. 3-27. CALL and RET instructions.

Intrasegment CALLs save only the offset address of the return location, as shown in Fig. 3-27A. Intrasegment RETurns POP this value off the stack and into the IP register. As shown in Fig. 3-27B, intersegment CALLs save both the offset address and the current code-segment value (found in the CS register). Intersegment RETurns POP the offset address off the stack and into the IP register, and then POP the code-segment value off the stack and into the CS register. Because the stack is used, it is possible to *nest* subroutines (i.e., call one subroutine from within another). The stack will ensure that we return to the point of the most recent CALL (see Fig. 3-28).

A CALL instruction always has one operand. This operand, the *call target*, specifies where control is to be transferred. It is specified by using any of the *JMP addressing modes* (Fig. 3-24) with the exception of *direct short*. No operand is required on RET instructions.

Interrupts

To be aware of events that take place externally, a microprocessor must be able to detect requests for its attention. For example, consider a microcomputer and its keyboard. We know that characters typed are received by the microprocessor via one of its i/o ports. But how does the microprocessor know when to read from the keyboard port? It is really quite simple; the keyboard sends a *signal* to the microprocessor whenever a key is struck. The microprocessor receives and decodes this signal. Realizing that the signal is from the keyboard, the microprocessor reads the character from the appropriate port.

The signal referred to above is called an *interrupt*, and the *interrupt mechanism* of the microprocessor is responsible for responding to it. It is important to realize that interrupts can take place at any time, and there is no way to predict what the microprocessor will be doing when they occur. This makes it necessary for the interrupt mechanism to provide two basic facilities. First, it must be possible to *disable* the microprocessor from being sensitive to the interrupt signal. Second, when an interrupt signal *is* received, the microprocessor must be able to save information about what it is currently doing. This is necessary so that it can resume whatever it was doing after the interrupt has been *serviced*.

The first requirement is satisfied by the 8088 *interrupt flag*, IF (Fig. 3-12). If the interrupt flag is clear (IF = 0), then the microprocessor will ignore any incoming interrupt signal. Only when the interrupt flag is set (IF = 1) will the microprocessor respond to interrupt requests. (There does exist a special *nonmaskable interrupt*, NMI, that will be recognized regardless of the state of IF.)

The second requirement of the interrupt mechanism is addressed by treating interrupts as though they were a special kind of subroutine call.

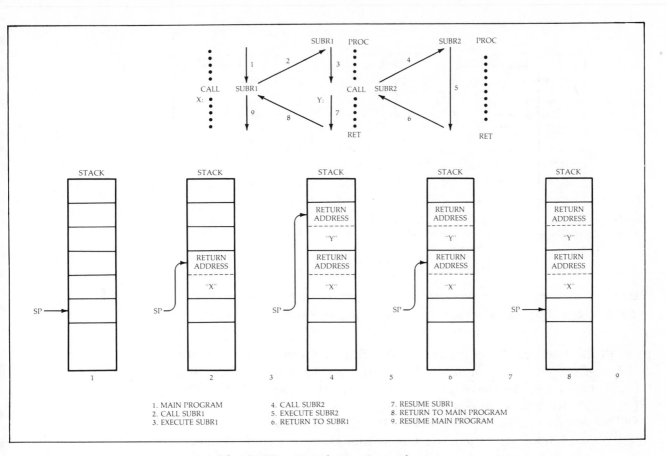

Fig. 3-28. Nesting subroutines.

Remember how we saved the return location by pushing it onto the stack during a CALL? When an interrupt is received, something very similar happens. First, the current 16-bit flags register is pushed onto the stack. The interrupt and trap flags, IF and TF, are cleared (this prevents a second interrupt from being received while the first is still being processed). Then the CS register (defining the current code segment) is pushed onto the stack. Finally, the offset address of the next instruction to have been executed (taken from the IP register) is pushed onto the stack. This process is illustrated in Fig. 3-29.

Once the current status of the processor has been saved, the interrupt mechanism transfers control to a special program at a specific address. This special program, called an *interrupt-service routine*, is responsible for handling the external event that has been signaled. When it completes this task, it returns control to whatever program was executing when the interrupt was received. This is accomplished with the *interrupt return* instruction, IRET. The IRET instruction restores the processor to the status it had

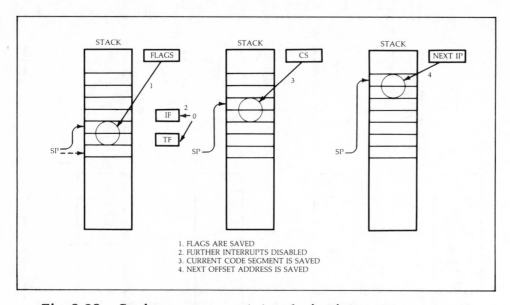

1. FLAGS ARE SAVED
2. FURTHER INTERRUPTS DISABLED
3. CURRENT CODE SEGMENT IS SAVED
4. NEXT OFFSET ADDRESS IS SAVED

Fig. 3-29.   Saving processor status during interrupt response.

prior to the interrupt by popping the IP, CS, and flags registers off the stack, in that order. Note that if the interrupt-service routine alters any other registers, it should save and restore them so that the integrity of the interrupted program is not compromised.

We have seen how the 8088 provides for the basic requirements of an interrupt mechanism. But there is one more important aspect of this mechanism to be studied. How does the processor determine where the interrupt-service routine is located? Early microprocessors simply dedicated a specific memory location (for example, 0000H) to this task. There is a problem with this approach, however, if more than one external device is capable of generating an interrupt signal. Since each of the devices will activate the same interrupt service routine, its first task must be to analyze the environment to determine which device wants attention.

The 8088 solves this problem by allowing us to identify each possible interrupt-signal source with a *type* code. The type code is specified by one byte; thus we can have up to 256 unique interrupt-signal sources. When the processor receives an interrupt signal, it also expects a one-byte type code. The interrupting device is expected to send the type code to the processor to identify itself. The processor, having received the type code, uses it to determine the location of the appropriate interrupt-service routine.

Fig. 3-30 illustrates this aspect of the interrupt mechanism. The lowest 1K of memory (physical addresses 00000H–003FFH) is reserved for a table of interrupt-service routine addresses. Each entry in the table is four bytes

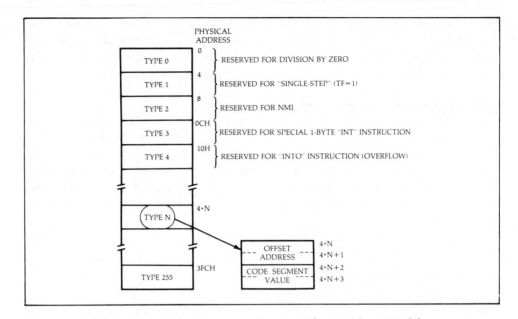

Fig. 3-30.   Interrupt-service routine address table.

long and contains a code-segment value and an offset-address value. The processor selects a table entry based upon the type code it has received. The code-segment value is placed into CS, and the offset-address value is placed into IP to transfer control to the interrupt-service routine. All we have to do is place the addresses of the appropriate interrupt-service routines into the proper table locations, and we will be all set to receive interrupts.

Notice that the first five table entries (corresponding to type codes 0–4) are reserved for specific interrupt conditions. For example, a type 0 interrupt will be signaled *by the microprocessor itself* if division by zero is attempted in a DIV or IDIV instruction.

We can, in fact, signal an interrupt with any type code desired from within the microprocessor by using the *interrupt* instruction, INT. For example, the instruction

```
INT 9
```

will signal a type 9 interrupt. This feature makes the interrupt mechanism useful for calling commonly or globally used routines. We will discuss this aspect later; for now, let us look at the rest of those reserved interrupt types.

The microprocessor will signal a type 1 interrupt after the completion of every instruction if the *trap flag*, TF, is set. This allows a "single-step" facility to be programmed. The special *nonmaskable interrupt* mentioned earlier will always generate a type 2 interrupt. The type 3 interrupt is special in that it can be signaled with a one-byte form of the INT instruction (all other INT instructions require a second byte to specify the type-code operand). The type 4 interrupt will be signaled by the *interrupt on overflow*, INTO, instruction if the overflow flag is set (OF = 1).

PROCESSOR-CONTROL INSTRUCTIONS

You can begin to relax now; we have saved the easiest instructions for last. The *processor-control* instructions are summarized in Table 3-3. The most significant instructions in this group allow us to set or clear the carry, direction, and interrupt flags directly. In addition, there is the *complement carry flag* instruction, CMC, which allows us to invert the current state of the carry flag.

Finally, there is the *halt* instruction, HLT. It causes the processor to stop executing instructions. We might use it if we had nothing to execute while waiting for an interrupt to be received.

Table 3-3. Processor-Control Instructions

Instruction Mnemonic(s)	Action Taken
CLC ("clear carry flag")	CF = 0
CLD ("clear direction flag")	DF = 0
CLI ("clear interrupt flag")	IF = 0
CMC ("complement carry flag")	CF = NOT(CF)
STC ("set carry flag")	CF = 1
STD ("set direction flag")	DF = 1
STI ("set interrupt flag")	IF = 1
HLT ("halt")	Processor stop executing instructions

IN CONCLUSION

The 8088 instruction set is large and complex, and proficiency can be gained only through experience in using it. To be able to write a complete program, however, there is much more that we must know. For example, how do we tell the assembler whether we want an instruction to use bytes or words? How does it know whether a CALL or RET instruction should be intrasegment or intersegment? These are the concerns that we shall turn our attention to next.

CHAPTER 4

BIOS, DOS, and the Macro Assembler

Our goal is to be able to write 8088 assembler-language programs that will run on the IBM Personal Computer. In this chapter, we will examine the three remaining elements that are necessary to achieve this. These are the *Basic Input Output System* (BIOS), the *Disk Operating System* (DOS), and the *Macro Assembler.*

The BIOS is a set of 8088 programs that are stored permanently in the Personal Computer. When the computer is turned on, these programs receive control and initialize the entire computer system. In addition, they provide the minimum software support necessary to control the various devices that may be attached to the computer.

The DOS is a control program that manages the various *resources* (memory, disk space, etc.) of the computer. It also provides the command language with which we can easily control the actions of the computer.

The *assembler* is a programming tool that we can use to convert our assembler-language programs into *object code.* The object code contains the actual bit patterns that the 8088 microprocessor recognizes as instructions and data.

TURNING IT ON

When we want to start using the Personal Computer, the normal procedure is to turn it on and insert a DOS diskette. After a few seconds, the machine beeps, the disk spins, and the DOS message "Enter Date" appears. What causes all of this to occur?

When power is first applied, the 8088 microprocessor enters its *reset* state. In this state, the CS register is set to FFFFH, and the IP register is set to 0000H. Thus the first instruction that the CPU will execute is at physical memory location FFFF0H. This area of physical memory is allocated to ROM (read only memory) chips within the Personal Computer.

The BIOS is contained in this ROM area and thus gets control when the computer is turned on. It interrogates the various i/o ports of the computer to determine which devices are attached. It initializes all of these devices, causes the speaker to beep, and then sets up the interrupt-service routine address table (Fig. 3-30). This table will contain the addresses of the device-support routines that are within the BIOS itself. We will therefore be able to access these routines in our own programs via the INT instruction.

If the BIOS determines that a disk drive is attached to the system, it will *bootstrap* the DOS. The bootstrap process consists of reading a predefined area of the disk into a predefined area of memory and then passing control to that area. The DOS diskette contains a *bootstrap program* that gets loaded and executed by this process. The bootstrap program reads in the rest of the DOS program from the disk; in this fashion the DOS gets control. The DOS will initialize additional entries in the interrupt-service routine address table before issuing the "Enter Date" message.

At this point, the main memory of the Personal Computer is organized as shown in Fig. 4-1A. Note that the DOS program is divided into two sepa-

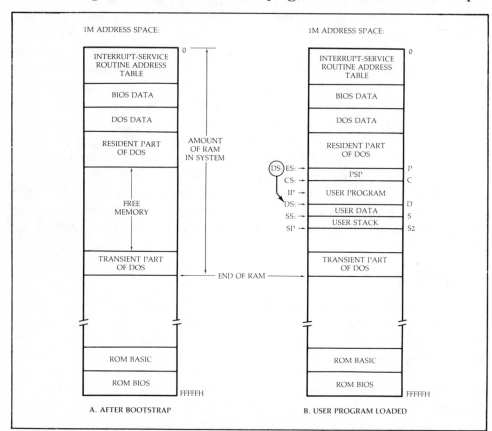

Fig. 4-1. DOS memory map.

rate parts. These parts bracket the "free memory" area that is available for our own programs.

RUNNING OUR OWN PROGRAM

We can now perform a series of steps, as shown in Fig. 4-2, to create our own executable program. Note that for each program we create, there will eventually be three disk files. In the case of the program named PROG1, we will begin by creating a *source file* named PROG1.ASM. We can use the *line editor program*, EDLIN, to create this file. It will contain all of the assembler-language statements that make up our program.

The *assembler program*, ASM, is then used to convert the source file into an *object file*, named PROG1.OBJ. If there are any syntax errors in our program, the assembler will inform us of them at this time. We will then have to go back to step 1 to correct them.

Finally, the *linker program*, LINK, is used to convert the object file into an *execution file*, named PROG1.EXE. This file can be loaded and run by DOS, simply by typing in the command PROG1.

When instructed in this fashion to load and execute a user program, the DOS complies as follows (refer to Fig. 4-1B). Starting at the first free memory address, DOS builds a control block known as the *program segment prefix* (PSP). The PSP contains information about the program to be run. It also provides the program with an interface back to the DOS. We will examine the PSP in more detail shortly.

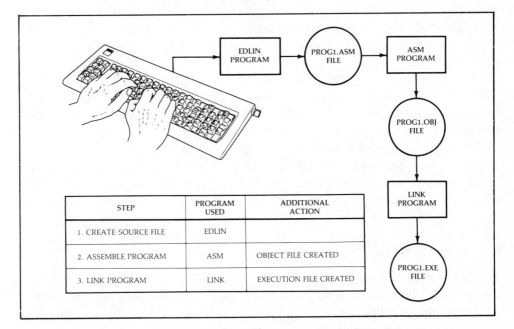

STEP	PROGRAM USED	ADDITIONAL ACTION
1. CREATE SOURCE FILE	EDLIN	
2. ASSEMBLE PROGRAM	ASM	OBJECT FILE CREATED
3. LINK PROGRAM	LINK	EXECUTION FILE CREATED

Fig. 4-2. Creating a program.

After creating the PSP, DOS reads the program from our execution file into memory. It places our code segment, which contains all of the instructions in our program, right after the PSP. This is followed by our data segment, which contains all of our variables. Finally, our stack segment is loaded into memory after the data segment.

The DOS now sets the DS and ES segment registers to point to the beginning of the PSP (location "P" in Fig. 4-1B). It sets the CS register to point to our code segment (location "C"), and the SS register to point to our stack segment (location "S"). The SP register is set to the size of our stack (location "S2"). The IP register is set to a specified offset address within our code segment. In this fashion, we can begin execution of our program at any desired point.

To be able to address our variables, however, we must first set the DS register to point to our data segment (location "D"). Controlling the addressability of information that is in various different segments will be an important consideration during all of our programming. In the next section, we will learn how to instruct the assembler to perform this and other tasks.

PSEUDO-OPERATIONS

There are two kinds of assembler-language statements. Until now we have been primarily concerned with *machine instruction* statements. In this type of statement, the opcode mnemonic represents an 8088 machine instruction (i.e., MOV). The other type of statement contains an opcode mnemonic that *does not* correspond to any 8088 machine instruction. Such mnemonics are thus referred to as *pseudo-operations*, or *pseudo-ops* for short.

To underscore the difference between these two types of statements, labels placed on regular (machine instruction) statements are always followed by a colon, whereas labels placed on pseudo-op statements never use a colon.

The most commonly used pseudo-ops are summarized in Table 4-1. Some pseudo-ops cause object code to be generated (i.e., DB, DW), whereas others simply control the way in which it is generated. We will need to use all of the pseudo-ops listed in even the simplest assembler-language program.

Data-Definition Pseudo-Ops

The data-definition pseudo-ops, DB and DW, allow us to allocate memory for our variables. They also allow us to assign a symbolic name to the memory address allocated, and to specify an initial value to be placed into the associated memory area.

Table 4-1. Pseudo-Operations

Mnemonic	Meaning
DB	Define byte(s)
DW	Define word(s)
PROC	Define procedure
ENDP	End procedure
SEGMENT	Define segment
ENDS	End segment
ASSUME	Establish segment register addressability
END	End program

The operand of these statements may be specified as a numeric value in any one of several bases, or as an ASCII character string. This is illustrated in Fig. 4-3, where each statement listed will cause the same byte of data to be assembled.

Several successive memory locations may be allocated with a single statement by specifying multiple operands, separated by commas. Note that if a symbolic label is used in this case, it refers only to the *first* memory address allocated.

Suppose we want to reserve a large number of bytes and initialize all of them to the same value. This can be accomplished by specifying a repetition factor and the "DUP" operator, as follows:

```
VAR1   DB   100 DUP(0)   ;100 BYTES OF ZERO
VAR2   DW   50 DUP(0)    ;50 WORDS OF ZERO
```

Although both of these statements will reserve a 100-byte area and fill it with zeros, there is an important difference between them. The assembler maintains a *type attribute* for each variable defined in the program. Because it was defined using DB, variable VAR1 has a type attribute of BYTE. Variable VAR2, however, was defined using DW and thus has a type attribute of WORD.

To understand why type attributes are necessary, consider the following three statements:

```
ADD SI,5     ;ADD 5 TO SI
ADD AL,5     ;ADD 5 TO AL
ADD VAR1,5   ;ADD 5 TO VAR1
```

Fig. 4-3. DB examples.

```
DB     65         ;DECIMAL
DB     41H        ;HEX
DB     01000001B  ;BINARY
DB     'A'        ;ASCII
```

The assembler knows to generate a 16-bit ADD instruction for the first statement because the SI register is a *word* register. Similarly, it knows to generate an 8-bit ADD for the second statement because the AL register is a *byte* register. In the third statement, however, the assembler must rely on outside information to determine whether to generate an 8- or 16-bit ADD. It is in these cases that the type attribute of the variable referenced is used. It is very important to realize that the way we define our data variables will affect the generation of code that references them.

Procedures

The pseudo-ops PROC and ENDP are used to divide the instruction statements that make up our program into blocks known as *procedures*. Each procedure is assigned a type attribute which can be either NEAR or FAR. In this manner, we inform the assembler whether to use intrasegment or intersegment CALL and RET instructions.

A label appearing on any instruction statement within a FAR procedure will be given a type attribute of FAR, as will the label on the PROC statement itself. Conversely, a label appearing on any instruction statement within a NEAR procedure will be given a type attribute of NEAR. When the assembler encounters a CALL statement, it inspects the type attribute of the operand. Those CALLS to FAR labels are intersegment, whereas CALLs to NEAR labels are intrasegment. If RET instructions appear within a FAR procedure, they are assembled as intersegment. Conversely, they are assembled as intrasegment if they appear within a NEAR procedure.

```
MAIN        PROC        FAR
            .
            .
            .
            CALL        SUBR1           ; INTRASEGMENT
            .
            .
            RET                         ; INTERSEGMENT,
    ;                           TERMINATE MAIN PROGRAM.
            .
SUBR1       PROC        NEAR
            .
            .
            .
            RET                     ; INTRASEGMENT
SUBR1       ENDP
MAIN        ENDP
```

Fig. 4-4.   Defining procedures.

Fig. 4-4 illustrates how this mechanism can be used. The main procedure of any program is usually defined as FAR. This is because it will be entered from another code segment where its invoking program (i.e., DOS) is located. If the program makes CALLs to internal subroutines (i.e., SUBR1), they will most likely be defined as NEAR, since they will reside within the same code segment as the main program. These internal subroutines will return to the main program via intrasegment RETs. The main program can be terminated by returning to its caller (DOS) via an intersegment RET. Notice that procedures may be *nested*. The innermost procedure definition will always determine the attribute of the statements within it.

Segment Definition and Addressing

Just as the PROC and ENDP statements divided the program into procedures, the SEGMENT and ENDS statements divide the program into segments. Most programs will contain at least three segment definitions. The three basic segments that we will always use are the *code segment*, which contains our program instructions, the *data segment*, which contains our variables, and the *stack segment*, which reserves space for the stack.

Fig. 4-5 shows how these segments are typically defined. The label field of the SEGMENT statement specifies the name to be assigned to the segment. The operand PARA specifies that the segment should begin at a standard paragraph (i.e., 16-byte) boundary in memory (see Fig. 3-4). The operand STACK is used to identify the stack segment specifically, while the operand PUBLIC is used for the code- and data-segment definitions.

```
STACK      SEGMENT    PARA STACK 'STACK'
           DB         1024 DUP (OFFH)       ;1K STACK SPACE
STACK      ENDS
DATA       SEGMENT    PARA PUBLIC  'DATA'
VAR1       DB         ...
           .
           .          variable definitions
           .
DATA       ENDS
CODE       SEGMENT    PARA PUBLIC 'CODE'
MAIN       PROC       FAR
           .
           .
           .          program instructions
           .
           .
           .
MAIN       ENDP
CODE       ENDS
```

Fig. 4-5. Defining segments.

```
1.     STACK      SEGMENT    PARA STACK 'STACK'
2.                DB         1024 DUP (OFFH)        ;1K STACK SPACE
3.     STACK      ENDS
4.     DATA       SEGMENT    PARA PUBLIC 'DATA'
                  .
                  .     variables
                  .
10.    DATA       ENDS
11.    CODE       SEGMENT    PARA PUBLIC 'CODE'
12.    MAIN       PROC       FAR
13.                ASSUME     CS:CODE
14.                PUSH       DS          ;SAVE PSP SEGMENT ADDRESS
15.                MOV        AX,0        ;PUSH AN OFFSET OF ZERO..
16.                PUSH       AX          ;...ONTO THE STACK
17.                MOV        AX,DATA     ;GET DATA SEGMENT ADDRESS
18.                MOV        DS,AX       ;...INTO DS REGISTER
19.                ASSUME     DS:DATA     ;ESTABLISH DATA SEGMENT..
            ;                             ...ADDRESSABILITY
                  .
                  .     program
                  .
                  .
30.                RET                    ;RETURN CONTROL TO DOS
31.    MAIN       ENDP
32.    CODE       ENDS
33.    END        MAIN
```

Fig. 4-6. Defining segment addressability—standard program prologue.

Note that we have placed the data segment before the code segment. This is very important because it allows us to define all of our variables before they are referenced by program instructions. We have already seen cases where the assembler must know the type attribute of a variable to be able to generate object code properly. By placing the data segment before the code segment, we ensure that the assembler never has a problem with this.

Once we have defined our segments, we must establish the means whereby the data within them can be addressed. This is done with the ASSUME pseudo-op. It tells the assembler that it can *assume* that a particular segment register points to a particular segment. The assembler cannot generate object code for program instructions until this has been done. The standard approach for defining segment addressability is shown in Fig. 4-6.

In Fig. 4-6, statement 13 tells the assembler that it can assume that the CS register points to the segment named CODE. We know this to be true because when DOS passes control to our program it will point the CS register at our code segment. In a similar fashion, we would like to be able to tell the assembler that the DS register points to our data segment (this is necessary if we are to access our variables there). However, a quick glance back at Fig. 4-1B shows that when our program starts, DOS has pointed the DS register at the PSP and not at our data segment. To establish addressability of our variables, we move the address of the data segment into the AX register (statement 17), and from there into the DS register (statement 18). We can now tell the assembler to assume that the DS register points to the data segment (statement 19). From this point on, we can reference our variables with program instructions, and the assembler will know that it can address them through the DS register. Note that the stack segment never requires an ASSUME statement.

Fig. 4-6 also illustrates the use of the END pseudo-op. This statement is used to signal the end of the source file to the assembler. In addition, the operand on the END statement specifies where execution of the program should begin. This value is placed in the IP register when DOS starts the program. In the example shown, we have indicated that we wish program execution to start with the first instruction of procedure MAIN.

DOS LINKAGE CONVENTIONS

The question now arises, "Why are statements 14, 15, and 16 present in Fig. 4-6?" The answer lies in the program segment prefix (PSP) and its reason for existing.

When DOS passes control to our program, various fields within the PSP have been initialized as shown in Table 4-2. The first two bytes of the PSP contain an "INT 20H" instruction. When our program has completed, it must execute this instruction *at this location* in order to return control to DOS. To ensure our ability to do this, we save the segment address of the PSP (passed to us by DOS in the DS register) on top of the stack (Fig. 4-6, statement 14). Statements 15 and 16 then push an offset value of zero onto the stack. This sets up the stack so that an intersegment (i.e., FAR) RET instruction will transfer control to the "INT 20H" instruction within the PSP. Statement 30, being within the FAR procedure "MAIN," generates an intersegment RET and thus terminates our program.

Table 4-2. The Program Segment Prefix (PSP)

Field at PSP +	Field Length (Bytes)	Field Description
0	2	"INT 20H" Instruction
2	2	Total Memory Size (in 16-byte increments)
5	5	FAR JMP to DOS Function Handler
5CH	16	1st Parameter Formatted as FCB
6CH	16	2nd Parameter Formatted as FCB
80H	1	Length of Parameter
81H	?	Parameter

The PSP also allows us to pass information, in the form of parameters, to our program. We can specify such parameters on the command line with which we invoke our program, for example:

```
PROG1 PARAM1 PARAM2
```

The characters that make up the parameter are placed in the PSP at offset 81H by DOS. The length of the parameter string will be stored at offset 80H. In addition, since the parameters often represent filenames, they will be formatted into *file control blocks* at offsets 5CH and 6CH. The use of file control blocks (FCBs) will be explained in a later chapter.

A SAMPLE PROGRAM

Now let us put everything that we have learned together and create a real 8088 program for the IBM PC. Our first program will be a simple message-retrieval system. It will be capable of storing 10 different messages, numbered 0 through 9. To retrieve a message, we will invoke the program and specify the desired message number as a parameter. The program will simply display the selected message on the screen and then return to DOS.

A listing of the program, which we will call MESSAGE, appears in Fig. 4-7. To simplify the program, we have decided to make each message exactly 30 characters long. The message table, consisting of the ten predefined messages, is placed in the data segment (statements 120–210). Other data variables include a byte containing the value 30 (THIRTY) for use in a MUL instruction, a 128-byte area to move the input parameter into (PARM), and an error-message string (ERRMSG).

Our code segment begins with the standard program prologue. Instead of establishing normal data-segment addressability, however, we use the extra segment (ES) to address our variables initially. The DS register is retained as a pointer to the PSP. This allows us to move the input parameter from the PSP into our own variable area by using the *move string* function (statements 410–440). Once this has been accomplished, we can establish normal data-segment addressability for our variables (statements 480–490).

We can now proceed to analyze the input parameter, within our data segment at label PARM. The input parameter will contain all of the characters that we type in after the program name when we start the program. In this application, we will type a single space after the program name, and follow it with a single character from 0 to 9 to indicate the message desired. The expected parameter length is therefore 2. Statements 530–540 check for this and branch to an error routine (ERROR) if any other parameter length is indicated. The parameter itself is fetched into the AL register in statement 550. In statements 560–590, we convert AL from an

```
00020 ; SAMPLE PROGRAM 1 - MESSAGE RETRIEVAL
00030 ;
00040 STACK     SEGMENT PARA STACK 'STACK'
00050           DB       256 DUP (0)         ;256 BYTES OF STACK SPACE
00060 STACK     ENDS
00070 ;
00080 DATA      SEGMENT PARA PUBLIC 'DATA'
00090 THIRTY    DB       30                  ;VALUE FOR MUL INSTRUCTION
00100 PARM      DB       128 DUP (0)         ;MOVE PARAMETER TO HERE
00110 ; MESSAGE TABLE:
00120 MSG0      DB       'I LIKE MY IBM PC----------------'
00130 MSG1      DB       '8088 PROGRAMMING IS FUN---------'
00140 MSG2      DB       'TIME TO BUY MORE DISKETTES-----'
00150 MSG3      DB       'THIS PROGRAM WORKS-------------'
00160 MSG4      DB       'TURN OFF THAT PRINTER!---------'
00170 MSG5      DB       'I HAVE MORE MEMORY THAN YOU----'
00180 MSG6      DB       'THE PSP CAN BE USEFUL----------'
00190 MSG7      DB       'BASIC WAS EASIER THAN THIS-----'
00200 MSG8      DB       'DOS IS INDISPENSABLE-----------'
00210 MSG9      DB       'LAST MESSAGE OF THE DAY--------'
00220 ; ERROR MESSAGE:
00230 ERRMSG    DB       'ERROR !!! INVALID PARAMETER !!'
00240 DATA      ENDS
00250 ;
00260 CODE      SEGMENT PARA PUBLIC 'CODE'
00270 START     PROC     FAR
00280 ;
00290 ; STANDARD PROGRAM PROLOGUE EXCEPT RETAIN DS AS PTR TO PSP
00300 ;
00310           ASSUME   CS:CODE
00320           PUSH     DS         ;SAVE PSP SEG ADDR
00330           MOV      AX,0
00340           PUSH     AX         ;SAVE RET ADDR OFFSET (PSP+0)
00350           MOV      AX,DATA
00360           MOV      ES,AX      ;ESTABLISH EXTRA SEG ADDRESSABILITY
00370           ASSUME   ES:DATA
00380 ;
00390 ; MOVE PARAMETER AREA FROM PSP TO OUR DATA SEGMENT
00400 ;
00410           MOV      SI,80H     ;SOURCE STRING OFFSET (WITHIN PSP)
00420           MOV      DI,OFFSET PARM ;DEST. STRING OFFSET
00430           MOV      CX,128     ;STRING LENGTH TO MOVE
00435           CLD                 ;SET 'FORWARD' STRING OPERATIONS
00440           REP      MOVSB      ;MOVE PARM INTO OUR DATA AREA
00450 ;
00460 ; ESTABLISH NORMAL DATA SEGMENT ADDRESSABILITY
00470 ;
00480           MOV      DS,AX
00490           ASSUME   DS:DATA
00500 ;
```

Fig. 4-7. Sample program—message retrieval.

Continued on next page.

```
00510 ; CHECK FOR VALID PARAMETER AND CONVERT IT TO NUMERIC VALUE
00520 ;
00530           CMP      PARM,2   ;IS PARAMETER LENGTH = 2 ?
00540           JNZ      ERROR    ;BRANCH IF NOT
00550           MOV      AL,PARM+2 ;GET PARAMETER ITSELF
00560           SUB      AL,'O'   ;CONVERT FROM ASCII TO BINARY
00570           JC       ERROR    ;BRANCH IF NOT NUMERIC ( < 'O' )
00580           CMP      AL,9     ;CHECK FOR VALID NUMERIC
00590           JA       ERROR    ;BRANCH IF NOT VALID ( > '9' )
00600 ;
00610 ; SELECT APPROPRIATE MESSAGE FROM MESSAGE TABLE
00620 ;
00630           MOV      BX,OFFSET MSGO   ;POINT TO FIRST MESSAGE
00640           MUL      THIRTY ; AX = AL * 30
00650           ADD      BX,AX    ;POINT TO DESIRED MESSAGE
00660           CALL     DISPLAY ;DISPLAY THE MESSAGE AT [BX]
00670           RET              ;RETURN TO DOS
00680 ;
00690 ; DISPLAY ERROR MESSAGE FOR INVALID PARAMETER:
00700 ;
00710 ERROR:    MOV      BX,OFFSET ERRMSG
00720           CALL     DISPLAY ;DISPLAY THE MESSAGE AT [BX]
00730           RET              ;RETURN TO DOS
00740 ;
00750 ; SUBROUTINE TO DISPLAY A MESSAGE ON THE SCREEN.
00760 ; ENTER WITH BX -> MESSAGE TO BE DISPLAYED.
00770 ; MESSAGE IS ASSUMED TO BE 30 CHARACTERS LONG.
00780 ;
00790 DISPLAY PROC     NEAR
00800           MOV      CX,30    ;NUMBER OF CHARACTERS TO DISPLAY
00810 DISP1:    MOV      AL,[BX] ;GET NEXT CHARACTER TO DISPLAY
00820           CALL     DISPCHAR ;DISPLAY IT
00830           INC      BX       ;POINT TO NEXT CHARACTER
00840           LOOP     DISP1    ;DO IT 30 TIMES
00850           MOV      AL,ODH   ;CARRIAGE RETURN
00860           CALL     DISPCHAR
00870           MOV      AL,OAH   ;LINE FEED
00880           CALL     DISPCHAR
00890           RET              ;RETURN TO CALLER OF 'DISPLAY'
00900 DISPLAY ENDP
00910 ;
00920 ; SUBROUTINE TO DISPLAY A CHARACTER ON THE SCREEN.
00930 ; ENTER WITH AL = CHARACTER TO BE DISPLAYED.
00940 ; USES VIDEO INTERFACE IN BIOS.
00950 ;
00960 DISPCHAR PROC     NEAR
00970           PUSH     BX       ;SAVE BX REGISTER
00980           MOV      BX,O     ;SELECT DISPLAY PAGE O
00990           MOV      AH,14    ;FUNCTION CODE FOR 'WRITE'
01000           INT      10H      ;CALL VIDEO DRIVER IN BIOS
01010           POP      BX       ;RESTORE BX REGISTER
```

Fig. 4-7 (cont). Sample program—message retrieval.

Continued on next page.

```
01020            RET                ;RETURN TO CALLER OF 'DISPCHAR'
01030 DISPCHAR ENDP
01040 START    ENDP
01050 CODE     ENDS
01060          END      START
```

Fig. 4-7 (cont). Sample program—message retrieval.

ASCII character to a binary value and check to be sure that it is in the range 0–9.

We now have the input parameter in AL as a binary number from 0 to 9. This value must be used to select the corresponding entry in the message table. To accomplish this, we initialize the BX register as a *pointer* to the first entry in the message table (statement 630). Note the use of the special assembler *operator*, OFFSET. It provides us with the *offset address* of the label MSG0. We then multiply the input parameter by 30 and add it to this pointer (statements 640–650). This results in the BX register pointing to the appropriate message-table entry. We then call a subroutine to display the message on the screen and return to DOS via an intersegment RET.

Two subroutines as well as a BIOS routine are actually used to display the message on the screen. The primary subroutine, DISPLAY, is coded in statements 750–900. It is called from the main program with the BX register pointing to the message to be displayed. This subroutine assumes that the message is 30 characters long. This value is loaded into the CX register so that a LOOP instruction can be used to repeat a section of code once for each character in the message. Each time through the loop (statements 810–840), the next character in the message is fetched to the AL register and displayed by a call to subroutine DISPCHAR. The BX register is used as the message pointer and is incremented by one after each character is displayed. Once the message has been displayed, we must position the display cursor on the leftmost column of the next line on the screen. This is accomplished by "displaying" the ASCII control characters *carriage return* (0DH) and *line feed* (0AH).

Subroutine DISPCHAR (statements 920–1030) is called to display the character in the AL register on the screen. Note that we save the BX register on the stack at the beginning of DISPCHAR and restore it before returning. This is necessary because BX is used in one manner by the caller of DISPCHAR and is used by DISPCHAR itself in another manner. To actually get the character onto the screen, DISPCHAR calls the *video driver program* within the BIOS. We mentioned earlier that the BIOS contained various routines for controlling i/o devices and that these routines were accessible through different interrupt type codes. Some of the more commonly used BIOS routines are listed in Table 4-3, along with the

Table 4-3. BIOS Routines

Invoke via	Input Requirements	Registers Altered	Output/Results
INT 10H	DISPLAY OUTPUT AH=0, AL=mode: AL=0: 40×25 bw AL=1: 40×25 color AL=2: 80×25 bw AL=3: 80×25 color	AX, SI, DI, BP	Set display mode specified by AL register
	AH=2, BH=0, DH=row, DL=column	AX, SI, DI, BP	Set cursor on screen to position specified. Row 0, column 0 is upper left corner
	AH=14, BX=0, AL=character	AX, SI, DI, BP	Display character specified on screen at current cursor position and advance cursor
INT 13H	DISKETTE I/O		(See Chapter 8)
INT 14H	SERIAL I/O		(See Chapter 7)
INT 16H	KEYBOARD INPUT		
	AH=0	AX	Read character from keyboard into AL reg
	AH=1	AX	Set ZF=0 if any key has been struck, otherwise ZF=1
	AH=2	AX	Return shift key status in the bits of the AL register: Bit 7 = insert key Bit 6 = caps lock Bit 5 = num lock Bit 4 = scroll lock Bit 3 = alt shift Bit 2 = ctl shift Bit 1 = left shift Bit 0 = right shift
INT 17H	PRINTER OUTPUT		
	AH=0, DX=0, AL=character	AH	Print character specified in AL reg
	AH=1, DX=0	AH	Initialize printer
	AH=2, DX=0	AH	Return printer status in the bits of the AH register: Bit 7 = 1 if busy Bit 6 = acknowledge signal Bit 5 = 1 if out of paper Bit 4 = select signal Bit 3 = 1 if error Bits 2–1 = unused Bit 0 = 1 if timeout

required calling conventions. For DISPCHAR, we use interrupt type code 10H with a function code of 14 in AH. The BX register must be set to zero, and the character to display is assumed to be in AL.

CREATING THE PROGRAM

A basic line-editing utility, called EDLIN is included with DOS by IBM. Using this program, type in the statements shown in Fig. 4-7, and create a source file named MESSAGE.ASM. (Instructions for using the EDLIN program will be found in the IBM DOS manual.)

Now load in the assembler program with the command ASM. The assembler will prompt you for the name of the source file. You should reply with the name MESSAGE; the assembler will assume the filename extension "ASM." The assembler will now prompt for the name of the object file to be created. You can simply reply with the ENTER key, as this will cause a default name of MESSAGE.OBJ to be used. In a similar fashion, reply to the next two prompts with just the ENTER key. After you have replied to all the prompts, the assembly process begins.

During the assembly process, the source file MESSAGE.ASM will be read twice. For this reason, the assembler is known as a *two-pass* assembler. The assembler determines the location and type attributes of each label in the program during the first pass. The object-code file is actually created during the second pass. Errors may be detected on either pass and will be listed on the display. If an error message is given, use the EDLIN program to correct the error in the source file and then run the assembly again.

A successful assembly will result in the creation of the object file MESSAGE.OBJ. Although the file contains all of our program instructions in machine-readable form, it is not in a format that can be loaded into memory by DOS. At this time, we must use the linker program (LINK) to convert the object file into an execution file. Like EDLIN, LINK and instructions for its use are included with IBM's DOS.

At first glance, the LINK program with its many features and options appears complex and unwieldy. For our purposes, however, it is actually very easy to use. Invoke the program by typing in the command LINK. The linker will prompt you for the name of the object file(s) that will serve as its input. Reply with the name MESSAGE; the linker will assume a filename extension of "OBJ." The linker will now prompt you for the name of the "run file"; reply again with the name MESSAGE. The linker will automatically add the extension name "EXE" onto the run-file name. You can reply to each of the subsequent seven prompts by simply pressing the ENTER key. The linker begins processing after the last prompt has been answered.

```
A>ASM
The IBM Personal Computer Assembler
Version 1.00 (C)Copyright IBM Corp 1981

Source filename [.ASM]: MESSAGE
Object filename [MESSAGE.OBJ]:
Source listing  [NUL.LST]:
Cross reference [NUL.CRF]:

Warning Severe
Errors  Errors
O       O

A>LINK
IBM Personal Computer Linker
Version 1.00 (C) Copyright IBM Corp 1981
Object Modules: MESSAGE
Run File: MESSAGE
List File [MESSAGE.MAP] :
Libraries [ ] :
Publics [No]:
Line Numbers [No]:
Stack size [Object file stack]:
Load Low [Yes]:
DSAllocation [No]:

A>TYPE MESSAGE.MAP

 Start  Stop   Length  Name             Class

 00000H 0005BH 005CH   CODE             CODE
 00060H 0022AH 01CBH   DATA             DATA
 00230H 0032FH 0100H   STACK            STACK

Program entry point at 0000:0000

A>
```

Fig. 4-8. Assemble-link procedure.

The linker reads in the MESSAGE.OBJ file and creates the MESSAGE.EXE file. In addition, it creates another file called MESSAGE.MAP, which contains information about the size of our program. After the linker has completed processing, we can obtain this information by entering the command.

        TYPE MESSAGE.MAP

The complete assemble-link procedure is illustrated in Fig. 4-8. Unless otherwise noted, this procedure should be used for all of the example programs that follow. You should note that the total length of each of our segments can be obtained from the map file produced by the linker.

Now that we have created our program, let us try it out. Type in the command

        MESSAGE 3

This will cause the execution file named MESSAGE.EXE to be loaded and run. The parameter "3" will be passed to the program by DOS. As a result, you should see our third message, "THIS PROGRAM WORKS----------" appear on the screen. Try out the program with several different input values. Try giving the program invalid input values and observe how they are handled.

THE BIOS ROUTINES

A central component of our message program was the BIOS routine that allowed us to display data on the screen of the computer. All programs must ultimately perform some amount of i/o, and the BIOS routines provide a convenient way of accomplishing this. Let us look at them more closely.

Table 4-3 summarizes the more commonly used BIOS routines. Notice that each input/output device type is assigned a unique interrupt code. Thus we can control the display device with an INT 10H, whereas the printer device would be accessed via an INT 17H. For each interrupt type, the AH register is used to specify the primary function to be performed. Other registers are used to specify additional information, if required. Whenever you use any of these routines, be sure to note which registers will be altered. If a register that you are using will be altered, you must save it before, and restore it after, the BIOS call.

Suppose we want to modify the message program so that, instead of expecting an input parameter, it waits for an input value to be typed on the keyboard. This can be accomplished simply by deleting statements 390-440 and 510–540. Replace statement 550, which obtains the input value, with the following two statements:

```
MOV AH,0   ;FUNCTION = READ CHARACTER
INT 16H    ;CALL BIOS KEYBOARD ROUTINE
```

Now assemble and link the modified program. Run it by typing in the execution-file name. The computer should now be waiting for you to strike a key. Hit the "1" key. You should receive message number 1, "8088 PROGRAMMING IS FUN-------."

ASSEMBLER OPERATORS

In the example of Fig. 4-7, we introduced the concept of an *assembler operator*. The 8088 assembler operators are listed in Table 4-4. They are

Table 4-4. Assembler Operators

Operator	Function
OFFSET	Extracts the offset address component of a label.
SEG	Extracts the segment address component of a label.
PTR	Preceded by either BYTE, WORD, NEAR, or FAR to override the type attribute of a label.
SHORT	Forces the "short" format for intrasegment direct jump target addressing.

used to extract or modify the attributes of a label that we wish to reference. Normally, when the assembler encounters a label reference, it uses the defined attributes of the label to assemble the statement. For example, if we define the label SLOT as:

```
SLOT DW 28
```

then the statement:

```
MOV AX,SLOT
```

will assemble into an instruction that fetches into AX the word at the memory location symbolically defined as SLOT. Suppose, however, that we wish to load into AX the offset address of this memory location instead of its contents. In this case, we would use the operator OFFSET to extract the offset address attribute of the label SLOT. The statement would read as follows:

```
MOV AX,OFFSET SLOT
```

In a similar fashion, we can use the operator SEG to extract the segment address attribute of a label, e.g.:

```
MOV AX,SEG SLOT
```

This is the value that must be in the appropriate segment register when the label is used. Note that if a label is defined on a segment definition statement, then any reference to that label automatically references the segment address (see statements 4 and 17 of Fig. 4-6).

A more sophisticated assembler operator is the PTR operator. It is used to override the defined type attribute of a label. For example, suppose we wish to access the byte at the memory location defined as SLOT above. If we attempt to use the statement:

```
MOV AL,SLOT
```

the assembler will give us an error, stating that we are trying to reference a *word* variable as if it were a *byte*. The correct approach is as follows:

```
        MOV AL,BYTE PTR SLOT
```

In this statement, we are requesting the assembler to override the type attribute of the label SLOT to BYTE. The PTR operator can be used to force a type attribute of either BYTE or WORD for data variables; it can also be used to force a type attribute of NEAR or FAR for program labels. For example, the statement:

```
        JMP FAR PTR STEP9
```

will cause an intersegment jump to label STEP9 to be assembled, even though STEP9 may have been defined as a NEAR label (i.e., within a NEAR procedure).

Some instructions actually *require* the use of the PTR operator. For example, suppose we wish to move the constant value 5 into a memory location pointed to by the BX register. We cannot write the statement as:

```
        MOV [BX],5
```

because the assembler would not know whether to generate a byte or word move instruction. This statement must be coded as either:

```
        MOV BYTE PTR [BX],5
```

or:

```
        MOV WORD PTR [BX],5
```

depending on whether we wish to move a byte or a word.

The SHORT operator is used to force the short format of intrasegment jump target addressing. Most of the time, unconditional jumps to labels will be within the same segment. They will therefore be assembled using the intrasegment direct addressing mode (refer back to Fig. 3-24). As you

```
HI:             . . . . .       . . . . .
                . . . . .       . . . . .
                . . . . .       . . . . .
                JMP             HI              ;ASSEMBLER KNOWS TO
        ;                                       ...USE SHORT FORMAT

                . . . . .       . . . . .
                . . . . .       . . . . .
                . . . . .       . . . . .
                JMP             SHORT HELLO     ;MUST TELL
        ;                                       ...ASSEMBLER TO
        ;                                       ...USE SHORT FORMAT
                . . . . .       . . . . .
                . . . . .       . . . . .
HELLO:          . . . . .       . . . . .
                . . . . .       . . . . .
```

Fig. 4-9. Use of the short operator.

may recall, there is a byte-saving format of this mode, known as "short," that can be used when the jump target is within a narrow range of the JMP instruction itself. If you code a JMP instruction to a label which *precedes* it in the source file, then the assembler will know whether it is within range for a "short" jump and will act accordingly. If, however, you code a JMP instruction to a label which has not yet been defined, then the assembler cannot determine whether it is within "short" range or not. In this case, the assembler will always use the normal, 16-bit direct addressing mode *unless* you override with the SHORT operator. Use the SHORT operator when jumping to a label that you know is only a few instructions further down in the program, as shown in Fig. 4-9.

CHAPTER 5

The PC System Board

The *system board* of the IBM Personal Computer contains the 8088 micro-processor chip, ROM chips that contain the BIOS, some amount of main memory, and several other support chips. An understanding of the organi-zation of the system board, coupled with our growing knowledge of 8088 assembler language, will allow us to exercise a fine degree of control over the entire microcomputer system.

THE BUS CONCEPT

An overview of the system board is shown in Fig. 5-1. The heart of the board is, of course, the 8088 microprocessor. It is contained in a single integrated circuit that has 40 pins. By sending and receiving electrical sig-nals over these pins, the 8088 communicates with its environment. For example, if the processor wants to read the contents of memory at location 123H, it will emit this value on the address pins. Control signals from other pins will be emitted to indicate that a *read from memory* is desired. The support logic on the system board must decode these signals and route the request to the appropriate memory chip. The resulting data must then be fed back into the 8088 within a specific time period.

To complicate matters, the same pins are used to emit address informa-tion and to send or receive data. A timing scheme is employed to determine how to interpret the contents of these pins at any specific moment. Such a scheme is referred to as *multiplexing.* A primary function of the system board is to *demultiplex* and buffer the information that flows into and out of these pins. Once this has been done, we have available separate sets of signal lines for address and data. These are referred to as the *address bus* and the *data bus*, respectively. Another chip on the system board, the *8288 Bus Controller*, decodes and buffers the signals from the control pins into the *control bus*.

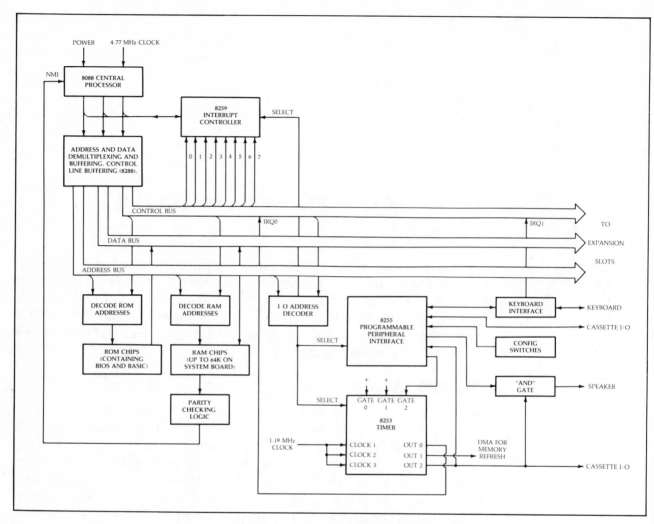

Fig. 5-1.   The system board.

Taken together, the address, data, and control buses form the "spinal cord" of the microcomputer system. Any device or component that must communicate with the central processor (8088) can do so by simply tying in to these buses. Each of the five expansion slots on the system board is prewired to the buses. As a result, an adapter card plugged into any of these slots has immediate access to the processor. The information carried by each bus is outlined in Table 5-1.

MAIN MEMORY SUPPORT

Fig. 5-1 illustrates how main memory is supported by the system board. Several logic chips are used to decode the contents of the address bus. For

Table 5-1.   The Personal-Computer Buses

Bus	Information Carried
Data	8-bit data byte going to or from i/o devices and memory.
Address	20-bit physical address used to select a specific memory location. The low-order 8 or 16 bits may also be used to select a specific i/o address.
Control	Consists of several discrete signals, including: 1. Memory read 2. Memory write 3. I/o read 4. I/o write 5. Interrupt requests (8 levels)

addresses within a specific range, a bank of ROM (read-only memory) chips is enabled. Addresses within a different range are decoded and used to select RAM (random-access, or read/write, memory). Read-only memory is mapped to the highest addresses within the one-megabyte address space of the 8088, whereas RAM starts at the lowest address (i.e., zero). This is illustrated by the system memory map of Fig. 5-2. Note that special logic

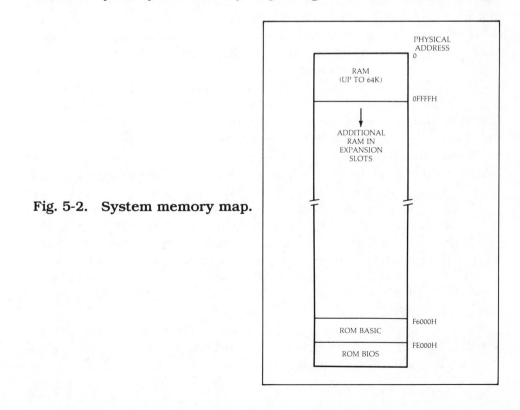

Fig. 5-2.   System memory map.

has been included to detect parity errors in read/write memory. Such errors are reported to the processor via its *nonmaskable interrupt* input, NMI.

We normally think of main memory as being uniquely controlled by the central processor. That is, the program running in the processor determines when and where to read from, or write into, memory. This is most certainly a workable view, but it does have disadvantages. For example, consider the task of reading a large block of data from a disk drive into memory. Using the conventional view of memory, we would write a program loop. Each time through the loop we would read a byte from the appropriate input port into a register, and then store the contents of the register into memory. Two other registers would also be used: one to control the number of loop iterations and the other to act as a pointer into the memory block being filled. Here the processor is simply being used as a middleman, moving the data from the i/o device to main memory. This can be considered a waste of the processor's time (after all, it should be *computing*). Such inefficiency can be avoided by providing an alternate mechanism for controlling main memory. This alternate mechanism is known as *direct memory access*, or DMA for short.

The system board provides a DMA mechanism in the form of the *8237 DMA Controller* chip. (Because of its complexity, the DMA mechanism has not been shown in Fig. 5-1.) To use DMA, the processor programs this chip with an *iteration count* and a *memory start address*. The i/o device is then commanded to begin the read (or write) operation. For each byte to be read (or written), the i/o device sends a *data request* signal to the DMA controller. The DMA controller then takes control of the address and data buses away from the central processor and uses them to effect the data transfer. This mechanism allows the processor to start an i/o operation and then do somthing else while the operation is taking place.

The 8237 chip provides four *channels* of DMA; i.e., four independent DMA operations can be programmed and can take place at the same time. One of these channels is constantly in use to provide *memory refresh* to the RAM chips. Memory refresh is necessary because the RAM chips can hold data for only a short time before they "forget" it. The DMA channel is programmed to read from each memory location and then write back to it in a continuous, never-ending loop. In this way, each memory location is refreshed just before it "forgets" its contents. The other three DMA channels are available for specific i/o devices. One of these is used by the diskette interface.

For more information about the DMA mechanism, consult the *IBM Personal Computer Technical Reference,* as well as Intel's product specification for the 8237 DMA Controller.

SYSTEM SUPPORT DEVICES

In addition to the 8237, the system board utilizes several other control chips to provide basic system functions. The most important of these are the 8259 Interrupt Controller chip, the 8255 Programmable Peripheral Interface chip, and the 8253 Timer chip. Fig. 5-1 shows that each of these chips is connected to the system as an i/o device (connections between these devices and the data bus have been omitted for clarity). The processor is therefore capable of accessing and controlling them via its i/o ports. Table 5-2 lists the actual i/o port addresses for each control chip. Note that more than one i/o port is allocated to each control chip.

Each of these chips is actually a microprocessor in its own right. Unlike the 8088, however, these microprocessors have been designed to accomplish very specific tasks. The 8253, for example, is capable of counting and/or timing events that can be signaled either by hardware or software. It can also be used to keep time and thus serve as a "clock."

Although their capabilities are limited and specific, these chips are nonetheless *programmable.* Each contains one or more internal registers. We can program a control chip by writing values into its registers (via 8088 OUT instructions to the appropriate port addresses). Similarly, the status of a chip can be obtained by reading the contents of its registers (8088 IN instruction). Armed with an understanding of how these chips operate, we will be able to control them from within our 8088 assembler-language programs.

Table 5-2. I/O Addresses for System Support Devices

8259 Interrupt Controller	
20H	Interrupt Command Register
21H	Interrupt Mask Register
8253 Timer	
40H	Timer Channel 0 Latch Register Access Port
41H	Timer Channel 1 Latch Register Access Port
42H	Timer Channel 2 Latch Register Access Port
43H	Timer Command Register
8255 Programmable Peripheral Interface	
60H	Input Port "PA"
61H	In/Output Port "PB"
62H	Input Port "PC"
63H	8255 Command Register (Set to 99H)

THE 8259 INTERRUPT CONTROLLER

The 8259 Interrupt Controller chip provides a vital support service for the central processor (8088). We have already seen how external events can be signaled to the central processor via its interrupt mechanism. In a typical Personal Computer system, such interrupt signals can originate from several different places (i.e., keyboard, disk drive, etc.). The 8088, however, has only one input line on which to receive an interrupt signal. The 8259 chip is therefore employed to manage the various interrupt sources and present a single, controllable interrupt signal to the central processor.

As configured for use in the PC, the 8259 chip can accept up to eight independent interrupt signals, numbered 0 through 7. For each interrupt it receives, the 8259 can present an interrupt signal to the 8088. Furthermore, it presents to the 8088 a unique *interrupt type code* for each of the eight interrupt sources. This allows us to assign a unique interrupt-service routine to each different interrupt source. The eight signal inputs to the 8259 are wired onto the control bus so that any device tied into the bus system can access this interrupt mechanism. On the control bus, the signals are named IRQ0 through IRQ7.

Because each signal is independent, provision must be made for the possibility of two or more signals occurring at the same time. The 8259 manages such an event by holding on to the secondary interrupt(s) while the processor services the first. When that interrupt has been serviced, the next one is signaled to the processor. For events that occur at exactly the same moment, the 8259 passes them to the processor in a *priority* order, where interrupt source 0 has the highest priority and interrupt source 7 has the lowest. One very important consequence of this scheme is that the processor (8088) must indicate to the controller (8259) when it has completed the servicing of each interrupt. This must be kept in mind whenever an interrupt-service routine is written.

Because it has been designed for use in many different applications, the 8259 is an extremely complex chip. Fortunately for us, however, most of this complexity is handled by the BIOS, which programs the proper configuration information into the 8259 on power-up. The 8259 is thus configured to signal interrupt type codes 08H–0FH to correspond with interrupt sources 0–7. The standard device allocations for each of these interrupt sources are listed in Table 5-3. Note that the two highest-priority interrupts, IRQ0 and IRQ1, are wired directly on the system board. The rest of the interrupt sources are obtained from adapter cards plugged into the expansion slots.

From our point of view, programming the 8259 consists of two basic actions. See Fig. 5-3. First, we can enable or disable each interrupt source independently by writing a value into the *interrupt mask register,* or IMR.

Table 5-3. Interrupt Sources

8259 Input	Type Code	Device
IRQ0	08H	Timer (Channel 0)
IRQ1	09H	Keyboard
IRQ2	0AH	Color Graphics Interface
IRQ3	0BH	Unused
IRQ4	0CH	Serial (RS-232) Interface
IRQ5	0DH	Unused
IRQ6	0EH	Diskette
IRQ7	0FH	Printer

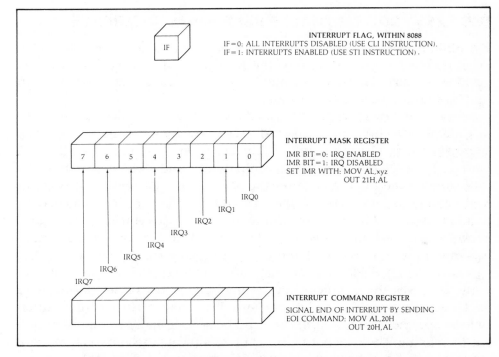

Fig. 5-3. Controlling the interrupt mechanism.

The IMR is a one-byte register within the 8259 that we can access via i/o port 21H. Each bit in the IMR corresponds to the interrupt source with its bit number (i.e., bit 0—IRQ0, bit 1—IRQ1, etc). If a bit in the IMR is 0, then its corresponding interrupt source is enabled. A signal appearing on that input to the 8259 will cause an interrupt to be sent to the 8088. If the IMR bit is 1, then the interrupt source is disabled (or *masked*) and cannot generate an interrupt. For example, suppose we wish to disable interrupts from all devices except the keyboard. This would be accomplished as follows:

```
MOV AL,0FDH
OUT 21H,AL
```

Keep in mind that the state of the *interrupt flag* within the 8088 will ultimately determine whether or not any interrupt signal is received.

The second 8259 programming action that we must be concerned with is the signaling of the end of an interrupt service routine. This is accomplished by sending the "end of interrupt" (EOI) command, represented by 20H, to the interrupt command register within the 8259. Coincidentally, this one-byte register is accessed via i/o port 20H. That is all there is to controlling the interrupt mechanism! A complete example will appear later in this chapter.

THE 8255 PROGRAMMABLE PERIPHERAL INTERFACE

The 8255 is a general-purpose i/o interface chip that can be configured in many different ways. It is used on the system board to support a variety of devices and signals. These include the keyboard, speaker, configuration switches, and several other signals.

The chip contains three ports, called PA, PB, and PC. These are mapped to i/o addresses 60H, 61H, and 62H, respectively. In addition, there is a one-byte command register on the chip, accessed via i/o address 63H. On power-up, the BIOS initializes this chip by sending a value of 99H to the command register. This configures the 8255 so that PA and PC are considered input ports and PB is considered an output port. The meaning of each port is defined in Fig. 5-4. Note that additional logic on the system board allows us to select alternate inputs to ports PA and PC by setting certain bits in output port PB. In addition, we can read back the last value that was written to port PB by performing an input operation on port PB.

Fig. 5-5 gives an example of how we might make use of this hardware to read the settings of the configuration switches. There are two configuration switches on the system board; each can be set manually to represent any one-byte value. They are normally set up to indicate the various hardware options installed in the Personal Computer system. If, for example, our program needed to know how many disk drives were attached to the system, it could examine the two high-order bits of switch 1. This is accomplished by the program instructions of Fig. 5-5. Note that to enable the configuration-switch information onto port PA, we must first set bit 7 of port PB.

THE KEYBOARD

The system board provides an interface to the Personal Computer keyboard via the interrupt mechanism and ports PA and PB of the 8255 chip. This hardware is normally supported and controlled by programs running in the BIOS so that we do not have to be concerned with it. We simply

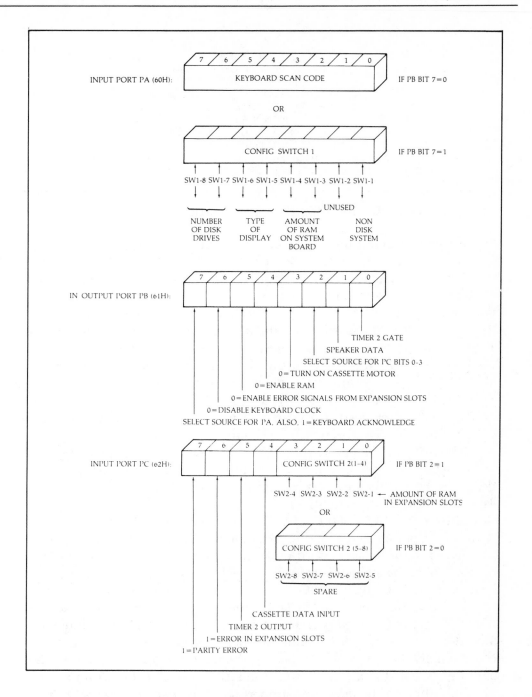

Fig. 5-4. 8255 port allocations.

access the keyboard via BIOS INT 16H, as shown in the last chapter. By understanding the hardware, however, we can write our own keyboard-support software, with certain interesting advantages.

```
        IN      AL,61H      ;GET PRESENT VALUE OF PORT PB
        OR      AL,80H      ;FORCE BIT 7 ON
        OUT     61H,AL      ;SET PORT PB BIT 7 = 1 ;
                             CONFIG SW1 NOW GATED TO PORT PA
        IN      AL,60H      ;READ PORT PA = CONFIG SWITCH 1
        NOT     AL          ;INVERT BITS
        MOV     CL,6        ;SET UP SHIFT AMOUNT
        SHR     AL,CL       ;ISOLATE BITS 7,6 OF AL
  ; NOW AL = NUMBER OF DISK DRIVES ATTACHED TO SYSTEM,
  ; AS OBTAINED FROM CONFIG SWITCH 1, POSITIONS 8,7.
```

Fig. 5-5.   Reading the configuration switches.

Within the keyboard itself is a small microprocessor that scans for and detects any change in state of the keys. This processor receives its basic power and clock signals from the system board. We can disable the clock signal going to the keyboard by setting bit 6 of port PB to 0. This will prevent the keyboard from operating. In addition, we can send an *acknowledge signal* to the keyboard by setting bit 7 of port PB to 1. To ensure that the keyboard is properly enabled, we must set bits 7 and 6 of port PB to 0 and 1, respectively. In this state, the keyboard will generate an interrupt signal (IRQ1) whenever any key is depressed or released. It will then transmit a one-byte *scan code* to the system board and wait for the acknowledge signal to be returned. The scan code will be a number between 1 and 83 that uniquely identifies which key changed state (there are 83 keys on the keyboard). The high-order bit (bit 7) of the scan code indicates whether the key was depressed or released. It will be 0 if the key was depressed, and it will be 1 if the key was released. Fig. 5-6 identifies the scan code associated with each key on the keyboard.

It is the responsibility of the keyboard-support software to detect the keyboard interrupt and to respond to it as follows. First, the scan-code value transmitted to the system board must be obtained by reading from 8255 port PA. Then, the acknowledge signal must be sent back to the keyboard by momentarily setting bit 7 of port PB. The scan code itself may be interpreted in any manner desired. Thus, the meaning of each key can be defined, or even dynamically changed, by software. A more important consideration, however, stems from the fact that the keyboard interrupt occurs *asynchronously* with respect to the main program running in the computer. What this means is that the striking of a key (and its subsequent handling by the keyboard-support software) can occur at any time, and it is totally independent of when the main program may wish to receive keyboard input. Our keyboard support routine is therefore required to *buffer,* or save, any keyboard input that it receives. To accomplish this, we employ a "first-in, first-out" buffer, also referred to as a *circular queue.*

```
                     FUNCTION KEYS (LEFT SECTION)

     "F1"—59              "F5"—63              "F9"—67
     "F2"—60              "F6"—64              "F10"—68
     "F3"—61              "F7"—65
     "F4"—62              "F8"—66


        LETTER, NUMBER, AND PUNCTUATION KEYS (CENTER SECTION)

     "1"—2                "Y"—21               "'"—40
     "2"—3                "U"—22               "`"—41
     "3"—4                "I"—23               "\"—43
     "4"—5                "O"—24               "Z"—44
     "5"—6                "P"—25               "X"—45
     "6"—7                "["—26               "C"—46
     "7"—8                "]"—27               "V"—47
     "8"—9                "A"—30               "B"—48
     "9"—10               "S"—31               "N"—49
     "0"—11               "D"—32               "M"—50
     "-"—12               "F"—33               ","—51
     "="—13               "G"—34               "."—52
     "Q"—16               "H"—35               "/"—53
     "W"—17               "J"—36               "*" (PrtSc)—55
     "E"—18               "K"—37               SPACE BAR —57
     "R"—19               "L"—38
     "T"—20               ";"—39


                 NUMERIC KEYPAD AREA (LEFT SECTION)

     "7"—71               "5"—76               "3"—81
     "8"—72               "6"—77               "0"—82
     "9"—73               "+"—78               "."—83
     "—"—74               "1"—79
     "4"—75               "2"—80


              CONTROL KEYS (CENTER AND LEFT SECTIONS)

     Esc        —1        Tab        —15       Right SHIFT —54
     Backspace —14        Enter      —28       Alt         —56
     Num Lock  —69        Ctrl       —29       Caps Lock   —58
     Scroll Lock —70      Left SHIFT —42
```

Fig. 5-6. Keyboard scan codes (listed in decimal).

Scan codes received from the keyboard are converted into the appropriate ASCII character codes and then placed onto this queue. When the main program wishes to obtain keyboard input, it calls an auxiliary routine within the keyboard-support software. This routine takes the characters off the queue, *in the order in which they were received,* and passes them to the main program. The size of the queue determines the maximum number of characters that can be buffered at any time. This represents the number of keystrokes that you can "type ahead" of the main program.

In Fig. 5-7, a complete program that sets up and utilizes its own key-board-support software is presented. The program is kept relatively simple by omitting features normally handled by BIOS keyboard support, such as upper/lower-case alphabetics, "shift" and "shift-lock" keys, and special control-key combinations. The main program consists of two parts. Part one modifies the interrupt-service–routine address table to point to our own keyboard interrupt routine. It is also responsible for initializing the necessary hardware interfaces by sending commands to the 8259 and 8255 chips. Once this has been accomplished, we enter part two, a simple loop that reads keyboard input and displays it on the screen. The other

```
00030 ; EXAMPLE OF CUSTOM KEYBOARD SUPPORT SOFTWARE
00040 ;
00050 STACK     SEGMENT PARA STACK 'STACK'
00060           DB       256 DUP (0)       ;256 BYTES OF STACK SPACE
00070 STACK     ENDS
00080 ;
00090 DATA      SEGMENT PARA PUBLIC 'DATA'
00100 BUFFER    DB       10 DUP (0)         ;TEN BYTE KEYBOARD BUFFER
00110 BUFPTR1 DW         0                  ;POINTS TO START OF BUFFER
00120 BUFPTR2 DW         0                  ;POINTS TO END OF BUFFER
00130 ; NOTE: WHEN BUFPTR1 = BUFPTR2 , THEN THE BUFFER IS EMPTY.
00140 ; SCANTABLE CONVERTS SCAN CODES RECEIVED FROM THE KEYBOARD
00150 ;   INTO THEIR CORRESPONDING ASCII CHARACTER CODES:
00160 SCANTABLE DB     0,0,'1234567890-=',8,0
00170           DB     'QWERTYUIOP[]',0DH,0
00180           DB     'ASDFGHJKL;',0,0,0,0
00190           DB     'ZXCVBNM,./',0,0,0
00200           DB     ' ',0,0,0,0,0,0,0,0,0,0,0,0,0,0
00210           DB     '789-456+1230.'
00220 DATA      ENDS
00230 ;
00240 CODE      SEGMENT PARA PUBLIC 'CODE'
00250 START     PROC    FAR
00260 ;
00270 ; STANDARD PROGRAM PROLOGUE
00280 ;
00290           ASSUME  CS:CODE
00300           PUSH    DS        ;SAVE PSP SEG ADDR
00310           MOV     AX,0
00320           PUSH    AX        ;SAVE RET ADDR OFFSET (PSP+0)
00330           MOV     AX,DATA
00340           MOV     DS,AX     ;ESTABLISH DATA SEG ADDRESSABILITY
00350           ASSUME  DS:DATA
00360 ;
00370 ; PART1: SETUP OUR OWN KEYBOARD INTERRUPT SERVICE ROUTINE
00380 ;
00390           CLI               ;DISABLE ALL INTERRUPTS
00400           MOV     AX,0
00410           MOV     ES,AX     ;POINT EXTRA SEGMENT AT THE...
00420 ;                 ...INTERRUPT SERVICE ROUTINE ADDRESS TABLE
00430           MOV     DI,24H  ;OFFSET OF ENTRY FOR TYPE CODE 09H
00440           MOV     AX,OFFSET KBINT ;OFFSET OF OUR SERVICE ROUTINE
00445           CLD                     ;SET 'FORWARD' STRING OPERATIONS
00450           STOSW               ;PLACE IT IN THE TABLE
00460           MOV     AX,CS         ;SEG OF OUR SERVICE ROUTINE
00470           STOSW               ;PLACE IT IN THE TABLE
00480           MOV     AL,0FCH ;ENABLE TIMER AND KYBD IRUPTS
00490           OUT     21H,AL  ;WRITE INTERRUPT MASK REGISTER
00500           STI               ;ENABLE INTERRUPTS TO THE 8088
00510 ;
```

Fig. 5-7. Custom keyboard-support program.

Continued on next page.

```
00520 ; PART2: READ FROM KEYBOARD AND DISPLAY CHARS ON SCREEN
00530 ;
00540 FOREVER: CALL    KBGET    ;WAIT FOR A CHARACTER FROM THE KEYBOARD
00550          PUSH    AX       ;SAVE THE CHARACTER
00560          CALL    DISPCHAR ;DISPLAY THE CHARACTER RECEIVED
00570          POP     AX       ;RESTORE THE CHARACTER
00580          CMP     AL,ODH   ;WAS IT A CARRIAGE RETURN?
00590          JNZ     FOREVER  ;BRANCH IF NOT
00600          MOV     AL,OAH   ;YES IT WAS, WE MUST ALSO DISPLAY...
00610          CALL    DISPCHAR ;...A LINE FEED!
00620          JMP     FOREVER  ;STAY IN THIS LOOP FOREVER
00630 ;
00640 ; CALL KBGET TO WAIT FOR A CHARACTER TO BE RECEIVED FROM
00650 ;  THE KEYBOARD.  THE CHARACTER IS RETURNED IN REG AL.
00660 KBGET    PROC    NEAR
00670          PUSH    BX                ;SAVE REGISTER BX
00680          CLI                       ;DISABLE INTERRUPTS
00690          MOV     BX,BUFPTR1        ;START OF BUFFER
00700          CMP     BX,BUFPTR2        ;IS BUFFER EMPTY?
00710          JNZ     KBGET2            ;->NO
00720          STI                       ;RE-ENABLE INTERRUPTS
00730          POP     BX                ;RESTORE REGISTER BX
00740          JMP     KBGET             ;WAIT UNTIL SOMETHING IN BUFFER
00750 ; THERE IS SOMETHING IN THE BUFFER, GET IT :
00760 KBGET2:  MOV     AL,[BUFFER+BX]    ;GET CHAR AT BUFFER START
00770          INC     BX                ;INCREMENT BUFFER START
00780          CMP     BX,10             ;HAVE WE WRAPPED AROUND?
00790          JC      KBGET3            ;BRANCH IF NOT
00800          MOV     BX,0              ;YES, WRAP AROUND
00810 KBGET3:  MOV     BUFPTR1,BX        ;INDICATE NEW START OF BUFFER
00820          STI                       ;RE-ENABLE INTERRUPTS
00830          POP     BX                ;RESTORE REGISTER BX
00840          RET                       ;RETURN FROM KBGET
00850 KBGET    ENDP
00860 ;
00870 ; KBINT IS OUR OWN KEYBOARD INTERRUPT SERVICE ROUTINE:
00880 ;
00890 KBINT    PROC    FAR
00900          PUSH    BX       ;SAVE ALL ALTERED REGISTERS!!
00910          PUSH    AX
00920 ;
00930 ; READ THE KEYBOARD DATA AND SEND THE ACKNOWLEDGE SIGNAL:
00940 ;
00950          IN      AL,60H   ;READ KEYBOARD INPUT
00960          PUSH    AX       ;SAVE KEYBOARD INPUT
00970          IN      AL,61H   ;READ 8255 PORT PB
00980          OR      AL,80H   ;SET KEYBOARD ACKNOWLEDGE SIGNAL
00990          OUT     61H,AL   ;SEND KEYBOARD ACKNOWLEDGE SIGNAL
01000          AND     AL,7FH   ;RESET KEYBOARD ACKNOWLEDGE SIGNAL
01010          OUT     61H,AL   ;RESTORE ORIGINAL 8255 PORT PB
01020 ;
```

Fig. 5-7 (cont).   Custom keyboard-support program.

Continued on next page.

```
01030 ; DECODE THE SCAN CODE RECEIVED:
01040 ;
01050           POP      AX       ;REGAIN THE KEYBOARD INPUT (AL)
01060           TEST     AL,80H   ;IS IT A KEY BEING RELEASED?
01070           JNZ      KBINT2   ;BRANCH IF YES, WE IGNORE THESE
01080           MOV      BX,OFFSET SCANTABLE ;SCAN CODE - ASCII TABLE
01090           XLATB             ;CONVERT THE SCAN CODE TO AN ASCII CHAR
01100           CMP      AL,0     ;IS IT A VALID ASCII KEY?
01110           JZ       KBINT2   ;BRANCH IF NOT
01120 ;
01130 ; PLACE THE ASCII CHARACTER INTO THE BUFFER:
01140 ;
01150           MOV      BX,BUFPTR2        ;GET POINTER TO END OF BUFFER
01160           MOV      [BUFFER+BX],AL    ;PLACE CHAR IN BUFFER AT END
01170           INC      BX                ;INCREMENT BUFFER END
01180           CMP      BX,10             ;HAVE WE WRAPPED AROUND?
01190           JC       KBINT3            ;BRANCH IF NOT
01200           MOV      BX,0              ;YES, WRAP AROUND
01210 KBINT3:   CMP      BX,BUFPTR1        ;IS BUFFER FULL?
01220           JZ       KBINT2            ;BRANCH IF YES, WE LOSE THIS CHAR
01230           MOV      BUFPTR2,BX        ;INDICATE NEW END OF BUFFER
01240 ;
01250 ; NOW INDICATE "END OF INTERRUPT" TO THE INTERRUPT CONTROLLER:
01260 ;
01270 KBINT2:   MOV      AL,20H            ;SEND "EOI" COMMAND...
01280           OUT      20H,AL            ;...TO 8259 COMMAND REGISTER
01290           POP      AX                ;RESTORE ALL ALTERED REGISTERS!!
01300           POP      BX
01310           IRET                       ;RETURN FROM INTERRUPT
01320 KBINT     ENDP
01330 ;
01340 ; SUBROUTINE TO DISPLAY A CHARACTER ON THE SCREEN.
01350 ; ENTER WITH AL = CHARACTER TO BE DISPLAYED.
01360 ; USES VIDEO INTERFACE IN BIOS.
01370 ;
01380 DISPCHAR PROC     NEAR
01390           PUSH     BX       ;SAVE BX REGISTER
01400           MOV      BX,0     ;SELECT DISPLAY PAGE 0
01410           MOV      AH,14    ;FUNCTION CODE FOR 'WRITE'
01420           INT      10H      ;CALL VIDEO DRIVER IN BIOS
01430           POP      BX       ;RESTORE BX REGISTER
01440           RET               ;RETURN TO CALLER OF 'DISPCHAR'
01450 DISPCHAR ENDP
01460 ;
01470 START     ENDP
01480 CODE      ENDS
01490           END      START
```

Fig. 5-7 (cont).   Custom keyboard-support program.

major component of the program is our custom keyboard-support software. This also consists of two parts; they are KBINT, the keyboard interrupt-service routine, and KBGET, called from the main program to obtain keyboard input.

Let us look at the program in more detail. Statements 400 through 470 set the address of our own keyboard interrupt-service routine (KBINT) into the appropriate entry in the interrupt-service—routine address table. Recall that the keyboad interrupt signal is sent to the IRQ1 input of the 8259. The 8259 has been programmed to identify this interrupt source with a type code of 09H. The correct address-table entry therefore begins at physical address 09H*4, or 00024H. Note that we disable interrupts (CLI) before altering the data in the address table. A catastrophic error could occur if an interrupt were to be received while the address table is being modified. Once the address table is modified, we program the interrupt-mask register of the 8259 to allow interrupts only from lines IRQ0 and IRQ1 (the timer and the keyboard, respectively). We then enable interrupts (STI) and enter the second part of the main program.

The second part (statements 540 through 620) is an infinite loop that calls routine KBGET to obtain characters input from the keyboard. Each character so received is echoed to the display screen by the DISPCHAR routine that we developed in the last chapter. Note the special code provided to detect the ENTER key (ASCII carriage return). This is necessary because a carriage return sent to an output device should always be followed by a line feed. If this is not done, we will find ourselves typing over the previous line of text.

If we strike a key while this loop is running, a type 09H interrupt will occur. This will cause our KBINT procedure to be activated. As you may recall, the 8088 interrupt response will also save the address of the instruction that was executing, save the flags, and disable further interrupts. The first responsibility of KBINT is to save any additional registers that it will use in servicing the interrupt (statements 900 and 910). It then reads in the scan code of the key that was depressed and sends back the acknowledge signal (statements 950 through 1010). If the scan code indicates that a key was being released (bit 7 = 1), then no further action is taken (statements 1060 and 1070). Otherwise, the XLATB instruction is used to convert the scan code into its corresponding ASCII character. The XLATB instruction requires that BX point to a translation table in the data segment. We therefore load BX with the offset address of SCANTABLE, which we have defined in our data segment. For each keyboard scan code that we wish to acknowledge, we have placed the appropriate ASCII code value into the corresponding position in SCANTABLE. Scan codes that we wish to ignore, such as those assigned to the function keys, F1—F10, are translated into a value of zero. After the translation, we test for a value of zero. If we have such a value, then the key is ignored (statements 1100 and 1110).

Assuming a valid key has been struck, we now have its ASCII code in the AL register. We must place this byte onto the circular queue so that it is available to the main program. This is accomplished by statements 1150 through 1230. The queue itself is defined in the data segment, with the name BUFFER. It has the capacity to hold up to ten keystrokes. Two pointers, named BUFPTR1 and BUFPTR2, are used to keep track of the data in the queue. They point to the beginning and end of the valid data in the queue, respectively. Data is added onto the queue by placing it at the position pointed to by BUFPTR2, and then incrementing BUFPTR2. Data is taken off the queue by removing it from the position pointed to by BUFPTR1, and then incrementing BUFPTR1. When both pointers are equal, this indicates that there is no data in the queue. When incremented past the end of the queue, each pointer "wraps around" back to the beginning of the queue. This approach, illustrated in Fig. 5-8, ensures that we always retrieve data from the queue in the same order in which it was placed onto the queue. Notice that, in our implementation, we simply ignore (lose) a character if it is received when the queue is full.

Once the data has been placed onto the queue, we complete the interrupt response by sending the "end of interrupt" signal to the 8259 (statements 1270 and 1280). We then restore all saved registers and return to the main program, at its point of interruption, via an IRET instruction.

The main program relies on the KBGET routine (statements 640 through 850) to retrieve keyboard data from the circular queue. This routine waits until there is some data in the queue (as indicated by BUFPTR1 not equal to BUFPTR2). It then fetches that data, advances BUFPTR1, and returns the data value to its caller. Note that we must disable interrupts while the queue pointers are being manipulated. If this is not done, a keyboard inter-

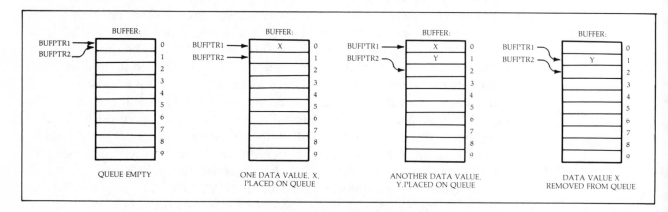

Fig. 5-8. Circular-queue operations.

rupt may occur while we are trying to take data off the queue. We cannot allow data to be placed onto the queue at the same time that it is being taken off the queue, because this could cause us to overlook a queue-full condition.

If you type in this program, assemble it, and run it, you will be able to type most characters on the keyboard and have them echoed on the display screen. The only control keys that will function are "Backspace" and "Enter." Most other control keys will be ignored. Most important, however, is the fact that the control-key combinations CONTROL-BREAK and CONTROL-ALT-DEL are totally disabled. These functions are normally detected by the BIOS keyboard support. Since we have not provided such detection in our own program, we have effectively "locked up" the machine; the only way to exit from our program is to *turn the machine off*. This demonstrates the power and control that an assembler-language programmer can exert over his computer.

THE 8253 TIMER

The 8253 Timer chip can perform a number of different timing and/or counting functions. Within the chip are three independent counters, numbered 0, 1, and 2. Each of these three *timer channels* can be programmed to operate in one of six different modes, referred to as mode 0 through mode 5. Once they have been programmed, all of the channels can perform their designated counting or timing operations simultaneously. As you can imagine, some very sophisticated operations can be performed with this device.

A block diagram of the 8253 is presented in Fig. 5-9. Note that the hardware related to each timer channel is identical. Each channel contains a 16-bit *latch* register and a 16-bit *counter* register. Each channel also has two dedicated input signals, called *clock* and *gate*, as well as an output signal, *out*. In general, we program a count value into the latch register. From there, it is transferred into the counter register. Each time a pulse appears on the clock input, the value in the counter register is decremented by one. When the counter register reaches zero, a signal is generated on the out line. The mode to which we program the timer channel will determine exactly how each of these operations takes place.

The 8253 is programmed by writing commands into its one-byte–wide *command register*. In addition, each channel has a dedicated, one-byte–wide i/o port that is used to read and write the contents of its corresponding latch register. The i/o-port addresses used by the 8253 on the system board are listed in Table 5-2 and are shown in parentheses on Fig. 5-9.

The programming of a timer channel is always initiated by writing a command to the command-register port, 43H. The format of this command

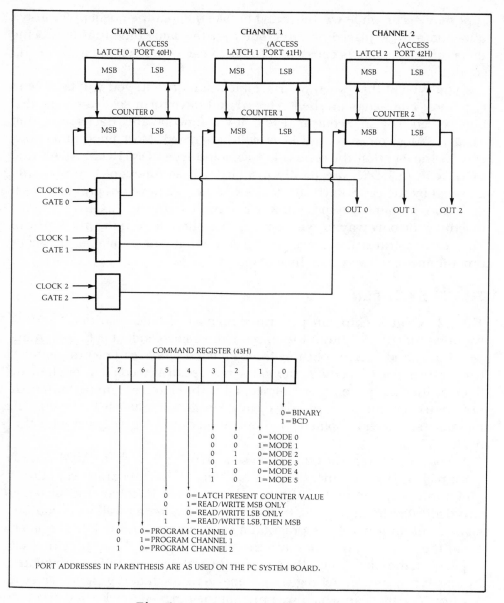

Fig. 5-9.   Block diagram of 8253.

is shown in Fig. 5-9. The two high-order bits are used to select which timer channel is being programmed. The rest of the bits in the command define how that channel will operate and how we will communicate with its latch register. Because the latch register is 16 bits wide and its access port is only 8 bits wide, we may need two i/o accesses to read or write the latch register. To access the entire latch register, we set both bits 5 and 4 in the command register to 1. We can then read the latch register by issuing two successive IN instructions, the first of which will return the least significant byte (LSB) of the latch register. The second IN instruction will return the most significant byte (MSB) of the latch register. Similarly, we can write the latch register (in LSB–MSB order) with two successive OUT instructions. If we need to access only the LSB or MSB half of the latch register, we can use a single IN or OUT instruction after selecting the desired half via bits 5 and 4 of the command register. The mode in which the timer channel will operate is set by bits 3, 2, and 1 of the command register; we will look at these in more detail shortly. Finally, bit 0 of the command register determines whether the counter register will decrement in binary or BCD format. For our purposes, we will always use binary format, and so bit 0 will always be 0.

Each of the six timer modes is described in detail in Table 5-4. For each of these modes, the signal on the clock input determines the rate at which the counter will decrement. The gate input signal can be used to enable or disable the clock signal into the counter, or it can be used to signal the start of the counting operation, depending on the mode. The result of any counting operation is a signal appearing on the out line. This signal can be

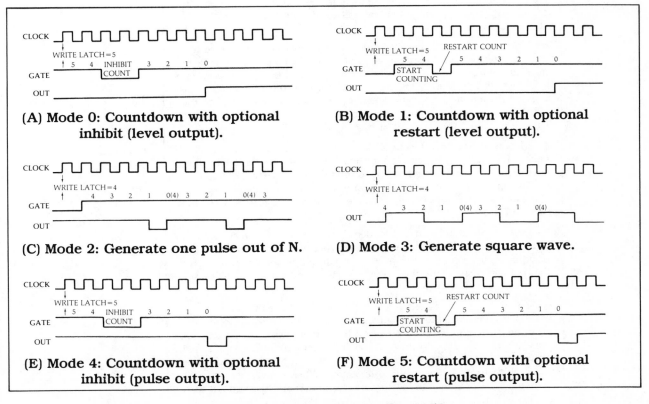

(A) Mode 0: Countdown with optional inhibit (level output).

(B) Mode 1: Countdown with optional restart (level output).

(C) Mode 2: Generate one pulse out of N.

(D) Mode 3: Generate square wave.

(E) Mode 4: Countdown with optional inhibit (pulse output).

(F) Mode 5: Countdown with optional restart (pulse output).

Fig. 5-10. Timing diagrams for 8253.

a single pulse, a constant level, or a periodically repeating signal, depending on the mode. Fig. 5-10 illustrates the operation of each mode through the use of timing diagrams. Note that modes 0 and 1 are similar to modes 4 and 5, respectively. To indicate completion of the timing event, the former provide a high level on the out line, whereas the latter provide a low pulse on the out line. Modes 2 and 3 are useful for providing periodic signals.

Table 5-4. 8253-Timer Modes

Mode	Description
0	As soon as the latch register is loaded, its contents are transferred into the counter register, the out signal goes low (0), and the counter begins decrementing. A low signal (0) on the gate input will inhibit the counting. When the counter reaches zero, the out signal will go high (1) and remain in that state. The counter will continue to decrement below zero.
1	When the latch register is loaded, its contents will be transferred to the counter register, and the out signal will go low (0). Counting will not begin until the gate input is brought high (1). If the gate input is brought low (0), the counting will stop—in this case, when the gate input is brought high again, the counter register will be *reloaded* with the original count from the latch register, and counting will resume. When the counter reaches zero, the out signal will go high and remain in that state.
2	As soon as the latch register is loaded, its contents are transferred to the counter register, the out signal goes high, and the counter begins decrementing. When the counter reaches one, the out signal goes low for one clock period. The counter register is then reloaded from the latch register, and the operation repeats. The mode will produce a 0 pulse on the out line for one clock cycle out of every N clock cycles, where N is the value loaded into the latch register.
3	This mode is identical to mode 2 except that the out signal is high for half of the total count specified by the latch register and is low for the other half. It can therefore be used to produce a square-wave signal on the out line. The frequency of the square wave will be equal to the frequency of the input clock signal, divided by the value programmed into the latch register.
4	As soon as the latch register is loaded, its contents are transferred to the counter register, the out signal goes high, and the counter begins decrementing. A low signal on the gate input will inhibit the counting. When the counter reaches zero, the out signal will go low for one clock cycle and then go back to high.
5	As soon as the latch register is loaded, its contents are transferred to the counter register, and the out signal goes high. Counting will not begin until the gate input is brought high. If the gate input is brought low (0), the counting will stop—in this case when the gate input is brought high again, the counter register will be *reloaded* with the original count from the latch register, and counting will resume. When the counter reaches zero, the out signal will go low for one clock cycle and then go back to high.

Mode 2 will provide one low pulse on the out line for every N pulses on the clock input, where N is the count value that we program into the latch register. Note that the gate input can be used to inhibit this operation temporarily. Mode 3 generates a symmetrical square wave on the out line. Its frequency will be equal to the frequency of the clock input signal, divided by the count value that we program into the latch register.

In each of these modes, the latch register acts as a holding place for the count value destined for the counter register. When operating in mode 1, 2, 3, or 5, the counter register can actually be reloaded several times from the latch register. There are cases where we might want to reverse this process and load the latch register from the counter register. Suppose we have started a timing operation and we would like to know how far it has progressed (it has not yet completed). This can be accomplished by writing a command to the command register with bits 7 and 6 selecting the timer channel to be interrogated and bits 5 and 4 both set to zero. Such a command will cause the current value of the counter register to be loaded into the latch register. Once this has been done, we can read the value out of the latch register via its access port. This operation can be performed even as the counter register is decrementing!

To be able to use the 8253 in the Personal Computer, we must understand how it has been configured on the system board. Referring to Fig. 5-1, we can see that each timer channel has been dedicated to a specific use within the PC system. The output of channel 0 is connected to the IRQ0 line and thus can be used to generate a level 0 interrupt (type code 08H). The output of channel 1 is used to issue the *data request* signal periodically to the DMA channel responsible for memory refresh. The output of channel 2 is routed to the internal speaker to generate sound effects; it can also be sampled via bit 5 of 8255 input port PC (62H).

The clock input of each channel is tied to a 1.19318-MHz signal. The period of each clock cycle is therefore $1/1.19$ MHz = 840 nanoseconds (one nanosecond = 0.000000001 second = 10^{-9} second). The gate inputs to channels 0 and 1 are tied to a positive (high) signal and are thus always enabled. We can control the gate input to channel 2 via bit 0 of 8255 output port PB (61H). Upon power-up, the BIOS initializes channel 0 to operate in mode 3 with a count value of 0000H. This is the maximum count value possible and results in 65536 counting iterations before zero is reached again. The output of channel 0 will therefore be a square wave of frequency 1.19 MHz/65536 = 18.2 Hz. A level 0 interrupt, if enabled, will thus occur 18.2 times a second, or once every 55 milliseconds. This periodic interrupt is used by the BIOS to keep track of the time of day. The BIOS maintains the time of day in 55-millisecond increments. The time-of-day clock is kept in memory as a 32-bit binary number and can be read or set by calling BIOS via INT 1AH (see Table 5-5).

Table 5-5. BIOS "Time-of-Day" Routine

Invoke via	Input Requirements	Registers Altered	Output/Results
INT 1AH	AH = 0	AX, CX, DX	Returns current value of the time of day counter: CX = Most significant word of count. DX = Least significant word of count. AL = 0, if count has not passed 24 hours since the last time it was read. Otherwise AL is not zero.
	AH = 1, CX = Most significant word of count. DX = Least significant word of count.	None	Sets the time-of-day counter to the value specified in the CX and DX registers.

Note: The time of day is counted in 55-millisecond increments.

Timer channel 1 is programmed by the BIOS to operate in mode 2. A count value of 18 is used, and so DMA memory refresh pulses are issued every 15 microseconds. This channel should never be altered, since to do so would jeopardize the integrity of our main memory. Channel 2 is available to be used in any manner we desire. If we wish to program a timer interrupt, and we do not care about the BIOS time-of-day clock, then we can reprogram channel 0. Channel 0 should not be altered, however, if disk i/o is going to be used. The disk motor timing is dependent on the BIOS time-of-day clock.

An example of 8253 programming is shown in Fig. 5-11. This program turns the Personal Computer into a fairly accurate desk clock. The time of day is maintained in ASCII format in the six variables TENHOUR, HOUR, TENMIN, MINUTE, TENSEC, and SECOND. These variables are defined in that order in the data segment, with bytes containing the character ":" inserted between HOUR and TENMIN, and MINUTE and TENSEC. Thus the eight-character string starting at location TENHOUR will be in the familiar format hh:mm:ss. We initialize this string with the program parameter passed to us by DOS (statements 350 through 380). In this manner, we can "set" the clock when we start the clock program.

In statements 650 through 730, we reprogram timer channel 0 to issue an interrupt 100 times a second, or every 10 milliseconds. The count value is 1.19318 MHz/desired frequency = 11932.

A type 08H interrupt will thus occur 100 times a second. We modify the interrupt-service–routine address table so that our procedure, TIMER, gets

```
00030 ; 'DESK CLOCK' - ILLUSTRATES USE OF THE 8253 TIMER CHIP.
00040 STACK     SEGMENT PARA STACK 'STACK'
00050           DB      256 DUP (0)      ;256 BYTES OF STACK SPACE
00060 STACK     ENDS
00070 ;
00080 DATA      SEGMENT PARA PUBLIC 'DATA'
00090 COUNT100 DB       100      ;DIVIDE BY 100 SOFTWARE COUNTER
00100 TENHOUR DB        0        ;TENS DIGIT FOR HOUR
00110 HOUR      DB      0        ;ONES DIGIT FOR HOUR
00120           DB      ':'
00130 TENMIN  DB        0        ;TENS DIGIT FOR MINUTE
00140 MINUTE  DB        0        ;ONES DIGIT FOR MINUTE
00150           DB      ':'
00160 TENSEC  DB        0        ;TENS DIGIT FOR SECOND
00170 SECOND  DB        0        ;ONES DIGIT FOR SECOND
00180 DATA      ENDS
00190 ;
00200 CODE      SEGMENT PARA PUBLIC 'CODE'
00210 START     PROC    FAR
00220 ;
00230 ; STANDARD PROGRAM PROLOGUE EXCEPT RETAIN DS AS PTR TO PSP
00240 ;
00250           ASSUME  CS:CODE
00260           PUSH    DS       ;SAVE PSP SEG ADDR
00270           MOV     AX,0
00280           PUSH    AX       ;SAVE RET ADDR OFFSET (PSP+0)
00290           MOV     AX,DATA
00300           MOV     ES,AX    ;ESTABLISH EXTRA SEG ADDRESSABILITY
00310           ASSUME  ES:DATA
00320 ;
00330 ; MOVE 8 BYTE PARAMETER FROM PSP TO OUR DATA SEGMENT
00340 ;
00350           MOV     SI,82H   ;SOURCE STRING OFFSET (WITHIN PSP)
00360           MOV     DI,OFFSET TENHOUR ;DEST. STRING OFFSET
00370           MOV     CX,8     ;STRING LENGTH TO MOVE
00375           CLD              ;SET 'FORWARD' STRING OPERATIONS
00380           REP     MOVSB    ;MOVE PARM INTO OUR DATA AREA
00390 ;
00400 ; ESTABLISH NORMAL DATA SEGMENT ADDRESSABILITY
00410 ;
00420           MOV     DS,AX
00430           ASSUME  DS:DATA
00440 ;
00450 ; WAIT FOR A KEY TO BE STRUCK TO 'START' THE CLOCK:
00460 ;
00470           MOV     AH,0     ;SELECT BIOS FUNCTION = READ KEY
00480           INT     16H      ;CALL BIOS KEYBOARD ROUTINE
00490 ;
00500 ; SETUP OUR OWN TIMER INTERRUPT SERVICE ROUTINE:
00510 ;
```

Fig. 5-11. Desk-clock program.

Continued on next page.

```
00520               CLI              ;DISABLE ALL INTERRUPTS
00530               MOV      AX,O
00540               MOV      ES,AX    ;POINT EXTRA SEGMENT AT THE...
00550 ;                              ...INTERRUPT SERVICE ROUTINE ADDRESS TABLE
00560               MOV      DI,20H   ;OFFSET OF ENTRY FOR TYPE CODE 08H
00570               MOV      AX,OFFSET TIMER ;OFFSET OF OUR SERVICE ROUTINE
00580               STOSW                    ;PLACE IT IN THE TABLE
00590               MOV      AX,CS            ;SEG OF OUR SERVICE ROUTINE
00600               STOSW                    ;PLACE IT IN THE TABLE
00610 ;
00620 ; PROGRAM CHANNEL O OF THE 8253 TIMER TO REQUEST AN
00630 ;   INTERRUPT 100 TIMES A SECOND:
00640 ;
00650               MOV      AL,36H   ;TIMER COMMAND: SELECT CHANNEL O;
00660 ;                                            READ/WRITE LSB-MSB;
00670 ;                                            MODE 3; BINARY.
00680               OUT      43H,AL   ;SEND COMMAND TO 8253 COMMAND REG
00690               MOV      BX,11932 ;DESIRED COUNT VALUE FOR 100HZ RESULT
00700               MOV      AL,BL    ;SEND LSB OF VALUE FIRST
00710               OUT      40H,AL   ;SEND LSB TO LATCH REGISTER
00720               MOV      AL,BH    ;SEND MSB OF VALUE LAST
00730               OUT      40H,AL   ;SEND MSB TO LATCH REGISTER
00740 ;
00750 ; NOW PROGRAM 8259 INTERRUPT CONTROLLER TO ALLOW INTERRUPTS
00760 ;   FROM THE KEYBOARD AND THE TIMER:
00770 ;
00780               MOV      AL,OFCH  ;ENABLE TIMER AND KYBD IRUPTS
00790               OUT      21H,AL   ;WRITE INTERRUPT MASK REGISTER
00800               STI              ;ENABLE INTERRUPTS TO THE 8088
00810 ;
00820 ; DISPLAY TIME ON THE SCREEN, WAIT FOR IT TO CHANGE AND THEN
00830 ;   DISPLAY IT AGAIN.  LOOP HERE FOREVER:
00840 ;
00850 FOREVER: MOV      BX,OFFSET TENHOUR          ;START OF STRING TO DISPLAY
00860               MOV      CX,8                  ;STRING LENGTH
00870 DISPCLK: MOV      AL,[BX]                   ;GET CHARACTER FROM STRING
00880               CALL     DISPCHAR              ;DISPLAY IT ON SCREEN
00890               INC      BX                    ;POINT TO NEXT CHARACTER
00900               LOOP     DISPCLK               ;DO ALL 8 CHARACTERS
00910               MOV      AL,ODH                ;ISSUE A CARRIAGE RETURN
00920               CALL     DISPCHAR
00930               MOV      AL,SECOND        ;GET DIGIT THAT CHANGES MOST OFTEN
00940 WAIT:    CMP      AL,SECOND        ;HAS IT CHANGED?
00950               JZ       WAIT         ;WAIT UNTIL IT DOES CHANGE
00960               JMP      FOREVER      ;AND THEN REFRESH THE DISPLAY
00970 ;
00980 ; TIMER IS OUR OWN TIMER INTERRUPT SERVICE ROUTINE:
00990 ;
01000 TIMER    PROC     FAR
01010               PUSH     AX       ;SAVE ALL ALTERED REGISTERS!!
01020 ;
```

Fig. 5-11 (cont).   Desk-clock program.

Continued on next page.

```
01030. ; COUNT DOWN THE 'COUNT100' COUNTER AND GENERATE THE
01040  ;   'SOFTWARE SIGNAL' WHEN IT REACHES ZERO:
01050  ;
01060          DEC     COUNT100            ;DECREMENT THE COUNTER
01070          JNZ     TIMERX   ;IF IT HAS NOT YET REACHED ZERO, WE'RE ALL DONE!
01080          MOV     COUNT100,100     ;RESET THE COUNTER FOR NEXT TIME
01090  ;
01100  ; WE FALL THROUGH TO THE ROUTINE BELOW WHEN THE COUNTER
01110  ;   REACHES ZERO, THIS IS ONCE A SECOND:
01120  ;
01130          INC     SECOND          ;TICK CLOCK BY ONE SECOND
01140          CMP     SECOND,'9'      ;DO WE HAVE TO ADJUST TENSEC?
01150          JLE     TIMERX          ;BRANCH IF NOT, WE'RE DONE!
01160          MOV     SECOND,'0'      ;SECOND OVERFLOWS, RESET IT
01170          INC     TENSEC          ;AND CARRY OVER TO THE NEXT DIGIT
01180          CMP     TENSEC,'6'      ;HAS A MINUTE GONE BY?
01190          JL      TIMERX          ;BRANCH OF NOT, WE'RE DONE!
01200          MOV     TENSEC,'0'      ;RESET TENSEC
01210          INC     MINUTE          ;AND CARRY OVER TO NEXT (TICK MINUTES)
01220          CMP     MINUTE,'9'      ;DO WE HAVE TO ADJUST TENMIN?
01230          JLE     TIMERX          ;BRANCH IF NOT, WE'RE DONE!
01240          MOV     MINUTE,'0'      ;MINUTE OVERFLOWS, RESET IT
01250          INC     TENMIN          ;AND CARRY OVER TO THE NEXT DIGIT
01260          CMP     TENMIN,'6'      ;HAS AN HOUR GONE BY?
01270          JL      TIMERX          ;BRANCH OF NOT, WE'RE DONE!
01280          MOV     TENMIN,'0'      ;RESET TENMIN
01290          INC     HOUR            ;AND CARRY OVER TO NEXT (TICK HOURS)
01300          CMP     HOUR,'9'        ;HAVE WE GONE PAST 9 O'CLOCK?
01310          JA      ADJHOUR         ;BRANCH IF YES, WE MUST ADJUST TENHOUR
01320          CMP     HOUR,'3'        ;COULD WE HAVE JUST GONE PAST 12 O'CLOCK?
01330          JNZ     TIMERX          ;BRANCH IF NOT, WE'RE DONE!
01340          CMP     TENHOUR,'1'     ;DID WE JUST GO PAST 12 O'CLOCK?
01350          JNZ     TIMERX          ;BRANCH IF NOT, WE'RE DONE!
01360          MOV     HOUR,'1'        ;YES: SET 1 O'CLOCK
01370          MOV     TENHOUR,'0'     ;YES: SET 1 O'CLOCK
01380          JMP     SHORT TIMERX    ;WE'RE DONE!
01390 ADJHOUR: INC    TENHOUR         ;CARRY OVER FROM 9 O'CLOCK...
01400          MOV     HOUR,'0'        ;... TO 10 O'CLOCK
01410  ;
01420  ; NOW INDICATE "END OF INTERRUPT" TO THE INTERRUPT CONTROLLER:
01430  ;
01440 TIMERX: MOV     AL,20H          ;SEND "EOI" COMMAND...
01450          OUT     20H,AL          ;...TO 8259 COMMAND REGISTER
01460          POP     AX              ;RESTORE ALL ALTERED REGISTERS!!
01470          IRET                    ;RETURN FROM INTERRUPT
01480 TIMER   ENDP
01490  ;
01500  ; SUBROUTINE TO DISPLAY A CHARACTER ON THE SCREEN.
01510  ; ENTER WITH AL = CHARACTER TO BE DISPLAYED.
01520  ; USES VIDEO INTERFACE IN BIOS.
01530  ;
```

Fig. 5-11 (cont).   Desk-clock program.

Continued on next page.

```
01540 DISPCHAR PROC     NEAR
01550          PUSH     BX        ;SAVE BX REGISTER
01560          MOV      BX,0      ;SELECT DISPLAY PAGE O
01570          MOV      AH,14     ;FUNCTION CODE FOR 'WRITE'
01580          INT      10H       ;CALL VIDEO DRIVER IN BIOS
01590          POP      BX        ;RESTORE BX REGISTER
01600          RET                ;RETURN TO CALLER OF 'DISPCHAR'
01610 DISPCHAR ENDP
01620 START    ENDP
01630 CODE     ENDS
01640          END      START
```

Fig. 5-11 (cont). Desk-clock program.

control on this interrupt. This routine uses a software counter that operates just like the 8253 chip to divide the 100-Hz signal into a once-per-second software signal. The software counter is kept in our data segment and is called COUNT100. It is initialized to 100 and is decremented by one every time the interrupt is received (statements 1060 through 1080). When it reaches zero, we reset it to 100 and generate the software signal (fall through to statement 1130).

The once-per-second software signal thus activates a routine (statements 1130 through 1400) that "ticks" the clock. This is accomplished by incrementing the value in SECOND every time the routine is activated. If this causes SECOND to go above 9, then SECOND is reset to 0 and TENSEC is incremented. When TENSEC reaches 6 (representing 60 seconds), it is reset to 0 and MINUTE is incremented. This process continues as is necessary to maintain the entire 6-digit clock. Note that the logic in this routine has been designed to maintain the clock in conventional 12-hour format. An excellent exercise at this time would be to modify this routine so that the clock is maintained in 24-hour format.

After obtaining the DOS parameter and programming the timer and interrupt controller chips, the main program simply goes into a loop that displays the clock string on the screen whenever it changes (statements 850 through 960). Our familiar routine, DISPCHAR, is used to write to the display. Notice that a carriage return is sent after the string, but no line feed is sent. This allows us to overwrite the same location on the screen continually and thus give the impression of a ticking clock.

Type in the program as shown (use the filename CLOCK.ASM), and then assemble and link it. To execute the program, type in the command

```
CLOCK hh:mm:ss
```

where the current time is specified by the parameter. The clock will be set but will not start. To start the clock, strike any key on the keyboard (this lets you synchronize it to a standard time signal). The program will then display and maintain the time on the screen. When you are finished using this program, be sure to reboot the computer so that BIOS will regain control of the timer interrupt (necessary for disk i/o).

GENERATING SOUND EFFECTS

The system board provides us with enough hardware support to produce sound effects using two different methods. As illustrated in Fig. 5-1, the built-in speaker receives its input from the logical AND of two separate signals. One of these signals is the output of timer channel 2, and the other comes from bit 1 of 8255 output port PB. With appropriate programming, either the 8253 or the 8255 can be used to produce sound effects. In more complex applications, both devices can produce different sounds simultaneously.

The easiest way to generate sound is to program timer channel 2 to produce a square wave with a frequency within the audible spectrum (20 Hz–20 kHz). This is accomplished by using mode 3 and the appropriate latch-register value, as described earlier. If we then set both the timer 2 gate and speaker data signals high (bits 0 and 1 of port PB = 1), then the square wave will be gated into the speaker circuit. Because the speaker and its amplifier cannot respond to the sharp edges of the square wave, the waveform will be rounded off to produce a more pleasant-sounding sine wave (Fig. 5-12). The advantage to this method is that once the processor has started the sound, it can do something else while the sound is being played. To change tones, however, requires reprogramming the 8253 chip. The example given in Fig. 5-13 will produce a 600-Hz tone. The sound will be played until a key is struck, at which time the program will terminate.

The alternate method for generating sound is more complex, but it can also be more flexible. Instead of using the timer to produce the square-wave signal, we produce it ourselves by alternating the value of the speaker data bit. We control the duration of time that the bit is on or off by using a program *delay loop.* This effectively sets the frequency of the resulting square wave. The general approach is shown in Fig. 5-14. The

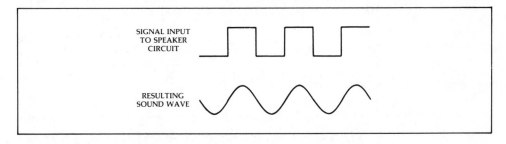

Fig. 5-12. The speaker signal.

```
00030 ; SOUND EFFECTS GENERATION USING METHOD 1 - THE 8253 TIMER.
00040 STACK     SEGMENT PARA STACK 'STACK'
00050         DB      256 DUP (0)      ;256 BYTES OF STACK SPACE
00060 STACK     ENDS
00070 DATA      SEGMENT PARA PUBLIC 'DATA'
00080 FREQ      DW      1989      ;COUNT VALUE NEEDED TO PRODUCE A
00090 ;                             600 HZ SQUARE WAVE.
00100 DATA      ENDS
00110 CODE      SEGMENT PARA PUBLIC 'CODE'
00120 START     PROC    FAR
00130 ;
00140 ; STANDARD PROGRAM PROLOGUE:
00150 ;
00160         ASSUME  CS:CODE
00170         PUSH    DS        ;SAVE PSP SEG ADDR
00180         MOV     AX,0
00190         PUSH    AX        ;SAVE RET ADDR OFFSET (PSP+0)
00200         MOV     AX,DATA
00210         MOV     DS,AX     ;ESTABLISH DATA SEG ADDRESSABILITY
00220         ASSUME  DS:DATA
00230 ;
00240 ; SETUP 8255 PORT PB TO ALLOW TIMER CHANNEL 2 OUT SIGNAL
00250 ;   TO BE GATED INTO THE SPEAKER CIRCUIT:
00260 ;
00270         IN      AL,61H    ;READ CURRENT STATE OF PORT PB
00280         OR      AL,3      ;TURN ON 'SPEAKER DATA' AND
00290 ;                           'TIMER 2 GATE' SIGNALS.
00300         OUT     61H,AL    ;WRITE NEW PORT PB VALUE
00310 ;
00320 ; PROGRAM CHANNEL 2 OF THE 8253 TIMER TO GENERATE A
00330 ;   600 HZ SQUARE WAVE:
00340 ;
00350         MOV     AL,0B6H ;TIMER COMMAND: SELECT CHANNEL 2;
00360 ;                                     READ/WRITE LSB-MSB;
00370 ;                                     MODE 3; BINARY.
00380         OUT     43H,AL  ;SEND COMMAND TO 8253 COMMAND REG
00390         MOV     BX,FREQ ;COUNT VALUE FOR DESIRED FREQUENCY
00400         MOV     AL,BL   ;SEND LSB OF VALUE FIRST
00410         OUT     42H,AL  ;SEND LSB TO LATCH REGISTER
00420         MOV     AL,BH   ;SEND MSB OF VALUE LAST
00430         OUT     42H,AL  ;SEND MSB TO LATCH REGISTER
00440 ;
00450 ; TONE IS NOW BEING PRESENTED TO SPEAKER, WAIT FOR ANY
00460 ;   KEY TO BE STRUCK TO TERMINATE THE SOUND:
00470 ;
00480         MOV     AH,0      ;SELECT BIOS FUNCTION = READ KEY
00490         INT     16H       ;CALL BIOS KEYBOARD ROUTINE
00500 ;
00510 ; A KEY HAS BEEN STRUCK: STOP THE SOUND:
00520 ;
```

Fig. 5-13. Sound-effects generation using method 1.

Continued on next page.

```
00530              IN        AL,61H   ;READ CURRENT STATE OF PORT PB
00540              AND       AL,0FCH  ;TURN OFF 'SPEAKER DATA' AND
00550 ;                               'TIMER 2 GATE' SIGNALS.
00560              OUT       61H,AL   ;WRITE NEW PORT PB VALUE
00570 ;
00580              RET                ;TERMINATE AND RETURN TO DOS
00590 START        ENDP
00600 CODE         ENDS
00610              END       START
```

Fig. 5-13 (cont). Sound-effects generation using method 1.

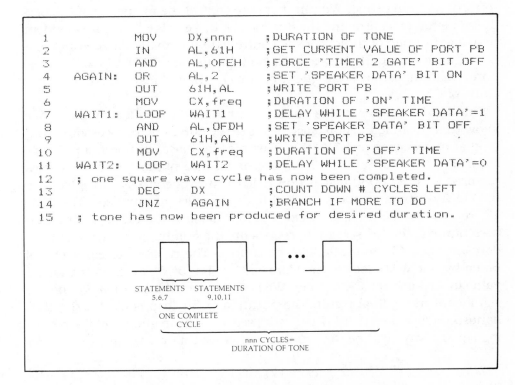

Fig. 5-14. Program-generated square wave.

DX register is initialized to the number of square-wave cycles that we wish to produce. This will determine the duration of the tone (i.e., how long it will play). We obtain the current state of port PB and force the timer 2 gate signal to zero. This disables the timer signal. The speaker data signal is turned on for the first half of the cycle by statement 5. The duration of time that the signal will remain on is determined by the count value loaded into CX. Statement WAITl then loops to itself for this duration. The second half of the cycle is then initiated by turning the speaker data signal off (statements 8 and 9). Once again, CX is loaded with the half-cycle duration count, and we delay at statement WAIT2. At this point, one complete square-wave cycle has been produced. We therefore count down the total cycle count in register DX and repeat the entire operation until DX reaches zero (statements 13 and 14).

The amount of time spent in the one-statement delay loops WAIT1 and WAIT2 is much longer than the time occupied by the execution of the other statements in this program. The duration of one half of our square-wave cycle is thus approximated by the duration of time spent in either of these loops. The duration of a complete cycle, also known as its *period,* is equal to twice this time. The frequency of the resulting signal is equal to the reciprocal of the period. We can therefore control the frequency of the produced signal by controlling the duration of these delay loops. It is evident that the duration of these loops is controlled by the value loaded into the CX register prior to their execution (statements 6 and 10). The only question remaining is, for a specific time delay, "How do we determine what value of CX to use?"

Finding the answer to this question is not as hard as it may seem. We know that the fundamental clock input to the 8088 microprocessor is running at a frequency of 4.77 MHz. This means that each 8088 clock cycle requires $1/4.77$ MHz = 210 nanoseconds. The number of clock cycles required by each 8088 instruction is listed in Appendix A. If we look up the LOOP instruction there, we will find two different numbers. The first, 17, represents the number of clock cycles taken if the LOOP instruction does branch, and the second, 5, represents the number of cycles taken if it does not (i.e., CX = 0 after decrementing). The number of clock cycles taken by our WAIT loop is therefore (cx * 17) + 5, where cx is the initial value loaded into the CX register. We now drop the 5 because it will not be significant in the final result. The duration of the loop is (cx * 17) * 210 nanoseconds = (cx * 17) * (210 * 10^{-9}) second. The frequency of the resulting square wave will be the reciprocal of twice this value, or

$$f = \frac{1}{2 * (cx * 17) * (210 * 10^{-9})}$$

Since we really want to determine a value to use for cx based upon a desired result frequency (f), we rearrange this formula using simple algebra and obtain:

$$cx = \frac{1}{2 * f * 17 * 210 * 10^{-9}} \\ \frac{10^{9}}{f * 7140}$$

We can now rewrite the program of Fig. 5-13 to produce the same 600-Hz tone by the second sound-generation method. From the formula we

```
00030 ; SOUND EFFECTS GENERATION USING METHOD 2 - PROGRAM GENERATED
00040 ;   SQUARE WAVE.
00050 STACK     SEGMENT PARA STACK 'STACK'
00060           DB      256 DUP (0)      ;256 BYTES OF STACK SPACE
00070 STACK     ENDS
00080 DATA      SEGMENT PARA PUBLIC 'DATA'
00090 FREQ      DW      233      ;CX VALUE NEEDED TO EFFECT A HALF
00100 ;                          CYCLE DELAY FOR A 600 HZ RESULT.
00110 DURA      DW      1200     ;NUMBER OF CYCLES TO PRODUCE FOR
00120 ;                          A TWO SECOND TOTAL TONE DURATION.
00130 DATA      ENDS
00140 CODE      SEGMENT PARA PUBLIC 'CODE'
00150 START     PROC    FAR
00160 ;
00170 ; STANDARD PROGRAM PROLOGUE:
00180 ;
00190           ASSUME  CS:CODE
00200           PUSH    DS       ;SAVE PSP SEG ADDR
00210           MOV     AX,0
00220           PUSH    AX       ;SAVE RET ADDR OFFSET (PSP+0)
00230           MOV     AX,DATA
00240           MOV     DS,AX    ;ESTABLISH DATA SEG ADDRESSABILITY
00250           ASSUME  DS:DATA
00260 ;
00270 ; GENERATE A 600 HZ TONE FOR TWO SECONDS:
00280 ;
00290           CLI              ;DISABLE ALL INTERRUPTS!!
00300           MOV     DX,DURA  ;DURATION OF TONE
00310           IN      AL,61H   ;GET CURRENT VALUE OF PORT PB
00320           AND     AL,0FEH  ;FORCE 'TIMER 2 GATE' BIT OFF
00330 AGAIN:    OR      AL,2     ;SET 'SPEAKER DATA' BIT ON
00340           OUT     61H,AL   ;WRITE PORT PB
00350           MOV     CX,FREQ  ;DURATION OF 'ON' TIME
00360 WAIT1:    LOOP    WAIT1    ;DELAY WHILE 'SPEAKER DATA'=1
00370           AND     AL,0FDH  ;SET 'SPEAKER DATA' BIT OFF
00380           OUT     61H,AL   ;WRITE PORT PB
00390           MOV     CX,FREQ  ;DURATION OF 'OFF' TIME
00400 WAIT2:    LOOP    WAIT2    ;DELAY WHILE 'SPEAKER DATA'=0
00410 ; ONE SQUARE WAVE CYCLE HAS NOW BEEN COMPLETED.
00420           DEC     DX       ;COUNT DOWN # OF CYCLES LEFT
00430           JNZ     AGAIN    ;BRANCH IF MORE TO DO
00440 ; TONE HAS NOW BEEN PRODUCED FOR DESIRED DURATION
00450           STI              ;TURN INTERRUPTS BACK ON
00460           RET              ;TERMINATE AND RETURN TO DOS
00470 START     ENDP
00480 CODE      ENDS
00490           END     START
```

Fig. 5-15.   Sound-effects generation using method 2.

have just derived, we obtain an initial CX value of 233 for a 600-Hz tone. Each cycle of the 600-Hz tone will last for 1/600 Hz = 1.66 milliseconds. We can therefore produce the tone for two seconds by producing 2 seconds / 1.66 milliseconds = 1200 complete cycles. The complete program is shown in Fig. 5-15.

Note that while it is generating a tone by this method, the processor cannot be doing anything else. Even interrupts must be disabled so that we can be sure of accurate timing of each half cycle. This is a major disadvantage over the timer method. The advantage to this approach, however, is that we can smoothly vary the resulting tone by dynamically modifying the delay-loop times. We can even generate an asymmetrical signal by using different time delays in the WAIT1 and WAIT2 loops. This allows an even wider range of sound effects to be produced.

SUMMARY

In this chapter, we have learned how to control the various support devices present on the Personal Computer system board. The complete Personal Computer usually includes devices such as displays and disk drives that are not controlled by system-board hardware. Instead, each of these devices is controlled by a dedicated *adapter* that plugs into an expansion slot on the system board. In the following chapters, we shall study the more commonly used adapters and learn how to control them.

CHAPTER 6

The Monochrome, Color/Graphics, and Printer Adapters

The *Monochrome* and *Color/Graphics Adapters* give the assembler-language programmer a great deal of control over the display used with the PC. Both of these adapters convert a section of memory into a display image. The 8088 has direct control over this section of memory. By understanding the way the memory is used to form a display image, we can change the image on the display screen at the speed of memory accesses.

The *Monochrome Display and Printer Adapter* also allows a printer with a standard parallel interface to be operated. If the Color/Graphics Adapter is used, then a separate *Parallel Printer Adapter* is available.

THE MONOCHROME DISPLAY

In this section, the control of the monochrome display will be discussed. The monochrome display is meant to be used with the Monochrome Display and Printer Adapter. The control of the printer will be discussed later. When running the example programs in this section, be sure that the configuration switch on the system board has been set to monochrome display mode (prior to power on).

The Monochrome Display Adapter supports an 80-column by 25-line screen image. Therefore, 80 * 25, or 2000, characters can be displayed at the same time. A representation of the screen image is shown in Fig. 6-1. Note that each display position can be represented by the coordinates row number and column number. Another way to describe each display position is with an address from 0 through 1999. This is shown in Fig. 6-2. Each display position can be calculated as (80 * row number) + column number. It takes 11 bits of information to describe a display position from 0 through 1999. The display position will be important when we learn how a section of memory is displayed on the screen.

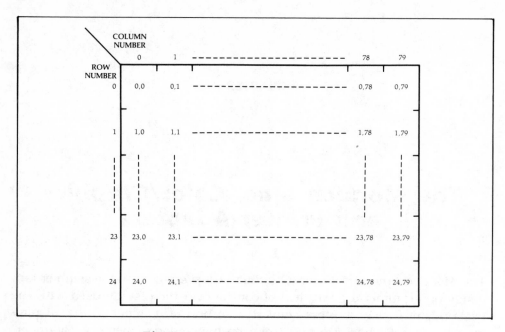

Fig. 6-1.   80-by-25 screen image.

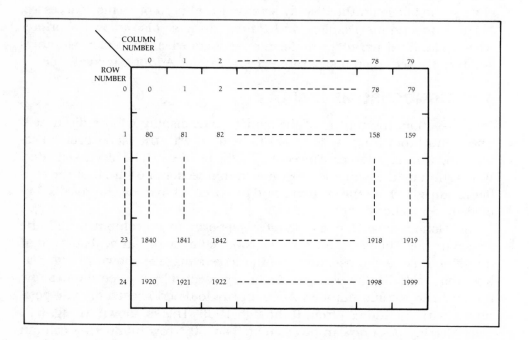

Fig. 6-2.   Display positions on an 80-by-25 screen.

Each character can be one of 256 possible images. A byte, which can contain one of 256 possible values (0–255), is used to represent a single character. Table 2-1 shows the images for characters with values from 20H to 7FH. We will write a program to display all the possible character images.

Each character also has a corresponding *display attribute*. The display attribute determines how the character is displayed. For example, a character image can be displayed as a white character on a black background *(normal video)* or as a black character on a white background *(reverse video)*. High intensity, blinking, and underlining are also available as display attributes. The display attribute for each character is represented by a byte of data. This is shown in Fig. 6-3. We will write a program to display a character with many different attributes.

The Monochrome Display Adapter contains 4K bytes of memory. This is enough memory to hold the display information for the 2000 characters that appear on the screen. Two bytes of information are needed for each character that is displayed. One byte contains the character code, and the other byte contains its display-attribute information.

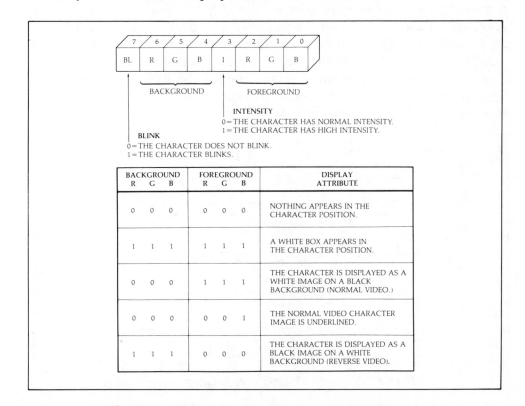

BACKGROUND R G B			FOREGROUND R G B			DISPLAY ATTRIBUTE
0	0	0	0	0	0	NOTHING APPEARS IN THE CHARACTER POSITION.
1	1	1	1	1	1	A WHITE BOX APPEARS IN THE CHARACTER POSITION.
0	0	0	1	1	1	THE CHARACTER IS DISPLAYED AS A WHITE IMAGE ON A BLACK BACKGROUND (NORMAL VIDEO.)
0	0	0	0	0	1	THE NORMAL VIDEO CHARACTER IMAGE IS UNDERLINED.
1	1	1	0	0	0	THE CHARACTER IS DISPLAYED AS A BLACK IMAGE ON A WHITE BACKGROUND (REVERSE VIDEO).

Fig. 6-3. Monochrome-display attribute byte.

The 4K of memory on the adapter board is addressable by the 8088 starting at physical location 0B0000H. By setting a segment register to 0B000H, we can view the memory on the adapter board as offset addresses 0—4K. Each even memory location on the adapter board contains a character representation, and each odd memory location contains the corresponding display attribute.

By appending a 0 or 1 to the 11-bit display position (Fig. 6-2), we get the 12-bit even or odd offset address on the adapter board. The high-order 11 bits of this 12-bit memory address determine which display position is being described, and the low-order bit determines whether this address contains a character representation or a display attribute. This is shown in Fig. 6-4. Therefore, memory addresses 0 and 1 describe display position 0, and memory addresses 2 and 3 describe display position 1.

We can easily derive which display position a memory address describes by dividing the address by 2. If the original address was even, it contained a character representation. If it was odd, it contained a character-display attribute.

Now that we understand how the memory on the adapter board maps to the display, we can write programs to modify the display image. A program that displays all possible characters is shown in Fig. 6-5. A blank column and row are placed between adjacent displayed characters. Hitting any key will blank the display and cause the program to return to DOS.

Let us look at this program in detail. The ES segment register is initialized to the first physical address of the memory on the adapter board in statements 210—230. Now the program can view the memory on the

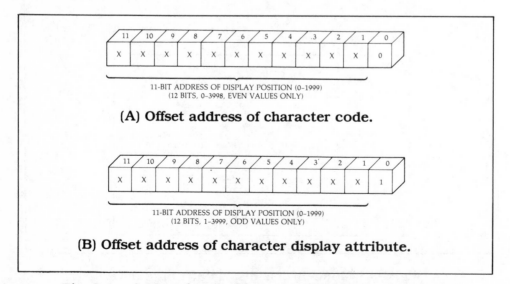

(A) Offset address of character code.

(B) Offset address of character display attribute.

Fig. 6-4.   Addressing the Monochrome Display Adapter.

```
00020 ; PROGRAM TO DISPLAY ALL THE CHARACTERS ON
00030 ; THE MONOCHROME DISPLAY
00040 ;
00050 ;
00060 STACK     SEGMENT PARA STACK 'STACK'
00070           DB      256 DUP(0)
00080 STACK     ENDS
00090 ;
00100 CODE      SEGMENT PARA PUBLIC 'CODE'
00110 START     PROC    FAR
00120 ;
00130 ;STANDARD PROGRAM PROLOGUE
00140 ;
00150           ASSUME  CS:CODE
00160           PUSH    DS        ;SAVE PSP SEG ADDRESS
00170           MOV     AX,0
00180           PUSH    AX        ;SAVE RET ADDRESS OFFSET (PSP+0)
00190 ;
00200 ;PART1: CLEAR THE DISPLAY
00210           MOV     AX,0B000H  ;SEGMENT ADDRESS OF MEMORY
00220 ;                             ON MONOCHROME DISPLAY ADAPTER
00230           MOV     ES,AX     ;SET UP ES SEGMENT REGISTER
00240 ;                            TO POINT AT BASE OF ADAPTER MEMORY
00250           MOV     DI,0      ;INITIAL OFFSET ADDRESS INTO SEGMENT
00260           MOV     AL,' '    ;BLANK CHARACTER TO FILL DISPLAY
00270           MOV     AH,07H    ;ATTRIBUTE BYTE FOR NORMAL DISPLAY
00280           MOV     CX,2000   ;NUMBER OF WORDS TO INITIALIZE
00290           CLD               ;SO STOSW GOES FORWARD IN MEMORY
00300           REP     STOSW     ;BLANK OUT THE DISPLAY
00310 ;
00320 ; PART2: FILL THE DISPLAY WITH 256 CHARACTERS WITH A
00330 ;        BLANK COLUMN AND LINE BETWEEN ALL CHARACTERS
00340 ;
00350           MOV     AL,0      ;AL ALWAYS HAS CHARACTER TO DISPLAY
00360           MOV     AH,0      ;AH ALWAYS HAS THE CURRENT COLUMN NUMBER
00370           MOV     DI,160    ;DI WILL CONTAIN THE OFFSET ADDRESS
00380 ;                            DI IS INITIALIZED TO POINT TO THE
00390 ;                            FIRST CHARACTER POSITION OF THE
00400 ;                            SECOND ROW.
00410 ;
00420 ; THIS IS THE MAJOR LOOP THAT FILLS THE SCREEN
00430 AGAIN:    MOV     ES:[DI],AL    ;PUT CHARACTER TO DISPLAY
00440 ;                                IN THE ADAPTER MEMORY
00450           ADD     DI,4      ;POINT TO THE NEXT CHARACTER POSITION
00460 ;                            TO FILL BY SKIPPING OVER THE CURRENT
00470 ;                            ATTRIBUTE BYTE AND THE ENTIRE NEXT
00480 ;                            COLUMN POSITION (2 BYTES).
00490           ADD     AH,2      ;UPDATE COLUMN POSITION
00500           CMP     AH,80     ;FINISHED THIS ROW?
00510           JB      SAME_LINE     ;IF COLUMN NUMBER BELOW 80
```

Fig. 6-5. Program to display all characters.

Continued on next page.

```
00520 ;                                    THEN STAY ON SAME LINE.
00530 ; IF THE PROGRAM GETS HERE THEN WE WANT TO SKIP A LINE
00540 ; ON THE DISPLAY.
00550          ADD       DI,160   ;MOVE ADDRESS POINTER PAST NEXT LINE
00560          MOV       AH,0     ;RESET COLUMN COUNTER TO 0
00570 ; COMMON POINT AFTER COLUMN AND LINE POSITION IS RESOLVED
00580 SAME_LINE: CMP    AL,255
00590          JE        FINISHED          ;256 CHARACTERS HAVE BEEN DISPLAYED
00600          INC       AL       ;UPDATE TO NEXT CHARACTER TO DISPLAY
00610          JMP       AGAIN
00620 ;
00630 ;
00640 ;PART 3:   AFTER DISPLAYING ALL THE CHARACTERS,
00650 ;          WAIT FOR A KEY TO BE STRUCK, THEN BLANK THE
00660 ;          DISPLAY AND RETURN TO DOS.
00670 ;
00680 FINISHED: MOV      AH,0     ;GET KEYBOARD INPUT CODE
00690          INT       16H      ;BIOS CALL
00700 ;WHEN CONTROL IS RETURNED WE MUST CLEAR THE SCREEN
00710          MOV       DI,0     ;INITIAL OFFSET ADDRESS
00720          MOV       AL,' '   ;BLANK CHARACTER
00730          MOV       AH,07H   ;ATTRIBUTE BYTE FOR NORMAL DISPLAY
00740          MOV       CX,2000
00750          REP       STOSW    ;BLANK OUT THE ADAPTER MEMORY.
00760          RET                ;RETURN TO DOS
00770 START    ENDP
00780 CODE     ENDS
00790          END       START
```

Fig. 6-5 (cont). Program to display all characters.

adapter board as offset addresses 0—4K. Whenever accessing the memory on the adapter board, the program must use the ES segment register.

The program blanks out the screen before filling it with characters (statements 250–300). The word register, AX, is stored 2000 times in the adapter memory. Note that AL contains the representation of the blank character and AH contains the display-attribute byte. The contents of AL are placed at even addresses, and the contents of AH are placed at odd addresses because the data is stored in the LSB/MSB format and the initial value of DI is even.

Statements 350–370 initialize the main loop variables. The current character that is being displayed is in AL. The current column number is in AH. The current offset address into the adapter memory is in DI. The first display position we want filled is the first column of the second row. This is display position 80, memory location 160 on the adapter.

Statement 430 moves the current character code into the adapter memory. The attribute byte does not have to be set because all the characters are to be displayed with the normal video attribute. This attribute byte already exists in all the odd memory locations.

There are two bytes of memory for each display position. In statement 450, we update DI by 4 because we want to skip a column between displayed characters. The column skipped already contains a blank character. If the end of the current line has been reached, then statement 550 updates DI by another 160. This causes the program to skip an entire line (80 display positions).

The program checks for a struck key after character code 255 has been displayed. When the keyboard BIOS call returns, we know a key was struck, so we blank out the screen again and return to DOS.

Type in the program and assemble, link, and run it. Some of the possible characters are very interesting. Notice the blinking cursor, which has remained where it was left when the program was invoked. We know how to control the contents of the screen, but we still don't know how to control the cursor. For this program, it would be best to remove the cursor from the screen. This subject will be covered in the next section.

Fig. 6-6 contains a program that displays the character "A" with eight different display attributes. The characters are displayed down the center of the screen, with a blank line between adjacent characters. As in the previous program, striking any key will return control to DOS.

Statements 110–180 contain the eight different attribute-display bytes that will be used with the character "A." This is the only information in the data segment. Register BX will be used to point at the current attribute byte.

Register ES is initialized, and the display is blanked out. The loop counter is set to 8 in statement 500. This will ensure that only eight bytes of attribute information from the data segment are used. Register DI, which contains an offset address into the adapter memory, is initialized to 240. This corresponds to display position 120, which is the center of the second line on the display. In statement 530, BX is initialized to point to the beginning of the display-attribute bytes. Finally, AL is initialized to the character code for "A."

Statements 570–630 contain the loop that displays the character in AL eight times. Each time, a different attribute byte is used, because BX is incremented in statement 620. When AX is stored in the memory location pointed to by the even offset address in DI, AL is stored at an even address and AH is stored at an odd address. Updating DI by 320 advances 160 display positions and causes the next character to appear two lines below the current character.

Once all the information is displayed, the program waits for a key to be struck before clearing the screen and returning to DOS. Type in the program and assemble, link, and run it. As in the previous program, we would prefer to remove the cursor from the screen. To be able to do this, we must take a closer look at the adapter board.

```
00020 ; PROGRAM TO DEMONSTRATE DIFFERENT DISPLAY ATTRIBUTES
00030 ; ON THE MONOCHROME DISPLAY
00040 ;
00050 ;
00060 STACK     SEGMENT PARA STACK 'STACK'
00070           DB      256 DUP(0)
00080 STACK     ENDS
00090 ;
00100 DATA      SEGMENT PARA PUBLIC 'DATA'
00110 ATTRIBUTES DB     07H     ;NORMAL
00120           DB      0FH     ;INTENSE
00130           DB      8FH     ;INTENSE/BLINKING
00140           DB      87H     ;BLINKING
00150           DB      01H     ;UNDERLINED
00160           DB      70H     ;REVERSE VIDEO
00170           DB      0F0H    ;REVERSE VIDEO/BLINKING
00180           DB      0F8H    ;REVERSE VIDEO/INTENSE/BLINKING
00190 DATA      ENDS
00200 ;
00210 CODE      SEGMENT PARA PUBLIC 'CODE'
00220 START     PROC    FAR
00230 ;
00240 ;STANDARD PROGRAM PROLOGUE
00250 ;
00260           ASSUME  CS:CODE
00270           PUSH    DS      ;SAVE PSP SEG ADDR
00280           MOV     AX,0
00290           PUSH    AX      ;SAVE RETURN ADDRESS OFFSET (PSP+0)
00300           MOV     AX,DATA
00310           MOV     DS,AX   ;ESTABLISH DATA SEGMENT ADDRESSABILITY
00320           ASSUME  DS:DATA
00330 ;
00340 ;PART 1: CLEAR THE DISPLAY
00350           MOV     AX,0B000H       ;SEGMENT ADDRESS OF MEMORY
00360 ;                                 ON THE MONOCHROME ADAPTER
00370           MOV     ES,AX   ;ES SEGMENT REGISTER WILL POINT
00380 ;                         TO THE MEMORY ON THE ADAPTER CARD
00390           MOV     DI,0    ;INITIAL OFFSET ADDRESS INTO SEGMENT
00400           MOV     AL,' '  ;BLANK CHARACTER TO FILL DISPLAY
00410           MOV     AH,07H  ;ATTRIBUTE BYTE FOR NORMAL DISPLAY
00420           MOV     CX,2000 ;NUMBER OF WORDS OF MEMORY TO INITIALIZE
00430           CLD             ;SO STOSW GOES FORWARD IN MEMORY
00440           REP     STOSW   ;BLANK OUT THE DISPLAY
00450 ;
00460 ;PART 2: WRITE THE CHARACTER 'A' WITH 8 DIFFERENT ATTRIBUTES
00470 ;        DOWN THE CENTER OF THE SCREEN WITH A BLANK LINE
00480 ;        IN BETWEEN EACH CHARACTER
00490 ;
00500           MOV     CX,8    ;LOOP COUNTER FOR 8 ATTRIBUTE BYTES
00510           MOV     DI,240  ;INITIAL OFFSET INTO DISPLAY MEMORY
```

Fig. 6-6. Program to demonstrate display attributes.

Continued on next page.

```
00520 ;                          FOR CENTER OF SECOND LINE
00530          MOV       BX,OFFSET ATTRIBUTES      ;POINTER TO THE
00540 ;                                            ATTRIBUTE BYTES
00550          MOV       AL,'A'   ;CHARACTER TO BE DISPLAYED
00560 ;LOOP TO DISPLAY 'A' WITH 8 ATTRIBUTES
00570 DISPLAY: MOV       AH,[BX]          ;GET NEW ATTRIBUTE BYTE
00580          MOV       ES:[DI],AX       ;MOVE CHARACTER CODE AND ATTRIBUTE
00590 ;                                   BYTE TO ADAPTER MEMORY
00600          ADD       DI,320           ;POINT TO DISPLAY POSITION
00610 ;                                   TWO LINES DOWN.
00620          INC       BX       ;POINT TO NEXT ATTRIBUTE BYTE
00630          LOOP      DISPLAY  ;DO IT FOR 8 ATTRIBUTE BYTES
00640 ;
00650 ;PART 3: AFTER DISPLAYING ALL THE ATTRIBUTES,
00660 ;        WAIT FOR A KEY TO BE STRUCK, THEN BLANK THE
00670 ;        DISPLAY AND RETURN TO DOS.
00680 ;
00690          MOV       AH,0     ;GET KEYBOARD INPUT CODE
00700          INT       16H      ;BIOS CALL
00710 ;WHEN CONTROL IS RETURNED WE MUST CLEAR THE SCREEN
00720          MOV       DI,0     ;INITIAL OFFSET ADDRESS
00730          MOV       AL,' '   ;BLANK CHARACTER
00740          MOV       AH,07H   ;ATTRIBUTE CODE FOR NORMAL DISPLAY
00750          MOV       CX,2000  ;NUMBER OF WORDS OF MEMORY TO INITIALIZE
00760          REP       STOSW    ;BLANK OUT THE SCREEN
00770          RET                ;RETURN TO DOS
00780 START    ENDP
00790 CODE     ENDS
00800          END       START
```

Fig. 6-6 (cont).   Program to demonstrate display attributes.

THE 6845 CRT CONTROLLER

If you look closely at the display, you can see that each character is made up of a collection of dots. As you get farther from the display, the characters appear to be solid. Each dot at the same vertical position on the screen is part of the same *scan line.* The number of scan lines (or vertical dots) that make up each character determines the height of the character. The display image is "painted" on the screen one scan line at a time.

For example, the characters in Fig. 6-7 are made up of seven scan lines. The width of each character is five dot positions, with two blank dot positions separating each character from the next. To display each character on the screen, the dots that make up the tops of all the characters would be displayed first. Then the dots that make up the second scan line of all the characters would be displayed. This would go on until the last row of dots is displayed. If there is another row of characters, they are displayed after a number of blank scan lines are displayed. This causes the separation between rows of characters.

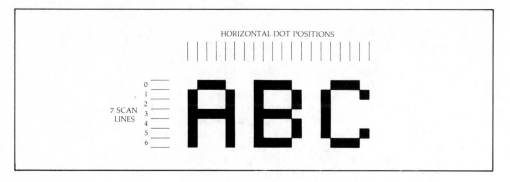

Fig. 6-7.   Character formation.

It is apparent that the process of displaying characters is quite complex. The dot patterns that make up each character must be accessed one row at a time. In addition, each character can have its own display attribute. The cursor must be placed at a specific location on the screen. All the complex video-signal information must also be generated. The timing relationships among all these events are critical.

Fig. 6-8 shows a block diagram of the Monochrome Display Adapter. The "heart" of the adapter is the 6845 CRT Controller, or CRTC. The 6845 selects each character code to be displayed from the adapter memory. It also must select which scan row of the character should be displayed. The video timing information and the cursor image are also generated by the 6845. When the 6845 selects a character code from memory, the adapter board also processes the appropriate display attribute.

The 6845 is a very complex and versatile chip. It can be used to create many different types and sizes of displays. Once it is initialized, the control of the chip is fairly simple. Fortunately, the adapter board and the 6845 are initialized for us when the PC is powered up (assuming correct config-uration-switch settings). By examining the programming of the 6845 after initialization, we can learn how to control the cursor.

Table 6-1 shows a list of the 6845 registers and their associated i/o addresses. Notice that all but one of the registers are at i/o address 3B5H. A register number must be placed in the address register (at i/o address 3B4H) before one of the registers at i/o address 3B5H can be accessed. For example, if we want to write to the cursor start register, we must first out-put a 10 to the address register at i/o address 3B4H. We can then output the desired value for the cursor start register to i/o address 3B5H.

The horizontal registers (0–3) determine the horizontal characteristics of the display. The number of characters per line and the width of each char-acter are determined by these registers. The vertical registers (4–9) deter-mine the vertical characteristics of the display. The number of characters per column and the number of scan lines per character are determined by

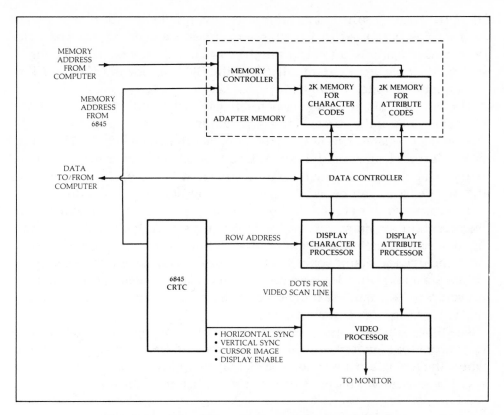

Fig. 6-8.   The Monochrome Display Adapter.

Table 6-1.   The 6845 Registers

PC I/O Address	6845 Register	Register Number	Description
3B4H	Address Register		Used to select all other registers.
3B5H	Horizontal Registers	0–3	Initialized to control the horizontal characteristics of the display.
	Vertical Registers	4–9	Initialized to control the vertical characteristics of the display.
	Cursor Start Cursor End	10 11	These registers define the cursor image (see Fig. 6-9).
	Start Address High Start Address Low	12 13	These registers determine which part of the adapter memory is used (see Fig. 6-11).
	Cursor Address High Cursor Address Low	14 15	These registers determine in which display position the cursor will appear (see Fig. 6-12).

these registers. For the monochrome display, the number·of scan lines per character is initialized to 14. Nine scan lines are used for the character dots, and five are used to separate the rows of characters. The horizontal and vertical registers are initialized by the BIOS at power-up time, so we do not have to touch them.

The cursor start and end registers (registers 10 and 11) determine the characteristics of the cursor. This is shown in Fig. 6-9. Bits 5 and 6 of the cursor start register determine whether or not there is a cursor. The blink-rate bit settings must not be used. The adapter board generates the cursor blink, which cannot be turned off. As shown in Fig. 6-9, the remainder of the two registers can be used to set the cursor start and end addresses.

The values for the cursor start and end addresses determine which scan lines contain the cursor. Some examples are shown in Fig. 6-10. In this figure, a character with a height of 14 scan lines is represented. These scan lines include the blank space between rows of characters. By setting the cursor start and end addresses, the height and placement of the cursor are determined. The middle example in the figure shows how the cursor is initialized for the monochrome display.

The 6845 supports up to 16K of character-code memory. It takes 14 bits to address that amount of memory. The start-address registers determine where the first character code to be displayed appears in the adapter memory. The successive character codes are obtained from the adapter memory

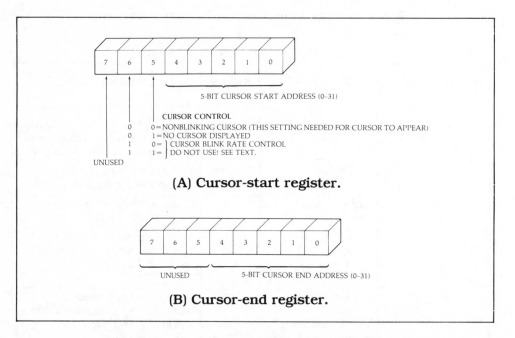

(A) Cursor-start register.

(B) Cursor-end register.

Fig. 6-9.   Cursor start and end registers.

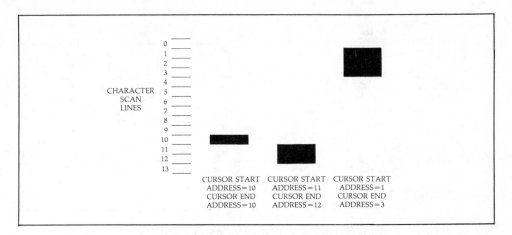

Fig. 6-10.   Different cursors.

by incrementing this starting address by one for each display position. These registers are shown in Fig. 6-11.

It is important to understand that the above memory offset does not take into account the attribute bytes. Therefore, the start address is 1/2 the adapter memory offset as viewed from the 8088. For example, the 8088 views the memory for character codes as all the even addresses from 0 to 4K. The 6845 views the memory for the character codes as all the addresses from 0 to 2K. This is because a 0 bit will be appended to the address generated by the 6845, thereby accessing the correct even address for the character code. When programming the 6845 address registers, we must consider the memory address from the point of view of the 6845.

The start-address registers are not important when programming the Monochrome Adapter. Since there is only 2K of memory for character codes and there are 2000 display positions on the monitor, all the adapter memory must be used at the same time. The start-address registers are

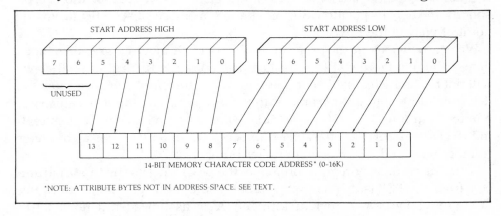
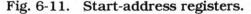

Fig. 6-11.   Start-address registers.

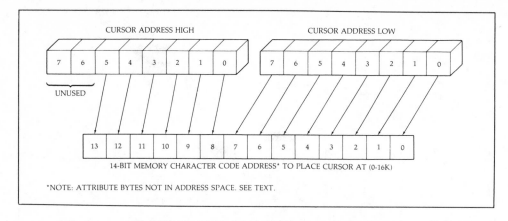

Fig. 6-12.   Cursor-address registers.

initialized to 0 for the Monochrome Adapter. This allows the 6845 to use the entire memory space. However, the Color Adapter has 8K of memory for character codes. More than one screen image of character codes can be stored in that amount of memory. By modifying the start-address registers, the portion of adapter memory that is displayed on the screen can be changed. This useful feature provides a capability known as *hardware scrolling*. We will examine this feature in greater detail when we look at the Color Adapter.

The cursor-address registers are shown in Fig. 6-12. The cursor can be placed over a specific character display position by putting the memory address of the appropriate character code into these registers. Again, this address is as viewed by the 6845. This is 1/2 the offset address of the character code as viewed from the 8088, which is equivalent to the display position for the monochrome display. For example, to move the cursor to the first column of the second row, we would set the cursor-address high register to 0 and the cursor-address low register to 80. This location corresponds to display position 80, or adapter memory offset 160 (from the point of view of the 8088).

We can now look at the program in Fig. 6-13. It moves a graphics block across the middle row of the display. The cursor is turned off so that we will not be distracted by it. The speed at which the graphics block moves is determined by an input parameter to the program. The input parameter is a letter from A to Z, with the resulting delay between movements being 10 milliseconds times the "character number." The letter "A" has a character number of 1, and "Z" has a character number of 26.

After the standard program prologue, the program gets the input parameter from the PSP (statements 220–230). If the input parameter does not fall in the range of A–Z, then an input of "A" is assumed (statements 240–340). When the parameter is entered, it must be a capital letter or it will

```
00010 ; FIG. 6-13.
00020 ;PROGRAM TO MOVE A GRAPHICS BLOCK ACROSS THE CENTER OF THE
00030 ;MONOCHROME DISPLAY IN DELAY INCREMENTS OF 10 MILLISECONDS
00040 ;TIMES AN INPUT PARAMETER OF A-Z.
00050 ;
00060 STACK     SEGMENT PARA STACK 'STACK'
00070          DB      256 DUP(0)
00080 STACK     ENDS
00090 ;
00100 CODE      SEGMENT PARA PUBLIC 'CODE'
00110 START     PROC    FAR
00120 ;
00130 ;STANDARD PROGRAM PROLOGUE. DS POINTS INTO PSP
00140 ;
00150          ASSUME  CS:CODE
00160          PUSH    DS       ;SAVE PSP SEGMENT ADDRESS
00170          MOV     AX,0
00180          PUSH    AX       ;SAVE RETURN ADDRESS OFFSET (PSP+0)
00190 ;
00200 ;PART 1: GET THE INPUT PARM AND VERIFY IT
00210 ;
00220          MOV     SI,82H   ;INPUT CHARACTER OFFSET WITHIN PSP
00230          MOV     BL,[SI]  ;GET INPUT CHARACTER
00240          CMP     BL,'A'
00250          JB      ERROR    ;IF LESS THAN 'A' THEN INVALID
00260          CMP     BL,'Z'
00270          JA      ERROR    ;IF GREATER THAN 'Z' THEN INVALID
00280          SUB     BL,'A'   ;BASE INPUT CHARACTER AT 0
00290          JMP     SHORT INIT    ;INITIALIZE THE DISPLAY
00300 ;IF THE PROGRAM GETS HERE THEN THERE WAS AN
00310 ;INVALID INPUT PARAMETER. SET BL AS IF THE INPUT PARM
00320 ;IS 'A' :
00330 ;
00340 ERROR:   MOV     BL,0
00350 ;
00360 ;PART 2: INITIALIZE THE DISPLAY BY
00370 ;        BLANKING OUT THE DISPLAY AND
00380 ;        REMOVING THE CURSOR FROM THE SCREEN
00390 ;
00400 INIT:    MOV     AX,0B000H      ;SEGMENT ADDRESS OF MEMORY
00410 ;                               ON MONOCHROME DISPLAY ADAPTER
00420          MOV     ES,AX    ;SET UP EXTRA SEGMENT REGISTER
00430          MOV     DI,0     ;INITIAL OFFSET ADDRESS INTO SEGMENT
00440          MOV     AL,' '   ;BLANK CHARACTER TO FILL DISPLAY
00450          MOV     AH,07H   ;ATTRIBUTE CODE FOR NORMAL DISPLAY
00460          MOV     CX,2000  ;NUMBER OF WORDS OF MEMORY TO INITIALIZE
00470          CLD              ;SO STOSW GOES FORWARD
00480          REP     STOSW    ;BLANK OUT THE DISPLAY
00490 ;ADDRESS THE CURSOR START REGISTER IN THE 6845
00500          MOV     DX,3B4H  ;ADDRESS OF ADDRESS REGISTER IN 6845
00510          MOV     AL,10    ;ADDRESS OF CURSOR START REGISTER
```

Fig. 6-13. Program to move a block across the screen.

Continued on next page.

```
00520             OUT      DX,AL    ;CURSOR START REGISTER SELECTED
00530             MOV      DX,3B5H  ;ADDRESS OF DATA REGISTERS IN 6845
00540             MOV      AL,20H   ;CODE TO TURN THE CURSOR OFF
00550             OUT      DX,AL    ;THE CURSOR IS NOW REMOVED
00560 ;
00570 ;PART 3: DISPLAY THE BLOCK AND MOVE IT ACROSS THE SCREEN
00580 ;
00590             CLI               ;DISABLE INTERRUPTS
00592             MOV      AL,0FDH  ;MASK OFF ALL BUT KEYBOARD INTERRUPTS
00594             OUT      21H,AL   ;WRITE 8259 INTERRUPT MASK REG
00596             STI               ;ENABLE SO THAT WE CAN QUIT VIA CTL-ALT-DEL
00600             INC      BL       ;BASE INPUT PARM AT 1
00610             MOV      DI,1920  ;OFFSET ADDRESS FOR BEGINNING OF
00620 ;                             THE 13TH LINE
00630             MOV      BH,BL    ;BH AND BL HAVE THE INPUT PARM
00640             MOV      AH,0     ;AH HAS THE COLUMN NUMBER
00650 ;
00660 ;THIS IS THE MAJOR DISPLAY LOOP
00670 ;
00680 FOREVER: MOV      BYTE PTR ES:[DI],0DBH ;MOVE THE GRAPHICS BLOCK
00690 ;                                CHARACTER TO THE ADAPTER MEMORY
00700 ; DELAY 10 MILLISECONDS TIMES THE NUMBER IN BL:
00710 DELAY:   MOV      CX,2800             ;LOOP COUNT FOR 10
00720 ;                                     MILLISECOND DELAY
00730 WAIT:    LOOP     WAIT     ;LOOP HERE FOR 10 MILLISECONDS
00740             DEC      BL
00750             JNZ      DELAY    ;IF BL NOT 0 THEN DELAY AGAIN
00760 ;WHEN WE GET TO HERE THE CORRECT DELAY HAS TAKEN PLACE
00770             MOV      BL,BH    ;RESTORE BL
00780             MOV      BYTE PTR ES:[DI],' ' ;BLANK OUT THE CURRENT
00790 ;                                DISPLAY POSITION
00800             INC      AH       ;UPDATE COLUMN POSITION
00810             CMP      AH,80    ;HAVE WE MOVED OFF THE LINE?
00820             JZ       NEW_LINE ;START THE LINE OVER AGAIN
00830             ADD      DI,2     ;UPDATE OFFSET ADDRESS TO
00840 ;                             POINT TO THE NEXT COLUMN
00850             JMP      FOREVER  ;DISPLAY NEXT COLUMN POSITION
00860 ;THE PROGRAM GETS HERE IF THE LINE MUST BE
00870 ;STARTED OVER AGAIN
00880 ;
00890 NEW_LINE: MOV     DI,1920  ;RESET DI TO POINT TO BEGINNING OF LINE
00900             MOV      AH,0     ;RESET COLUMN POSITION
00910             JMP      FOREVER  ;DISPLAY FIRST COLUMN POSITION
00920 ;
00930 START    ENDP
00940 CODE     ENDS
00950             END      START
```

Fig. 6-13 (cont).   Program to move a block across the screen.

not be accepted. The input parameter is then converted so that an A will be a 0. This value is kept in BL.

In statements 400–480, the display is blanked out and ES is initialized. The cursor is removed from the screen in statements 500–550. Notice that it takes two OUT instructions to access a 6845 register. Timer interrupts are disabled in statements 590–596. This is done so that our delay-loop timing will be accurate. It also means that we can still use a keyboard reset (CTL-ALT-DEL) to stop the program. Then BL is incremented by one. Now an input parameter of "A" is represented by a 1 in BL. In statement 630, BH is set to BL to save the input parameter value. The column number will be held in AH, so AH is initialized to 0.

The offset address into the adapter memory is held in DI. It is initialized to 1920, which corresponds to display position 960. This is the beginning of the 13th, or middle, line of the display.

The graphics block character (0DBH) is moved into the adapter memory in statement 680. Which display position gets set is determined by DI. Statements 710–750 form the delay loop. With 2800 as a starting value for CX, the program stays at statement 730 for about 10 milliseconds. The value in BL determines how many times the 10-millisecond delay is used.

Once the delay is complete, BL is restored, and the current display position is blanked out. The current column position is incremented. If the end of the line has not been reached, then DI is incremented by 2. Now DI points at the next column position on the same line. If the end of the line has been reached, then DI is reinitialized to point to the beginning of the display line, and the column counter is reset to 0. This causes the graphics block to be redisplayed at the beginning of the line.

Type in the program and assemble, link, and run it. When invoking the program, be sure to skip a space and type a capital letter from A to Z. Notice the different effects that can be created by changing the speed of the movement. Very high speeds are possible only through the use of assembler language.

A program that contains a "display driver" is shown in Fig. 6-14. It performs the same function as the INT 10H BIOS call with AH = 14, except that no beep code is recognized. One of the reasons why the program is very fast is that it is written specifically for the monochrome display. The display BIOS calls must handle all the different types of displays and configurations.

The variables COLUMN and ROW in the data segment are very important. They contain the current position for the cursor. The display program places most of the characters it receives at the current cursor position and then advances the cursor position by one column. If the end of a row is reached, then the cursor is advanced to the beginning of the next row.

If the display program receives a backspace character (08H), then the

```
00010 ; FIG. 6-14.
00020 ; THIS IS AN EXAMPLE OF A MONOCHROME DISPLAY DRIVER
00030 ; THAT EMULATES A TERMINAL
00040 ; CHARACTERS THAT ARE TYPED ARE SENT TO THE DISPLAY
00050 ; DRIVER TO BE DISPLAYED
00060 ; BACKSPACE CAUSES THE CURSOR TO MOVE BACK ONE COLUMN
00070 ; ON THE SAME LINE
00080 ; CARRIAGE RETURN CAUSES THE CURSOR TO MOVE TO THE BEGINNING
00090 ; OF THE SAME LINE
00100 ; LINE FEED CAUSES THE CURSOR TO MOVE DOWN ONE LINE IN THE
00110 ; SAME COLUMN POSITION
00120 ; IF A CARRIAGE RETURN IS DEPRESSED ON THE KEYBOARD THEN A
00130 ; CARRIAGE RETURN AND LINE FEED WILL BE SENT TO THE DISPLAY
00140 ; DRIVER
00150 ;
00160 STACK    SEGMENT PARA STACK 'STACK'
00170          DB      256 DUP(0)
00180 STACK    ENDS
00190 ;
00200 DATA     SEGMENT PARA PUBLIC 'DATA'
00210 COLUMN   DW      0         ;CONTAINS THE CURRENT COLUMN
00220 ROW      DB      0         ;CONTAINS THE CURRENT ROW
00230 TWO      DW      2         ;CONSTANT FOR MULTIPLY INSTRUCTION
00240 DATA     ENDS
00250 CODE     SEGMENT PARA PUBLIC 'CODE'
00260 START    PROC    FAR
00270 ;
00280 ;STANDARD PROGRAM PROLOGUE
00290 ;
00300          ASSUME  CS:CODE
00310          PUSH    DS        ;SAVE PSP SEGMENT ADDRESS
00320          MOV     AX,0
00330          PUSH    AX        ;SAVE RETURN ADDRESS OFFSET (PSP+0)
00340          MOV     AX,DATA
00350          MOV     DS,AX     ;ESTABLISH DATA SEGMENT ADDRESSABILITY
00360          ASSUME  DS:DATA
00370 ;
00380 ;PART 1: CLEAR THE DISPLAY AND INITIALIZE THE CURSOR
00390 ;
00400          MOV     AX,0B000H      ;SEGMENT ADDRESS OF MEMORY
00410 ;                               ON MONOCHROME DISPLAY ADAPTER
00420          MOV     ES,AX     ;SET UP EXTRA SEGMENT REGISTER
00430          MOV     DI,0      ;INITIAL OFFSET ADDRESS INTO SEGMENT
00440          MOV     AL,' '    ;BLANK CHARACTER TO FILL DISPLAY
00450          MOV     AH,07H    ;ATTRIBUTE CODE FOR NORMAL DISPLAY
00460          MOV     CX,2000   ;NUMBER OF WORDS OF MEMORY TO INITIALIZE
00470          CLD               ;SO STRING INSTRUCTIONS GO FORWARD
00480          REP     STOSW     ;BLANK OUT THE DISPLAY
00490          CALL    CURSOR    ;MOVE THE CURSOR TO THE INITIAL
00500 ;                          ROW AND COLUMN
00510 ;
```

Fig. 6-14.   Monochrome display-driver program.

Continued on next page.

```
00520 ;PART 2: THIS IS THE MAIN LOOP OF THE PROGRAM
00530 ;        THE KEYBOARD BUFFER IS READ.
00540 ;        WHATEVER IS TYPED IS SENT TO THE DISPLAY DRIVER
00550 ;        IF A CARRIAGE RETURN IS TYPED THEN A CARRIAGE
00560 ;        RETURN AND LINE FEED ARE SENT TO THE DISPLAY DRIVER
00570 ;
00580 MAIN:   MOV     AH,0     ;READ CHARACTER FROM KEYBOARD CODE
00590         INT     16H
00600 ;AL HAS THE CHARACTER THAT WAS TYPED
00610         PUSH    AX       ;SAVE THE CHARACTER
00620         CALL    DISPLAY  ;THE DISPLAY DRIVER DISPLAYS THE
00630 ;                         CHARACTER IN AL
00640         POP     AX
00650         CMP     AL,0DH   ;WAS A CARRIAGE RETURN THE LAST CHARACTER?
00660         JNE     MAIN     ;IF NOT THEN GET THE NEXT CHARACTER
00670         MOV     AL,0AH   ;IF A CARRIAGE RETURN WAS DISPLAYED
00680 ;                         THEN ALSO DISPLAY A LINE FEED.
00690         CALL    DISPLAY
00700         JMP     MAIN     ;GET THE NEXT TYPED CHARACTER
00710 ;
00720 ;
00730 ;PART 3: THIS IS THE DISPLAY DRIVER
00740 ;        ON ENTRY AL HAS THE CHARACTER WE WANT TO DISPLAY
00750 ;        BACKSPACE (08H), CARRIAGE RETURN (0DH), AND
00760 ;        LINE FEED (0AH) ARE PROCESSED AS DESCRIBED IN
00770 ;        THE BEGINNING OF THE PROGRAM
00780 ;
00790 DISPLAY PROC    NEAR
00800         CMP     AL,08H   ;BACKSPACE?
00810         JE      BS       ;IF BACKSPACE THEN JUMP
00820         CMP     AL,0DH   ;CARRIAGE RETURN?
00830         JE      CR       ;IF CARRIAGE RETURN THEN JUMP
00840         CMP     AL,0AH   ;LINE FEED?
00850         JE      LF       ;IF LINE FEED THEN JUMP
00860 ;IF THE PROGRAM FALLS THROUGH TO HERE THEN WE WANT TO
00870 ;DISPLAY THE CHARACTER IN AL.
00880 ;FIRST WE MUST GET THE CORRECT OFFSET ADDRESS FOR THE
00890 ;CURRENT CURSOR POSITION.
00900         MOV     BL,AL    ;SAVE THE CHARACTER TO DISPLAY IN BL
00910         MOV     AL,80
00920         MUL     ROW      ;AX HAS 80*ROW NUMBER
00930         ADD     AX,COLUMN
00940 ;AX NOW HAS THE DISPLAY POSITION. MULTIPLYING IT BY 2
00950 ;GIVES THE OFFSET ADDRESS FOR THE DISPLAY POSITION.
00960         MUL     TWO      ;AX HAS THE OFFSET ADDRESS FOR
00970 ;                         THE CHARACTER CODE.
00980         MOV     DI,AX    ;DI HAS THE OFFSET ADDRESS
00990         MOV     ES:[DI],BL    ;THE CHARACTER CODE IS NOW
01000 ;                         IN THE ADAPTER MEMORY. THE DISPLAY
01010 ;                         ATTRIBUTE CODE IS ALREADY SET TO NORMAL
01020 ;
```

Fig. 6-14 (cont). Monochrome display-driver program.

Continued on next page.

```
01030 ;NOW UPDATE THE CURSOR POSITION
01040          INC      COLUMN   ;INCREMENT THE COLUMN COUNT
01050          CMP      COLUMN,80
01060          JE       ENDLINE  ;IF THE NEW COLUMN COUNT IS EQUAL
01070 ;                           TO 80 THEN WE JUST WENT OFF THE
01080 ;                           RIGHT SIDE OF THE LINE.
01090 ;IF FALL THROUGH HERE THEN THE NEW CURSOR POSITION IS OK
01100          CALL     CURSOR   ;UPDATE THE CURSOR TO THE CURRENT
01110 ;                           ROW,COLUMN
01120          RET
01130 ;
01140 ;GO TO THE BEGINNING OF THE NEXT LINE
01150 ENDLINE: MOV      COLUMN,0           ;POSITION TO COLUMN 0
01160          JMP  SHORT LF    ;GO TO THE NEXT LINE WHICH IS THE
01170 ;                          SAME PROGRAM AS PROCESSING A LINE FEED
01180 ;
01190 ;BACKSPACE PROCESSING
01200 BS:      CMP      COLUMN,0
01210          JNE      BACKSP   ;IF NOT 0 THEN REALLY BACKSPACE
01220          RET               ;DON'T BACKSPACE IF ALREADY AT
01230 ;                           THE BEGINNING OF A LINE
01240 BACKSP: DEC       COLUMN
01250          CALL     CURSOR   ;UPDATE THE CURSOR TO REFLECT
01260 ;                           THE NEW ROW,COLUMN
01270          RET
01280 ;
01290 ;
01300 ;CARRIAGE RETURN PROCESSING
01310 CR:      MOV      COLUMN,0           ;NEW COLUMN POSITION
01320          CALL     CURSOR   ;RE-POSITION THE CURSOR
01330          RET
01340 ;
01350 ;
01360 ;LINE FEED PROCESSING
01370 LF:      CMP      ROW,24
01380          JE       SCROLL   ;IF ON LAST ROW THEN MUST SCROLL
01390 ;                           THE DISPLAY
01400          INC      ROW      ;INCREMENT ROW COUNT
01410          CALL     CURSOR   ;RE-POSITION THE CURSOR
01420          RET
01430 ;IF THE PROGRAM GETS HERE THEN THE CURSOR IS ALREADY ON
01440 ;THE LAST LINE. INSTEAD OF MOVING THE CURSOR, THE DISPLAY
01450 ;MUST BE SCROLLED UP ONE LINE AND THE BOTTOM LINE MUST BE
01460 ;BLANKED OUT. THE CURSOR CAN REMAIN WHERE IT IS.
01470 ;
01480 SCROLL: PUSH      DS       ;SAVE THE DATA SEGMENT REGISTER
01490          MOV      AX,0B000H ;SEGMENT ADDRESS OF MEMORY ON
01500 ;                           THE MONOCHROME DISPLAY ADAPTER
01510          MOV      DS,AX    ;ES=DS=SEGMENT ADDRESS OF ADAPTER MEMORY
01520          MOV      SI,160   ;SOURCE DISPLACEMENT. START MOVING
01530 ;                           FROM BEGINNING OF SECOND LINE
01540          MOV      DI,0     ;DESTINATION DISPLACEMENT. START MOVING
```

Fig. 6-14 (cont).   Monochrome display-driver program.

Continued on next page.

```
01550 ;                          TO BEGINNING OF FIRST LINE
01560          MOV     CX,1920 ;MOVE 24*80 WORDS=1920
01570 ;NOTE: THE DIRECTION FLAG IS ALREADY CLEARED FOR FORWARD MOVEMENT
01580          REP     MOVSW   ;MOVE 1920 WORDS OR 3840 BYTES
01590 ;THE DISPLAY HAS BEEN SCROLLED SO NOW BLANK OUT THE BOTTOM
01600 ;LINE. DI ALREADY HAS THE CORRECT OFFSET DISPLACEMENT
01610 ;FROM THE PREVIOUS MOVSW
01620          MOV     AL,' '  ;FILL WITH BLANK CHARACTER
01630          MOV     AH,07H  ;NORMAL DISPLAY ATTRIBUTE
01640          MOV     CX,80   ;MOVE 80 WORDS FOR ONE LINE
01650          REP     STOSW   ;BLANK OUT THE BOTTOM LINE
01660          POP     DS      ;RESTORE THE DATA SEGMENT REGISTER
01670          RET
01680 DISPLAY ENDP
01690 ;
01700 ;
01710 ;CURSOR MOVES THE CURSOR TO THE POSITION DESCRIBED
01720 ;IN THE ROW AND COLUMN VARIABLES
01730 ;
01740 CURSOR  PROC    NEAR
01750 ;CALCULATE THE DISPLAY POSITION BASED ON ROW,COLUMN
01760          MOV     AL,80
01770          MUL     ROW     ;AX HAS 80*ROW NUMBER
01780          ADD     AX,COLUMN
01790 ;AX NOW HAS THE DISPLAY POSITION FOR THE CURSOR
01800 ;IT MUST BE PLACED IN THE 6845 CURSOR H AND CURSOR L REGISTERS
01810 ;
01820          MOV     BX,AX   ;SAVE DISPLAY POSITION
01830          MOV     DX,3B4H ;ADDRESS OF 6845 ADDRESS REGISTER
01840          MOV     AL,14   ;ADDRESS OF CURSOR H REGISTER
01850          OUT     DX,AL   ;CURSOR H REGISTER ADDRESSED
01860          MOV     DX,3B5H ;ADDRESS OF 6845 DATA REGS
01870          MOV     AL,BH   ;NEW VALUE FOR CURSOR H
01880          OUT     DX,AL   ;CURSOR H REGISTER MODIFIED
01890          MOV     DX,3B4H ;ADDRESS OF 6845 ADDRESS REGISTER
01900          MOV     AL,15   ;ADDRESS OF CURSOR L REGISTER
01910          OUT     DX,AL   ;CURSOR L REGISTER ADDRESSED
01920          MOV     DX,3B5H ;ADDRESS OF 6845 DATA REGISTER
01930          MOV     AL,BL   ;NEW VALUE FOR CURSOR L
01940          OUT     DX,AL   ;CURSOR L REGISTER MODIFIED
01950 ;THE CURSOR IS NOW DISPLAYED AT THE NEW DISPLAY POSITION
01960          RET
01970 CURSOR  ENDP
01980 ;
01990 START   ENDP
02000 CODE    ENDS
02010          END     START
```

Fig. 6-14 (cont). Monochrome display-driver program.

cursor is moved backward one column on the line. No action takes place if the cursor is at the beginning of the line. If a carriage return (0DH) is received, then the cursor is moved to the beginning of the current line. If a line feed (OAH) is received, then the cursor is moved to the same column on the next line. The backspace, carriage return, and line feed are the only control characters that the display program recognizes.

After the display is filled with characters, the cursor cannot move down any more lines. Once the cursor is on the bottom line, the display is scrolled up instead of moving the cursor down. This means that the contents of the top line are replaced with the contents of the second line and the second line is replaced with the contents of the third line. This action continues until the next-to-last line is replaced with the last line; then the last line is blanked out. Now the cursor is in the correct column of a blank line. The entire scrolling operation can be accomplished with a single 8088 string operation.

After a standard prologue, the program initializes ES to point to the adapter memory. The display is then blanked out, and the cursor is positioned at the upper left-hand corner of the display. Let us take a closer look at the cursor-positioning subroutine.

The cursor-positioning subroutine is found in statements 1740–1970. When called, it moves the cursor to the display position described by the variables ROW and COLUMN in the data segment. It calculates the display position by multiplying the row number by 80 and adding the column number to it. Notice the fact that ROW is a byte variable and COLUMN is a word variable. This is due to the fact that we must add the column value to the result of the multiplication, which is a word value. Once the display position is calculated, the rest is easy. The display position is the correct value for the cursor-address registers of the 6845.

The main loop of the program is found in statements 580–700. These statements are not part of the display driver. Instead, they allow us to demonstrate the use of the display driver. The main loop gets a character from the keyboard and sends that character to the display driver. If the character is a carriage return, a line feed is also sent to the display driver. This way the cursor will be moved to the beginning of a new line when we hit the ENTER key.

The display routine is found in statements 730–1680. It also uses the cursor subroutine. It is called with AL containing the character to be displayed. The beginning of the routine checks for a control character. If it is not a control character, then statements 900–1160 are executed. First, the character must be placed in the adapter memory at the correct character-code address, which is twice the display-position value. This value is calculated in statements 910–960. The input character is then moved to memory in statement 990.

The cursor position must be updated after the character is placed in memory. The column value is incremented. If the end of the line has not been reached, then the CURSOR routine is called. If the end of the line has been reached, then the column value is set to 0 and the program jumps to the code that handles line feeds (statements 1150–1160).

If the input character is a backspace, then statements 1190–1270 are executed. If the current column position is already at the beginning of the line, then nothing has to be done. Otherwise, the column value is decremented, and the CURSOR subroutine is called.

If the input character is a carriage return, then the column value is forced to 0, and the CURSOR subroutine is called (statements 1300–1330).

If the input character is a line feed, then statements 1360–1680 are executed. This is the most complex part of the program because the screen may have to be scrolled. If the cursor is not on the last row, then all we have to do is increment the row value and call the CURSOR routine (statements 1400–1420). If the cursor is already on the last row, then the display must be scrolled.

The movement of the display is accomplished in statements 1480–1580. The DS segment register is saved and set to the beginning of the adapter memory. Register DI, which will contain the destination offset address, is set to 0. This way, the moved data is placed starting at the first row. Register SI, which will contain the source offset address, is set to 160. This address corresponds to the first column of the second row. Therefore, the "move string" instruction will start moving data from the second row to the first row. A value of 1920 is placed in CX. This causes 3840 bytes, or 24 rows of display information, to be moved up one row. The MOVSW in statement 1580 does the actual movement of the data. The SI and DI registers are incremented throughout the execution of the instruction because the direction flag was cleared at the beginning of the program. This demonstrates the fact that not only can we write to the adapter memory, but we can read from it as well!

After the display is scrolled, the DI register has the offset address of the display position for the first column of the last line. This last line is blanked out in statements 1620–1660. This completes the scroll operation. The cursor is already in the correct position.

Type in the program and assemble, link, and run it. We now have a custom display driver that we can use with any programs we may write. Adding any special control characters that may be needed for a custom application should be easy to do. This concludes our discussion of the monochrome display.

THE COLOR/GRAPHICS MONITOR ADAPTER

The Color/Graphics Monitor Adapter can be used to generate an alphanumeric or graphics display image. Color or black-and-white images can be created. The adapter can be used with a television set (with a user-supplied rf modulator) or with a direct-drive RGB monitor.

A 6845 CRTC is used in the Color/Graphics Adapter. This is the same CRT Controller chip that is used in the Monochrome Adapter. We can really see the power of this chip when we look at all the different modes that the Color/Graphics Adapter supports. The same 6845 is used for all the different modes. It is initialized differently for each mode.

The Color/Graphics Adapter contains 16K of memory. As with the Monochrome Adapter, the display image is formed from the contents of this adapter memory. From the point of view of the 8088, this memory resides starting at physical location 0B8000H. By setting a segment register equal to 0B800H, we can view the memory on the adapter as having offset addresses 0-16K. All of the memory is needed to support a single graphics image on the display. In the alphanumeric mode, 8K is used for character codes, and 8K is used for display-attribute information. Because all the memory is not required for a single alphanumeric display image, different parts of the memory can be used to store different display images. These parts of memory are called *pages*. We will see how to program the 6845 to display different pages of the adapter memory.

In alphanumeric, or A/N, mode, the adapter can be used to place character images on the screen. An 80-column by 25-line image is achievable with a monitor, but only a 40-column by 25-line image is achievable with a television set. Four pages of text can be stored in the adapter memory if an 80-by-25 image is used. Eight pages of text can be stored if a 40-by-25 image is used. The same display attributes (except for underlining) that are available with the Monochrome Adapter are available in the A/N mode if a black-and-white image is requested. If a color image is requested, then 16 foreground and 8 background colors are available. As shown in Fig. 6-15, the foreground color makes up the character image, while the background color surrounds the character. The 16 possible colors are shown in Table 6-2. The background colors may be from either the first eight or last eight colors. The blinking display attribute is still available with a color alphanumeric image. With a color alphanumeric image, one of 16 possible screen-border colors may be selected.

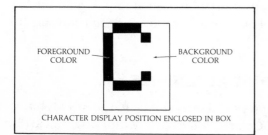

Fig. 6-15. Character foreground and background.

Table 6-2. Color Combinations With IRGB Bits

I	R	G	B	Color
0	0	0	0	Black
0	0	0	1	Blue
0	0	1	0	Green
0	0	1	1	Cyan
0	1	0	0	Red
0	1	0	1	Magenta
0	1	1	0	Brown
0	1	1	1	Light Gray
1	0	0	0	Dark Gray
1	0	0	1	Light Blue
1	0	1	0	Light Green
1	0	1	1	Light Cyan
1	1	0	0	Light Red
1	1	0	1	Light Magenta
1	1	1	0	Yellow
1	1	1	1	White

The adapter may also be set up to display graphics images. This is called the *All Points Addressable Graphics,* or *APA, mode.* There are two possible display resolutions available in this mode. In the medium-resolution mode, a color image with 320 horizontal by 200 vertical dots is displayed. The medium-resolution mode may be used with a television set. Each dot may be one of four colors. The first color may be one of the 16 possible colors shown in Table 6-2. This color is called the background color. The other three colors may be either red, green, and yellow or cyan, magenta, and white. Only one set of four colors is available for a given display image. In the high-resolution mode, a black-and-white image with 640 horizontal by 200 vertical dots is displayed.

Alphanumeric Mode

In the A/N mode, characters may be placed on the screen in either an 80-by-25 or a 40-by-25 format. As discussed above, black-and-white or color characters are available. We can use the BIOS call shown in Table 4-3 to initialize the 6845 and the adapter board. They may be initialized for either size display and black-and-white or color. For this BIOS call, we use an INT 10H with AH=0. The configuration switch on the system board should be set to indicate which type of display will be used.

After the BIOS call is used to initialize the type of display image, certain color characteristics must be initialized if a color display is requested. This is done through the *color-select register,* which is located at i/o address 3D9H. This register is shown in Fig. 6-16. The color of the screen border is

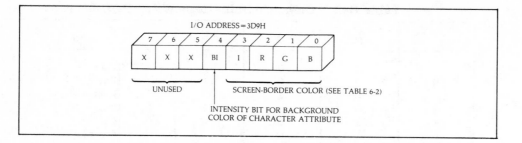

Fig. 6-16. Color-select register initialization (A/N mode).

selected with the low-order four bits. The color mapping for the IRGB bits is shown in Table 6-2. Bit 4 determines whether the background color of each character comes from the first or last eight entries of Table 6-2. This will be discussed further when character color attributes are covered.

As with the Monochrome Adapter, once we understand what a display position is, we can easily understand how to set memory to display a specific character with a certain color or attribute. For an 80-by-25 display image, the display position is (80 * row number) + column number. Fig. 6-2 shows the display positions for an 80-by-25 image. For a 40-by-25 display image, the display position is (40 * row number) + column number. This is shown in Fig. 6-17.

One byte of memory is used to store the character code, and another byte of memory is used to store the character display attribute. If a color image

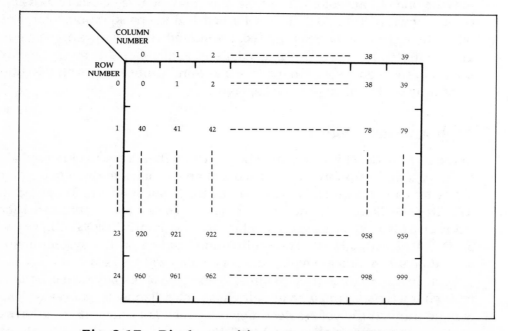

Fig. 6-17. Display positions on a 40-by-25 screen.

is requested, the character display attribute also contains the foreground and background color codes of the character. It takes two bytes of memory to represent a single display position.

The offset addresses of the two bytes of memory that represent a display position are the same as for the Monochrome Adapter. Character codes are stored in even addresses, and character attributes are stored in odd addresses. The offset address of the character code that represents a display position is twice the value of the display position. The character attribute is placed at the next offset address (which is odd). For the 40-by-25 display image, the display position can be represented by 10 bits. Therefore, the offset address can be represented by 11 bits. This is 1 bit less than the number of bits needed to address the 80-by-25 display. This should be expected because the number of characters displayed on the 40-by-25 screen is 1/2 the number of characters displayed on the 80-by-25 screen.

There is 8K of memory on the adapter board for character codes and 8K of memory on the adapter board for character display attributes. The 40-by-25 display requires only 1000 bytes of memory for character codes and 1000 bytes for character attributes. Therefore eight display images or *pages* can be stored in the adapter memory at the same time. Similarly, four pages can be stored simultaneously for the 80-by-25 display. The offset addresses for the different pages are shown in Fig. 6-18. There is 2K of memory per page for the 40-by-25 display and 4K of memory per page for the 80-by-25 display.

Previously, we learned how to calculate the offset address for a display position in page 0. The 6845 is initialized to display page 0 by the BIOS calls. To calculate the offset address of a display position in a different page, first calculate the offset address for page 0. Then add the offset address of the base of the desired page to the result. This is the correct offset address for the display position in the desired page. The segment register remains pointing at the base of the adapter memory. This is 0B8000H for the Color Adapter.

Fig. 6-18 shows the offset addresses for the different pages, assuming a maximum number of pages in the adapter memory. Actually, a page may start at any even offset address. The next 2K of memory will be displayed for a 40-by-25 display, and the next 4K of memory will be displayed for an 80-by-25 display. By advancing the beginning of the displayed page by one line of character images (80 bytes for the 40-by-25 display and 160 bytes for the 80-by-25 display), the display image can be scrolled. This is called *hardware scrolling* because the area of displayed memory is changed. This is different from the scrolling in the previous program (Fig. 6-14), where the characters were moved around in memory with a MOVSW.

How do we set the offset address of the page in memory to be displayed?

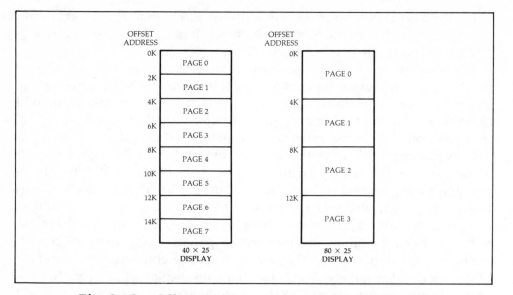

Fig. 6-18.   Offset addresses of pages in A/N mode.

The value in the start-address registers of the 6845 determines the offset address of the page in memory that is displayed. The start-address registers are shown in Fig. 6-11. As shown in Table 6-1, they are registers 12 and 13 in the 6845. For the Color Adapter, the i/o address of the address register in the 6845 is 3D4H, and the i/o address of all other registers is 3D5H.

When the monochrome display was discussed, we observed that the offset addresses from the point of view of the 8088 are not the same as the addresses from the point of view of the 6845. We have been viewing the offset addresses in the Color Adapter from the point of view of the 8088. This is the correct way to view the adapter memory when writing an 8088 program. However, remember that all adapter offset addresses must be divided by two before setting the 6845 registers. This is because the 6845 does not address the display-attribute bytes.

For example, suppose we want to display page 5 of the adapter memory. The adapter is initialized for a 40-by-25 display image. The base offset address of page 5 is 10K (2800H). Therefore, we would set the start-address registers of the 6845 to 5K (1400H), which is 1/2 of 10K. The offset addresses for the character codes and display-attribute bytes would start at 10K. The cursor-address registers, which determine where the cursor is displayed on the screen, would be set to 5K for display position 0. The cursor-address registers are always set to 1/2 the value of the offset address of the character code that we want the cursor to be positioned over. This is equivalent to the way we set up the cursor registers for the monochrome display, except that now more than one page of memory may

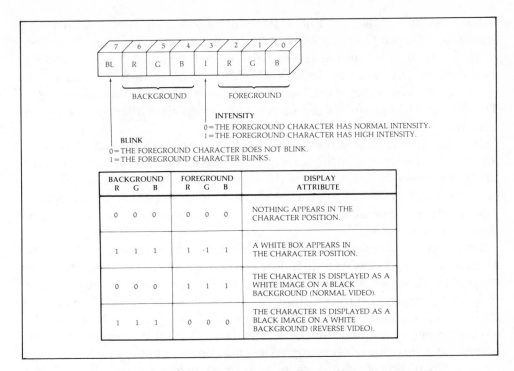

Fig. 6-19. Display-attribute byte for b-w A/N mode.

Fig. 6-20. Display-attribute byte for color A/N mode.

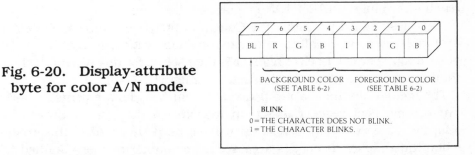

be displayed. Note that we can effectively turn off the cursor by setting the cursor-address registers equal to an address that is not in the page being displayed.

The display-attribute byte for a black-and-white image is similar to that used with the monochrome display. The correct setting for the black-and-white attribute byte is shown in Fig. 6-19. The attribute byte contains the color information for the character if a color image is displayed. This is shown in Fig. 6-20. The appropriate colors for the IRGB bits are shown in Table 6-2. Notice that there is no I bit for the background color. Bit 4 of the color-select register (Fig. 6-16) will determine whether the I bit is 0 or 1 for all background colors. Note that with a color image, the only display attribute besides color selection is blinking.

The program shown in Fig. 6-21 demonstrates the use of hardware scrolling. The program displays one of the first 128 possible character codes in the first column of each line. This requires 128 * 80, or 10240, bytes of adapter memory for a 40-by-25 display image. The cursor is placed at the beginning of the line that will hold the 64th character (a ''?''). The cursor will appear on the screen only when that display position is placed on the screen.

The display is scrolled down one line at a time until the last character appears in the middle of the screen. Then the display is scrolled up until the first character is at the top of the screen. The display is scrolled about once a second. The scrolling can be paused by hitting any key. The scrolling can then be resumed by hitting any key. A keyboard reset will return control to the system.

The data variables for the program are found in statements 220–250. The variable COUNT is used to hold a count of the number of lines that the display has been scrolled down. When this value reaches 116, it is time to reverse the direction of the scrolling until the value reaches 0. The variable BASE holds the current value of the start-address registers. By adding 40 to or subtracting 40 from this value, the new value for the registers can be computed. The value of 40 changes the offset address of the displayed page by exactly one line of characters for a 40-by-25 display image. The DIRECTION variable keeps track of the direction of the scrolling. When COUNT reaches its limits, DIRECTION is changed.

After a standard prologue, the Color Adapter is initialized. Statements 480–500 use a BIOS call to initialize the adapter for a 40-by-25 color display image. The color-select register is then set up for no border (black) and the first eight background colors (statements 510–540).

The memory of the adapter board is initialized in statements 560–660. The ES segment register is set up to point to the base address of the adapter memory. The ES register will be used throughout the program when the adapter memory is accessed. The adapter memory is filled with the blank character. The attribute byte that the memory is filled with will cause any character that is displayed to be green with a black background.

Statements 710–770 move the first 128 character codes (0–127) into the adapter memory. The memory positions that are filled map to the first column of every display line. As the display page is moved one line at a time, different characters will appear on the screen. They will always be in the first column because they are separated by 80 bytes (40 display positions). Of course, these numbers are correct only for a 40-by-25 display image.

In statements 820–940, the cursor is placed at the same display position as the 64th character code. The correct value for the cursor-address registers is 1/2 the value of the offset address for the 64th character code. This value is 40 * 63.

```
00020 ; THIS PROGRAM DEMONSTRATES THE USE OF HARDWARE SCROLLING.
00030 ; A 40 BY 25 COLOR IMAGE IS DISPLAYED ON THE SCREEN.
00040 ; CHARACTERS WITH CODES OF 0-127 ARE PLACED IN THE ADAPTER
00050 ; MEMORY SO THAT WHEN DISPLAYED, THEY ARE ALWAYS IN THE
00060 ; FIRST COLUMN OF A LINE.
00070 ; THE SCREEN IS SCROLLED DOWN ONE LINE A SECOND UNTIL THE
00080 ; 128TH CHARACTER IS IN THE MIDDLE OF THE SCREEN. THEN THE
00090 ; SCREEN IS SCROLLED UP UNTIL THE FIRST CHARACTER IS ON
00100 ; THE TOP LINE. THIS CONTINUES UNTIL THE PC IS RESET.
00110 ;
00120 ; HITTING ANY KEY WILL PAUSE THE SCROLLING UNTIL ANOTHER
00130 ; KEY IS HIT.
00140 ; THE CURSOR IS PLACED OVER THE ? CHARACTER.
00150 ;
00160 ;
00170 STACK     SEGMENT PARA STACK 'STACK'
00180           DB      256 DUP(0)
00190 STACK     ENDS
00200 ;
00210 DATA      SEGMENT PARA PUBLIC 'DATA'
00220 COUNT     DB      0         ;NUMBER OF LINES SCROLLED DOWN
00230 BASE      DW      0         ;THE CURRENT VALUE FOR THE
00240 ;                            START ADDRESS REGISTERS
00250 DIRECTION DB      0         ;THE SCROLL DIRECTION
00260 ;                            0=DOWN        1=UP
00270 DATA      ENDS
00280 CODE      SEGMENT PARA PUBLIC 'CODE'
00290 START     PROC    FAR
00300 ;
00310 ;STANDARD PROGRAM PROLOGUE
00320 ;
00330           ASSUME  CS:CODE
00340           PUSH    DS        ;SAVE PSP SEGMENT ADDRESS
00350           MOV     AX,0
00360           PUSH    AX        ;SAVE RET ADDRESS OFFSET (PSP+0)
00370           MOV     AX,DATA
00380           MOV     DS,AX     ;ESTABLISH DATA SEGMENT ADDRESSABILITY
00390           ASSUME  DS:DATA
00400 ;
00410 ;PART1: INITIALIZE THE DISPLAY ADAPTER
00420 ;        - BIOS CALL FOR 40 BY 25 COLOR DISPLAY
00430 ;        - INITIALIZE THE COLOR SELECT REGISTER
00440 ;        - CLEAR THE DISPLAY ADAPTER MEMORY
00450 ;        - FILL THE FIRST COLUMN POSITIONS WITH 128 CHARACTERS
00460 ;        - POSITION THE CURSOR OVER THE ?
00470 ;
00480           MOV     AH,0
00490           MOV     AL,1      ;40 BY 25 COLOR IMAGE
00500           INT     10H       ;ADAPTER INITIALIZED. PAGE 0 DISPLAYED
00510           MOV     DX,3D9H   ;ADDRESS OF COLOR SELECT REGISTER
00520           MOV     AL,0      ;BLACK BORDER.
```

Fig. 6-21. Hardware-scrolling program.

Continued on next page.

```
00530 ;                              I=0 FOR BACKGROUND COLORS
00540        OUT     DX,AL    ;COLOR SELECT REGISTERS INITIALIZED
00550 ;
00560        MOV     AX,0B800H        ;SEGMENT ADDRESS OF MEMORY
00570 ;                               ON COLOR ADAPTER
00580        MOV     ES,AX    ;SET UP EXTRA SEGMENT REGISTER
00590        MOV     DI,0     ;INITIAL OFFSET ADDRESS INTO SEGMENT
00600        MOV     AL,' '   ;BLANK CHARACTER TO FILL ADAPTER MEMORY
00610        MOV     AH,02H   ;THIS WILL BE THE ATTRIBUTE BYTE
00620 ;                        ALL CHARACTERS DISPLAYED WILL BE
00630 ;                        GREEN WITH A BLACK BACKGROUND
00640        MOV     CX,8000  ;INITIALIZE ALL OF MEMORY
00650        CLD              ;SO STOSW GOES FORWARD
00660        REP     STOSW    ;BLANK OUT THE ADAPTER MEMORY
00670 ;
00680 ;FILL EVERY 80TH BYTE (EVERY 40TH DISPLAY POSITION)
00690 ;WITH A CHARACTER FROM 0 TO 127
00700 ;
00710        MOV     AL,0     ;AL WILL HAVE CHARACTER
00720        MOV     DI,0     ;INITIAL OFFSET ADDRESS
00730 INIT:  MOV     ES:[DI],AL       ;MOVE CURRENT CHARACTER TO MEMORY
00740        ADD     DI,80    ;POINT TO NEXT LOCATION TO FILL
00750        INC     AL       ;INCREMENT CHARACTER TO DISPLAY
00760        CMP     AL,128
00770        JB      INIT     ;IF BELOW 128 THEN CONTINUE INITIALIZING
00780 ;
00790 ;THE ADAPTER MEMORY HAS BEEN INITIALIZED.
00800 ;NOW SET THE CURSOR ADDRESS REGISTERS
00810 ;
00820        MOV     BX,40*63 ;CURSOR ADDRESS FOR 64TH CHARACTER
00830        MOV     DX,3D4H  ;ADDRESS OF 6845 ADDRESS REGISTER
00840        MOV     AL,14    ;ADDRESS OF CURSOR ADDRESS HIGH REGISTER
00850        OUT     DX,AL    ;CURSOR ADDRESS HIGH REGISTER ADDRESSED
00860        MOV     DX,3D5H  ;ADDRESS OF 6845 DATA REGISTERS
00870        MOV     AL,BH    ;GET VALUE FOR CURSOR ADDRESS HIGH REGISTER
00880        OUT     DX,AL    ;SET CURSOR ADDRESS HIGH REGISTER
00890        MOV     DX,3D4H  ;ADDRESS OF 6845 ADDRESS REGISTER
00900        MOV     AL,15    ;ADDRESS OF CURSOR ADDRESS LOW REGISTER
00910        OUT     DX,AL    ;CURSOR ADDRESS LOW REGISTER ADDRESSED
00920        MOV     DX,3D5H  ;ADDRESS OF 6845 DATA REGISTER
00930        MOV     AL,BL    ;GET VALUE FOR CURSOR ADDRESS LOW REGISTER
00940        OUT     DX,AL    ;SET CURSOR ADDRESS LOW REGISTER
00950 ;
00960 ;
00970 ;PART 2:  SCROLL THE DISPLAY EVERY SECOND UNTIL A KEY IS HIT
00980 ;
00990 ;FIRST DELAY FOR A SECOND
01000 DELAY: MOV     AL,10
01010 TENTH: MOV     CX,28000         ;100 MS. DELAY COUNT
01020 DLOOP: LOOP    DLOOP            ;LOOP FOR 100 MS.
```

Fig. 6-21 (cont).   Hardware-scrolling program.

Continued on next page.

```
01030            DEC     AL
01040            CMP     AL,0
01050            JNE     TENTH    ;DELAY 100 MS. 10 TIMES
01060  ;
01070  ;NOW CHECK THE KEYBOARD FOR A DEPRESSED KEY
01080            MOV     AH,1     ;CODE FOR SETTING THE ZERO FLAG
01090            INT     16H
01100            JZ      SCROLL   ;IF NO KEY HIT THEN SCROLL DISPLAY
01110  ;CLEAR THE CHARACTER FROM THE KEYBOARD BUFFER
01120            MOV     AH,0     ;READ KEYBOARD BUFFER CODE
01130            INT     16H
01140  ;DO NOT CONTINUE SCROLLING UNTIL ANOTHER KEY IS HIT
01150            MOV     AH,0
01160            INT     16H
01170  ;WHEN FALL THROUGH, THE SCROLLING CAN PROCEED
01180  ;
01190  SCROLL:  MOV     BX,BASE ;CURRENT VALUE OF START ADDRESS REGISTERS
01200            CMP     DIRECTION,0    ;WHICH WAY TO SCROLL?
01210            JNE     BACKWARDS
01220  ;IF THE PROGRAM GETS HERE, THEN WE WANT TO SCROLL DOWN.
01230  ;BX HAS THE CURRENT VALUE FOR THE START ADDRESS REGISTERS
01240  ;
01250            INC     COUNT    ;INCREMENT SCROLLED LINES COUNT
01260            CMP     COUNT,116        ;MAXIMUM NUMBER OF LINES TO SCROLL DOWN
01270            JB      DOWN_OK
01280  ;IF THE PROGRAM GETS HERE, THEN WE WANT TO CHANGE
01290  ;THE SCROLL DIRECTION NEXT TIME
01300            MOV     DIRECTION,1      ;CHANGE THE DIRECTION VARIABLE
01310  DOWN_OK: ADD     BX,40            ;NEW VALUE FOR START ADDRESS REGISTERS
01320            MOV     BASE,BX          ;UPDATE VALUE IN MEMORY
01330  ;NOW CHANGE THE START ADDRESS REGISTERS TO THE VALUE IN BX
01340            JMP     SHORT UPDATE     ;COMMON UPDATE POINT
01350  ;
01360  ;IF THE PROGRAM GETS HERE, THEN WE WANT TO SCROLL UP
01370  ;BX HAS THE CURRENT VALUE FOR THE START ADDRESS REGISTERS
01380  ;
01390  BACKWARDS: DEC   COUNT    ;DECREMENT SCROLLED LINES COUNT
01400            CMP     COUNT,0 ;WILL WE HAVE SCROLLED COMPLETELY UP
01410            JNE     UP_OK
01420  ;IF THE PROGRAM GETS HERE, THEN WE WANT TO CHANGE THE
01430  ;SCROLL DIRECTION NEXT TIME THROUGH
01440            MOV     DIRECTION,0      ;CHANGE DIRECTION VARIABLE
01450  UP_OK:   SUB     BX,40    ;NEW VALUE FOR THE START ADDRESS REGISTERS
01460            MOV     BASE,BX ;UPDATE VALUE IN MEMORY
01470  ;
01480  ;COMMON POINT
01490  ;WHEN THE PROGRAM GETS HERE, WE WANT TO UPDATE THE
01500  ;START ADDRESS REGISTERS IN THE 6845 TO THE VALUE IN BX
01510  ;
01520  UPDATE:  MOV     DX,3D4H ;ADDRESS OF 6845 ADDRESS REGISTER
01530            MOV     AL,12    ;ADDRESS OF START ADDRESS HIGH REGISTER
01540            OUT     DX,AL    ;START ADDRESS HIGH REGISTER ADDRESSED
```

Fig. 6-21 (cont). Hardware-scrolling program.

Continued on next page.

```
01550              MOV      DX,3D5H  ;ADDRESS OF 6845 DATA REGISTERS
01560              MOV      AL,BH    ;GET VALUE FOR START ADDRESS HIGH REGISTER
01570              OUT      DX,AL    ;SET START ADDRESS HIGH REGISTER
01580              MOV      DX,3D4H  ;ADDRESS OF 6845 ADDRESS REGISTER
01590              MOV      AL,13    ;ADDRESS OF START ADDRESS LOW REGISTER
01600              OUT      DX,AL    ;START ADDRESS LOW REGISTER ADDRESSED
01610              MOV      DX,3D5H  ;ADDRESS OF 6845 DATA REGISTERS
01620              MOV      AL,BL    ;GET VALUE FOR START ADDRESS LOW REGISTER
01630              OUT      DX,AL    ;SET START ADDRESS LOW REGISTER
01640              JMP      DELAY    ;REPEAT THE PROCESS
01650     ;
01660 START        ENDP
01670 CODE         ENDS
01680              END      START
```

Fig. 6-21 (cont).   Hardware-scrolling program.

The major loop of the program starts with the code that delays for a second. The delay code is found in statements 1000–1050. After the delay, the keyboard is checked for a depressed key. Scrolling will be paused if a key is depressed. Scrolling will not resume until another key is depressed. These functions are accomplished in statements 1080–1160.

The scrolling is accomplished in statements 1190–1640. First the DIRECTION variable is checked to see whether the scrolling should be up or down. The current value of the start-address registers is placed in BX before the jump based on the scroll direction is made.

Statements 1250–1340 update the BASE value, assuming a downward scroll. A check is made to see whether the next scroll should be up instead of down. The new desired value for the start-address registers is left in BX, and control is transferred to a common point. Statements 1390–1460 perform the same function, except that the scrolling direction is up instead of down. In either case, the value for the start-address registers is modified by 40. This represents exactly one line of characters.

Statements 1520–1630 set the start-address registers to the value in BX. This actually causes the scrolling of the display. Statement 1640 jumps back to the delay code. This starts the cycle all over again.

Enter the program and assemble, link, and run it. Notice the way the cursor appears on the screen at the same time that the "?" character does. Try modifying the program to display different foreground and background colors and different character codes.

Graphics Mode

Besides the alphanumeric mode, the adapter can also be placed in the *graphics mode.* In the graphics mode, pictures may be drawn on the screen. Every picture is made up of a set of dots. The graphics mode allows us to draw individual dots on the screen. There are two screen resolutions available in the graphics mode. In the high-resolution mode, an image with 640 horizontal by 200 vertical dots may be produced; each dot may be either black or white. In the medium-resolution mode, an image with 320 horizontal by 200 vertical color dots may be produced. The vertical resolution for both modes is the same. The horizontal resolution for the high-resolution mode is twice as fine as the horizontal resolution for the medium-resolution mode. However, color dots can be produced in the medium-resolution mode.

In the medium-resolution mode, each dot may be one of four preselected colors. One of the colors may be preselected from the 16 colors in Table 6-2. This color is called the background color. The other three colors may be either red, green, and yellow or cyan, magenta, and white. Even though there are many different colors to choose from, only four may appear on the screen at the same time.

The Color Adapter board may be initialized to one of the resolutions described above by using the BIOS call shown in Table 6-3. It is the same BIOS call that we used to initialize the adapter for the A/N mode, except that the parameter in AL is different. When the board is initialized, the entire screen is filled with the background color.

Table 6-3. BIOS Calls for Graphics-Mode Initialization

Invoke via	Input Requirements	Registers Altered	Output/Results
INT 10H	AH = 0, AL = mode: AL = 4: 320 × 200 color AL = 5: 320 × 200 bw AL = 6: 640 × 200 bw	AX, SI, DI, BP	Set display mode specified by AL register. Configuration switch on system board must be set for color adapter.

If the adapter is initialized for the medium-resolution mode, the four possible colors must now be chosen. This is done by setting the color-select register at i/o address 3D9H. The settings for this register are shown in Fig. 6-22. The low-order four bits of the register determine the background color. The color that is determined by the IRGB bits is shown in Table 6-2. The other three preselected colors are determined by bit 5 of this register. Graphics images may be drawn on the screen once the color-select register has been initialized.

The contents of the adapter memory determine the image on the screen. The way the memory maps to the screen in the medium-resolution mode will now be discussed. The medium-resolution mode allows 320 by 200, or 64000, dots. Since the adapter has 16K of memory, four dots must be rep-

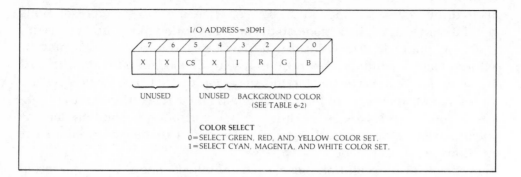

Fig. 6-22.   Color-select register initialization (graphics mode).

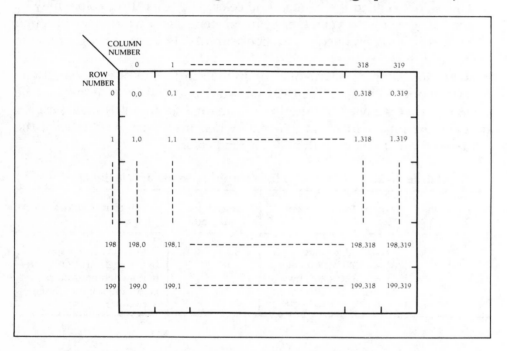

Fig. 6-23.   Dot coordinates in medium-resolution mode.

resented in one byte of adapter memory. This leaves two bits to represent each dot. Two bits can have four different combinations, which map to the four possible colors in the medium-resolution mode.

Each dot on the screen has a row and column coordinate. This is shown in Fig. 6-23. The memory that maps to the even row numbers starts at offset address 0. The memory that maps to the odd row numbers starts at offset address 2000H. It takes 80 bytes to represent a row of dots. Each byte is broken up into four sets of two bits each, as shown in Fig. 6-24. Each of these two-bit sets is called a *dot position*. The dot positions range

7	6	5	4	3	2	1	0
C1	C0	C1	C0	C1	C0	C1	C0

DOT POSITION 0   DOT POSITION 1   DOT POSITION 2   DOT POSITION 3

C1	C0	COLOR SET 0	COLOR SET 1
0	0	ONE OF 16 COLORS FOR BACKGROUND	
0	1	GREEN	CYAN
1	0	RED	MAGENTA
1	1	YELLOW	WHITE

Fig. 6-24.   Byte-to-dot mapping in medium-resolution mode.

from 0 to 3. Each dot position determines the color of a particular dot. The bit combination 00 is used to represent the background color.

To set a particular dot to a color, we must first get the offset address of the beginning of the 80 bytes that represent the row that contains the dot. Then the particular byte within the 80 bytes must be found. Then the correct two bits within that byte must be set to the bit combination that represents the desired color.

The row number of the desired dot coordinate is used to determine the offset address of the base of the 80 bytes. This is shown in Fig. 6-25. The lowest bit of the row number determines which half of memory to access. The value of the remaining 7 bits (0–99) is multiplied by 80 (the number of bytes that represent a row) to get the offset within the correct half of memory.

The column number is used to determine the correct byte and bits within the 80 bytes of interest. This is shown in Fig. 6-26. The column number is

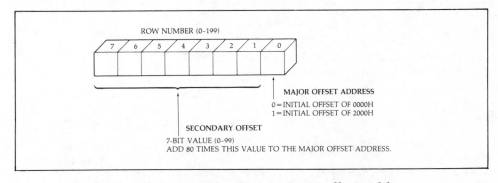

Fig. 6-25.   Obtaining the 80-byte offset address.

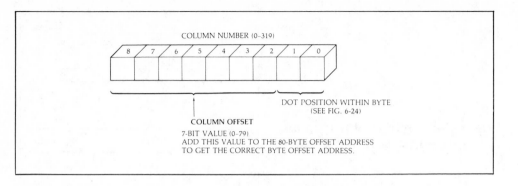

Fig. 6-26.   Determining bits to set in medium-resolution mode.

a nine-bit value ranging from 0 to 319. The high-order seven bits, which can range from 0 to 79, determine which byte within the 80 bytes (selected above) contains the correct bits to set. To access the correct byte, we can add the value of the offset address obtained from the row number to the value contained in these seven bits. The result will be the offset address for the correct byte to change.

The bits to use in the selected byte are determined by the low-order two bits of the column number. These low-order two bits form a value from 0 to 3. This value represents the dot position. If the low-order two bits of the column number are 00, then the high-order two bits of the selected byte must be changed. If the low-order two bits of the column number are 11, then the low-order two bits of the selected byte must be changed (see Fig. 6-24).

If we want to change a single dot on the screen, we must make sure that we do not change the color of the other dots that are represented in the same byte. When making a change, we must first read the appropriate byte from memory. The desired two bits can then be modified. After this is done, the byte can be written back to the correct offset address.

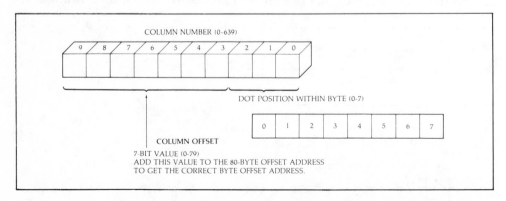

Fig. 6-27.   Determining which bit to set in high-resolution mode.

```
00020 ; THIS PROGRAM DISPLAYS A SET OF DOT COORDINATES
00030 ; AS RED ON A WHITE BACKGROUND
00040 ; IN THIS PROGRAM, THE COORDINATES FORM A TRIANGLE
00050 ; A GENERAL PURPOSE SUBROUTINE IS USED TO DRAW THE DOTS.
00060 ; THE MEDIUM RESOLUTION MODE OF THE COLOR ADAPTER IS USED
00070 ;
00080 ;
00090 STACK     SEGMENT PARA STACK 'STACK'
00100           DB      256 DUP(0)
00110 STACK     ENDS
00120 ;
00130 DATA      SEGMENT PARA PUBLIC 'DATA'
00140 COLOR     DB      10101010B        ;EACH 2 BIT CODE REPRESENTS RED
00150 MASKS     DB      11000000B        ;MASKS FOR EACH 2 BIT DOT POSITION
00160           DB      00110000B
00170           DB      00001100B
00180           DB      00000011B
00190 COUNT     DW      24        ;NUMBER OF COORDINATES IN LIST
00200 ;EACH SET OF COORDINATES IS COMPRISED OF A BYTE THAT
00210 ;CONTAINS THE VERTICAL ROW NUMBER AND A WORD THAT CONTAINS
00220 ;THE HORIZONTAL COLUMN NUMBER
00230 COORDINATES     DB      103      ;VERTICAL ROW NUMBER
00240           DW      154              ;HORIZONTAL COLUMN NUMBER
00250           DB      103
00260           DW      155
00270           DB      103
00280           DW      156
00290           DB      103
00300           DW      157
00310           DB      103
00320           DW      158
00330           DB      103
00340           DW      159
00350           DB      103
00360           DW      160
00370           DB      103
00380           DW      161
00390           DB      103
00400           DW      162
00410           DB      103
00420           DW      163
00430           DB      103
00440           DW      164
00450           DB      103
00460           DW      165
00470           DB      103
00480           DW      166
00490           DB      102
00500           DW      155
00510           DB      102
```

Fig. 6-28. Graphics program.

Continued on next page.

```
00520              DW       165
00530              DB       101
00540              DW       156
00550              DB       101
00560              DW       164
00570              DB       100
00580              DW       157
00590              DB       100
00600              DW       163
00610              DB       99
00620              DW       158
00630              DB       99
00640              DW       162
00650              DB       98
00660              DW       159
00670              DB       98
00680              DW       161
00690              DB       97
00700              DW       160
00710 EIGHTY       DB       80           ;CONSTANT FOR MULTIPLICATION
00720 DATA         ENDS
00730 ;
00740 CODE         SEGMENT PARA PUBLIC 'CODE'
00750 START        PROC     FAR
00760 ;
00770 ;STANDARD PROGRAM PROLOGUE
00780 ;
00790              ASSUME   CS:CODE
00800              PUSH     DS        ;SAVE PSP SEGMENT ADDRESS
00810              MOV      AX,0
00820              PUSH     AX        ;SAVE RETURN ADDRESS OFFSET (PSP+0)
00830              MOV      AX,DATA
00840              MOV      DS,AX     ;ESTABLISH DATA SEGMENT ADDRESSABILITY
00850              ASSUME   DS:DATA
00860 ;
00870 ;PART 1:  INITIALIZE THE COLOR ADAPTER BOARD
00880 ;
00890              MOV      AH,0      ;SET MODE CODE
00900              MOV      AL,4      ;320 BY 200 COLOR MODE
00910              INT      10H       ;ADAPTER INITIALIZED
00920 ;INITIALIZE THE COLOR SELECT REGISTER
00930              MOV      DX,3D9H ;ADDRESS OF COLOR SELECT REGISTER
00940 ·            MOV      AL,0FH    ;SELECT WHITE AS THE BACKGROUND COLOR
00950 ;                              AND SELECT THE COLOR GROUP WITH RED
00960              OUT      DX,AL     ;THE COLOR SELECT REGISTER IS INITIALIZED
00970 ;THE COLOR ADAPTER IS INITIALIZED. THE ADAPTER MEMORY IS
00980 ;INITIALIZED TO ZEROS (THE BACKGROUND COLOR) BY THE BIOS CALL.
00990              MOV      AX,0B800H        ;SEGMENT ADDRESS OF MEMORY
01000 ;                                      ON THE COLOR ADAPTER
01010              MOV      ES,AX     ;SET UP THE EXTRA SEGMENT REGISTER
01020 ;
```

Fig. 6-28 (cont).   Graphics program.

Continued on next page.

```
01030  ;PART 2: CALL THE DOT DISPLAY SUBROUTINE WITH THE NUMBER
01040  ;       OF COORDINATES IN COUNT
01050  ;
01060          MOV     CX,COUNT        ;CX HAS THE NUMBER OF
01070  ;                               COORDINATE SETS TO DRAW
01080          MOV     BX,OFFSET COORDINATES  ;BX HAS THE OFFSET
01090  ;                       ADDRESS OF THE BEGINNING OF THE
01100  ;                       LIST OF COORDINATES
01110  MAIN:   MOV     AL,[BX] ;AL HAS THE ROW NUMBER
01120          INC     BX      ;POINT TO COLUMN NUMBER
01130          MOV     DX,[BX] ;DX HAS THE COLUMN NUMBER
01140          ADD     BX,2    ;POINT TO NEXT COORDINATE
01150          CALL    DRAW    ;DRAW THE DOT DESCRIBED IN AL,DX
01160          LOOP    MAIN    ;DRAW COUNT NUMBER OF COORDINATES
01170  FOREVER: JMP    FOREVER ;AFTER DOTS DRAWN, NOTHING MORE TO DO
01180  ;
01190  ;
01200  ;DRAW SETS THE DOT DESCRIBED BY THE ROW NUMBER IN AL AND THE
01210  ;COLUMN NUMBER IN DX. THE DOT IS SET TO THE COLOR CODE
01220  ;CONTAINED IN THE VARIABLE COLOR
01230  ;REGISTERS ALTERED: AX,DX,DI,SI
01240  ;
01250  DRAW    PROC    NEAR
01260  ;FIRST CALCULATE THE 80 BYTE OFFSET ADDRESS
01270          SHR     AL,1    ;SHIFT ROW NUMBER ONE BIT TO RIGHT
01280  ;THE LOW ORDER BIT OF THE ROW NUMBER IS NOW IN THE CARRY FLAG.
01290  ;THE CORRECT 7 BIT VALUE TO MULTIPLY BY 80 IS LEFT IN AL.
01300  ;
01310          JC      ODD     ;THE LOW ORDER BIT WAS 1
01320  ;IF THE PROGRAM GETS HERE THEN THE LOW ORDER BIT WAS 0
01330          MOV     DI,0    ;MAJOR OFFSET ADDRESS IN DI
01340          JMP     SHORT COMMON
01350  ODD:    MOV     DI,2000H ;MAJOR OFFSET ADDRESS IN DI
01360  ;DI HAS THE CORRECT MAJOR OFFSET ADDRESS, WHICH IS
01370  ;DETERMINED BY THE ORIGINAL LOW ORDER BIT OF THE ROW NUMBER
01380  COMMON: MUL     EIGHTY          ;CALCULATE THE SECONDARY
01390  ;                       OFFSET, WHICH IS NOW IN AX
01400          ADD     DI,AX   ;DI NOW HAS THE OFFSET ADDRESS OF
01410  ;                       THE CORRECT 80 BYTE FIELD FOR THE ROW
01420  ;THE OFFSET WITHIN THE 80 BYTES MUST NOW BE CALCULATED
01430          MOV     SI,DX   ;SAVE THE COLUMN NUMBER IN SI
01440          SHR     DX,1
01450          SHR     DX,1    ;BY SHIFTING OUT THE TWO LOW ORDER
01460  ;                       BITS, DX NOW HAS THE CORRECT OFFSET
01470  ;                       WITHIN THE 80 BYTES
01480          ADD     DI,DX   ;DI NOW HAS THE CORRECT OFFSET ADDRESS
01490  ;                       FOR THE BYTE
01500          AND     SI,03H  ;SI NOW HAS THE VALUE FROM 0-3,
01510  ;                       WHICH REPRESENTS THE POSITION OF
01520  ;                       THE 2 BITS IN THE BYTE
01530  ;WE WILL NOW GET THE MASK WHICH REPRESENTS THE POSITION
```

Fig. 6-28 (cont).   Graphics program.

Continued on next page.

```
01540 ;OF THE 2 BITS IN THE BYTE. THE MASK WILL BE USED TO
01550 ;ISOLATE THE CORRECT COLOR BITS IN THE COLOR BYTE AND
01560 ;TO ISOLATE THE CORRECT 2 BITS TO CHANGE IN THE BYTE
01570 ;FROM THE ADAPTER MEMORY
01580         MOV     AL,[MASKS+SI]    ;GET CORRESPONDING MASK IN AL
01590         MOV     DH,COLOR         ;DH HAS THE RED COLOR CODE
01600 ;                       IN ALL ITS 2 BIT COLOR POSITIONS
01610         AND     DH,AL   ;DH NOW HAS THE RED COLOR CODE IN
01620 ;                       THE CORRECT 2 BIT POSITION.  ALL THE
01630 ;                       OTHER BITS IN DH ARE 0.
01640         NOT     AL      ;THE MASK IS COMPLEMENTED SO
01650 ;                       ALL THE ONES ARE ZEROS AND VICA VERSA
01660         MOV     AH,ES:[DI] ;GET THE CORRECT BYTE FROM THE
01670 ;                       GRAPHICS BOARD
01680         AND     AH,AL   ;AH NOW HAS THE BYTE FROM THE GRAPHICS BOARD
01690 ;                       WITH 0'S IN THE CORRECT 2 BIT POSITION
01700         OR      AH,DH   ;THE CORRECT 2 BIT POSITION HAS
01710 ;                       NOW BEEN FILLED WITH THE CODE FOR
01720 ;                       RED. ALL OTHER BITS REMAIN THE SAME
01730         MOV     ES:[DI],AH   ;MOVE THE NEW BYTE BACK TO
01740 ;                       THE CORRECT OFFSET ADDRESS
01750         RET             ;RETURN TO CALLER NOW THAT
01760 ;                       THE DOT HAS BEEN DRAWN
01770 DRAW    ENDP
01780 ;
01790 START   ENDP
01800 ;
01810 CODE    ENDS
01820         END     START
```

Fig. 6-28 (cont).   Graphics program.

The mapping for the 640-by-200 display image is similar to what we have just seen. There are still 80 bytes of memory needed to represent each row of dots. The base of the 80 bytes is calculated the same way as before. The only difference is that now the column number is a value from 0 to 639. Each byte represents 8 dots. One bit is used per dot. A 0 is used for black, and a 1 is used for white. There are not enough bits for any color information.

The selection of the correct bit to set within the 80 bytes is shown in Fig. 6-27. As before, the high-order seven bits determine the correct byte within the 80 bytes. The three low-order bits form a value from 0 to 7. This value determines which bit in the byte to set. The high-order bit is location 0, and the low-order bit is location 7.

Fig. 6-28 contains a program with a general-purpose subroutine that will set any dot position to a specific color. The subroutine works in the medium-resolution mode. The program calls the subroutine with a list of dot coordinates that we would like to draw. All the dots are set to red. The background is set to white.

The variables in the data segment are found in statements 140–710. The variable COLOR contains the two-bit code 10 in the four dot positions of the byte. This code represents red. This byte will be used to set a dot position to red. There are four mask bytes labeled MASKS. These bytes will be used to access the correct two bits of a byte. The selected two bits will represent a dot position in the byte. The first byte contained at the label MASKS represents dot position 0. The variable COUNT contains the number of coordinates that will be drawn. The coordinates are found starting at the label COORDINATES. Each coordinate consists of a byte that represents the row number of the dot and a word that represents the column number of the dot. There are 24 sets of coordinates in this list. They form an isosceles triangle. The variable EIGHTY is used with the MUL instruction.

After a standard prologue, the adapter board is initialized with the appropriate BIOS call. The color-select register is initialized in statements 930–960. The background color selected is white. The entire screen should now be white because when the adapter is initialized by the BIOS call, all of the adapter memory is set to 0. This value represents the background color in all the dot positions. The ES segment register is set up to point to the base of the adapter memory. Whenever the program wants to access the adapter memory, it will use ES.

Statements 1060–1170 call the DRAW subroutine with the 24 sets of coordinates. The DRAW subroutine is called with one set of coordinates at a time. The row number is put in AL, and the column number is put in DX. Throughout these statements, BX is used to point to the current set of coordinates in the data segment. Register CX is used to count down the number of coordinates already used. The program has finished the picture when CX reaches 0. The DRAW subroutine does not alter BX or CX.

The DRAW subroutine is found in statements 1250–1770. First, the major offset address is calculated and placed in DI. The major offset address represents which half of the adapter memory contains the correct byte to alter. This is determined by the low-order bit of the row number. By shifting AL one bit to the right, the low-order bit of the row number is placed into the carry flag. The carry flag is then tested, and the correct value is placed in DI (statements 1310–1350).

The remaining seven high-order bits of the row number are now properly positioned in AL to form a value from 0 to 99 (Fig. 6-25). This value is multiplied by 80, and the result is added to the major offset address. The offset address of the appropriate 80 bytes of memory is now in DI.

By reviewing Fig. 6-26, we can see how to get the offset within the 80 bytes. The offset is obtained by shifting the value of the column number two bits to the right. This result is added to DI. The offset address of the byte of adapter memory that must be altered is now in DI (statements

1440–1480). The original value of the column number is saved in SI before DX is destroyed by the shift.

The low-order two bits in SI determine which dot position within the byte must be altered. By ANDing SI with 3, a value of 0 to 3 remains in SI. This value represents the dot position desired. In statement 1580, AL is loaded with the mask byte that isolates the appropriate dot position. This mask byte is ANDed with the COLOR byte. A byte with the color code for red in only one dot position results. The rest of the dot positions contain zeros. This value is kept in DH (statement 1610).

The byte that must be altered is obtained from the adapter memory (statement 1660). It is ANDed with an inverted copy of the original mask byte. This causes the dot position that we want to alter to be set to 00. The rest of the dot positions remain unchanged. This result can now be ORed with the byte that contains the new color code in the correct dot position (statement 1700). The new color code has now been placed into the correct dot position. The other dot positions are not changed, since the color-code byte has zeros in all the other dot positions. The result can now be placed back into the adapter memory (statement 1730). At this point, the correct dot has been drawn, so the subroutine returns to the calling program.

Type in the program and assemble, link, and run it. Control can be returned to DOS with a keyboard reset. Try modifying the DRAW subroutine to set dots to a requested color (pass the color to DRAW as a parameter). Change the coordinates so that different images are drawn. This subroutine could be useful in any program that draws color graphics pictures.

THE PRINTER INTERFACE

The Personal Computer may be connected to a printer with a standard parallel interface. The *Monochrome Display and Printer Adapter* or the separate *Parallel Printer Adapter* may be used for this purpose. The signals of the parallel printer interface are shown in Table 6-4.

The operation of the parallel interface is quite simple. The printer will not accept any input unless the *select input* line is in the proper state. The *initialize printer* line is used to initialize the printer when the system is powered up. The correct signal must be on the line for at least 50 μs.

The data to be printed is placed on the eight *data-bit* lines. Then the *strobe* line is pulsed. The printer processes the data and then sends a pulse back on the *acknowledge* line. When the acknowledge pulse is received by the computer, another character may be sent to the printer. Instead of waiting for the acknowledge pulse, the computer may check the *busy* line. The computer may send characters to the printer as long as the printer is not busy. The *out-of-paper* input tells the computer that the printer is out of paper. The *select* input tells the computer that the printer is on line. The

Table 6-4. Parallel Printer Interface

Signal Name	Direction	Adapter Connector Pin Number
Data Bit 0	To Printer	2
Data Bit 1	To Printer	3
Data Bit 2	To Printer	4
Data Bit 3	To Printer	5
Data Bit 4	To Printer	6
Data Bit 5	To Printer	7
Data Bit 6	To Printer	8
Data Bit 7	To Printer	9
Strobe	To Printer	1
Select Input	To Printer	13
Auto Feed	To Printer	14
Initialize Printer	To Printer	16
Acknowledge	To Computer	10
Busy	To Computer	11
Out of Paper	To Computer	12
Select	To Computer	13
Error	To Computer	15

error input tells the computer that the printer is off line, out of paper, or in another error state. The busy status also reflects these error conditions.

Certain printers, including the IBM Matrix Printer and the Epson printers, are sensitive to the *auto feed* line. This line can be used to force the printer to generate an automatic line feed each time it prints a carriage return. This is not desirable under IBM DOS. Text files that are created under DOS have line feeds as well as carriage returns. If this signal is set incorrectly by the software, unintended double spacing will result.

The 8088 may input or output data to control or read the parallel printer interface lines. The i/o addresses are different for the Monochrome Display and Printer Adapter and the Parallel Printer Adapter. This is shown in Table 6-5. For example, when outputting the data to be printed, we would use i/o address 3BCH for the Monochrome Display and Printer Adapter or i/o address 378H for the Parallel Printer Adapter.

Fig. 6-29 shows how to control the output lines that go to the printer. These lines contain all the output control signals of the parallel printer port. The data that is output to the printer is sent to a different port. When

Table 6-5. I/O Addresses for Printer Adapters

Function	I/O Address on Monochrome Display and Printer Adapter	I/O Address on Parallel Printer Adapter
Output Data	3BCH	378H
Output Control	3BEH	37AH
Input Status	3BDH	379H

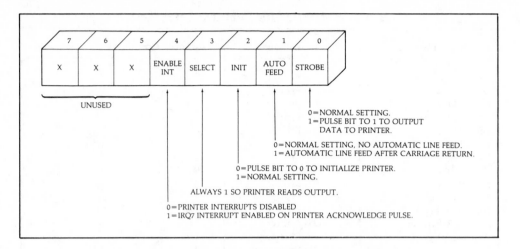

Fig. 6-29. Printer-adapter output control.

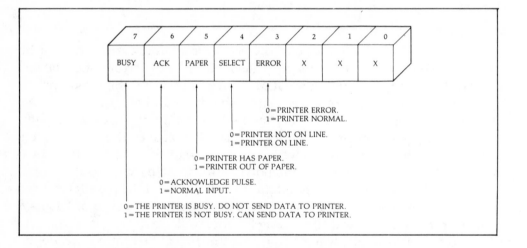

Fig. 6-30. Printer-adapter input control.

outputting data to this port, bit 3 must always be set to 1. Bit 1 should be 0 to inhibit the printer from generating automatic line feeds. Of course, if automatic line feeds are desirable, bit 1 should be set to 1.

Bit 4 can be used to enable printer interrupts. If bit 4 is set to 1, then when the adapter receives the printer acknowledge signal, an IRQ7 interrupt request will be generated. This interrupt can be used to tell a program that the printer is ready to accept another character. Usually, the busy signal input is used to determine when the printer is able to accept more data. This bit is normally set to 0.

When the printer is initialized, bit 2 is set to 0 for at least 50 microseconds. Then it is set back to 1. To initialize the printer, we would output a

```
; THIS SUBROUTINE PRINTS THE CHARACTER IN AL.
; I/O ADDRESSES FOR THE PARALLEL PRINTER ADAPTER ARE USED.
; CONTROL IS NOT RETURNED TO THE CALLER UNTIL THE PRINTER
; CAN ACCEPT THE CHARACTER. NO REGISTERS ARE CHANGED.
;
PRINT       PROC      NEAR
            PUSH      AX
            PUSH      DX          ;SAVE USED REGISTERS
; OUTPUT THE DATA:
            MOV       DX,378H     ;ADDRESS OF 'OUTPUT DATA' PORT
            OUT       DX,AL       ;OUTPUT THE CHAR TO BE PRINTED
; CHECK THE INPUT STATUS:
            MOV       DX,379H     ;ADDRESS OF 'INPUT STATUS' PORT
WAIT:       IN        AL,DX       ;READ PRINTER STATUS
            TEST      AL,80H      ;CHECK THE BUSY BIT
            JZ        WAIT        ;STAY IN LOOP UNTIL PRINTER NOT BUSY
; WHEN THE PROGRAM GETS HERE, THE PRINTER IS NOT BUSY:
            MOV       DX,37AH     ;ADDRESS OF 'OUTPUT CONTROL'PORT
            MOV       AL,ODH      ;STROBE BIT = 1
            OUT       DX,AL       ;STROBE THE PRINTER
            MOV       AL,OCH      ;STROBE BIT = O
            OUT       DX,AL       ;TURN PRINTER STROBE OFF
; RESTORE REGISTERS AND RETURN:
            POP       DX
            POP       AX
            RET
PRINT       ENDP
```

Fig. 6-31. Print routine.

08H to this port. Then, after waiting long enough, we would output a 0CH to this port. The printer would then be initialized.

When outputting data to the printer, the strobe bit must be set to 1 for a very short period of time. It must then be reset back to 0. The period of time is so short that the bit may be set and immediately reset. This action causes the printer to read the character on the data lines of the interface. This should be done only when the printer is not busy.

Fig. 6-30 shows how to read the input status from the printer. Before the data is strobed into the printer, the busy bit must be 1.

A BIOS call shown in Table 4-3 can be used to output data to the printer. When AH = 0 and DX = 0, an INT 17H will cause the character in AL to be printed. Bit 0 of the status return will be set to 1 if the printer was still busy after a long period of time. This is called a *time out* error.

Fig. 6-31 shows a routine that prints the character in AL. The routine assumes that the Parallel Printer Adapter is installed. Note that the routine does not return to the caller until the character can be strobed into the printer. Try writing a routine that will try to print a character, but will immediately return to the caller if the printer is not ready.

CHAPTER 7

Serial Communications

The communications adapter card, which plugs into an expansion slot, gives the PC the capability to communicate with other computers or devices using a standard RS232-C serial-communications interface. Before we explore how to control the communications adapter, a complete background on serial communications is presented.

SERIAL VERSUS PARALLEL

In the previous chapter, we saw how the PC is able to send data to the printer. Eight data lines and at least two control lines are required to perform the data transfer. A representation of this is shown in Fig. 7-1A. Note that with this method an entire byte of information can be transferred in the time it takes to transmit one bit because all the bits are transmitted at once on separate lines. This method is considered *parallel* communications because the data is transferred one byte (many bits) at a time. Besides being easy to program and understand, parallel communications supports a relatively fast transfer of data. So why bother with any other kind of communications protocol?

If we consider the case of two devices sitting next to each other, the answer is not obvious. But what happens when we move one of the devices to another floor or building? Not including electrical ground, we would need a cable with over 10 wires to carry on a one-way conversation or a cable with over 20 wires to carry on a two-way conversation. If we transmitted the data and control information one bit at a time, we could get by with one wire plus electrical ground to carry on a one-way conversation. This method is represented in Fig. 7-1B and is the basic concept behind *serial* communications. Serial communications is significantly slower than parallel communications because the bits that make up the data and control information must be transmitted one at a time.

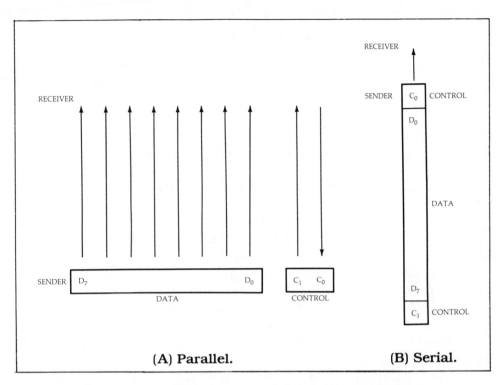

Fig. 7-1. Parallel versus serial data transmission.

An enormous amount of money could be saved in cable costs by using the serial concept. However, that is not the prime reason for the popularity of serial communications. We usually don't have to string a cable between two distant points to allow serial communications to take place. The cable is already there—the phone line. With a serial communications protocol and the proper interfacing equipment, a conversation can take place between any two devices over the telephone lines. With this in mind, it is not surprising that serial communications has become the standard way in which computers interface with the rest of the world.

THE ASYNCHRONOUS SERIAL PROTOCOL

The main concept behind the serial protocol is that all the data and control information necessary to transmit and receive a character of information must move over a single data line, one bit at a time. The way this is done is shown in Fig. 7-2.

When viewing Fig. 7-2, imagine that the bits of data flow as if they were traveling down a single wire. The width of each bit is determined by the data transmission speed, which is measured in bits per second. This speed is called the *baud rate*. If the data is being transmitted down the communi-

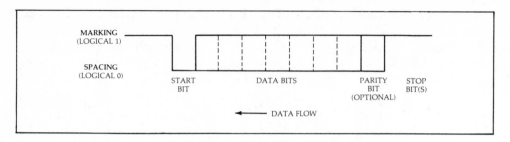

Fig. 7-2. Asynchronous serial data format.

cations line at 300 bits per second, then the speed of the transmission is 300 baud.

When no data is being transmitted on the line, the line is left in a logical 1 state, or a *marking state*. When we wish to transmit a character of data, the first bit to be transmitted is the *start bit*. The start bit is represented by a logical 0 state, or a *spacing state*, on the line. The duration of the start bit is determined by the baud rate. The receiver knows to expect a character of data when it notices the line change from a marking state to a spacing state—in other words, on reception of the start bit.

The data bits, which make up the character of information that is being transmitted, immediately follow the start bit. The number of data bits can be 5, 6, 7, or 8, but each character must contain the same number of data bits in the same transmission. The number of data bits is not fixed because many times the number of bits that make up a character of information that we wish to transmit is less than eight. By not fixing the size of the transmitted data, the speed of data transmission can be optimized. The data bits are transmitted least significant bit first and are reassembled on the receiving end to form the character of data that was transmitted.

An optional *parity bit* immediately follows the data bits. The type of parity selected must be consistent throughout the same transmission. If even parity is selected, then the number of logical 1 bits that make up the data bits and parity bit must be even; if odd parity is selected, then the number of logical 1 bits must be odd. As we will see later, the parity bit allows the receiver to detect certain types of transmission errors.

There are 1, 1.5, or 2 bits of marking (logical 1) following the parity bit (or data bits if no parity bit is present). These bits are called the *stop bits*. The stop bits represent the minimum amount of time that the line must be in a marking condition before the next start bit can appear. The number of stop bits must be consistent throughout the same transmission. If there is another character to be transmitted, then it will immediately follow the stop bits with its associated start bit. If another character is not immediately available to be transmitted, then the line will remain in a marking condition until there is another character to be transmitted.

Because data characters can start and stop arriving at any time, the serial communications protocol discussed above is an *asynchronous* protocol. After the stop bits of the last character have been received, the receiver does not begin to look for more data until a start bit is received. Until that time, the line should remain in a marking condition. This is different from a *synchronous* serial communications protocol, in which data characters are always being transmitted on the communications line.

In an asynchronous protocol, the receiver has to synchronize with the sender when the start bit of a new character is received. Since the baud rates of the sender and the receiver are set up to be the same, the receiver is able to pick off the start, data, parity, and stop bits from the line as a function of time; the beginning of the start bit is used as the synchronizing event. If there is a small difference between the clocks of the sender and receiver, an error may not result because the sender and receiver are resynchronized at the beginning of every character. The sender and receiver must also be set up for the same number of data bits, the same type of parity, and the same number of stop bits for the data reception to be successful.

THE UART

It would seem quite complex to write a program to send and receive data characters in an asynchronous serial communications environment. Fortunately, a dedicated microprocessor called a *Universal Asynchronous Receiver Transmitter*, or *UART*, is used to perform most of the serial-protocol conversion. The UART used in the PC is called the 8250 Asynchronous Communications Element.

A functional diagram of a UART is shown in Fig. 7-3. Modem (discussed later) and interrupt control signals have been omitted for clarity. The UART allows us to transmit and receive data serially without having to perform any parallel-to-serial or serial-to-parallel conversions. Before the UART can be used, it must first be told (via 8088 OUT instructions) the desired baud rate, the number of data bits, the type of parity, and the number of stop bits. Once the UART has been "programmed" with the desired serial-protocol characteristics, it can be used to transmit and receive serial data.

When we want to transmit a character of data, we check the UART status (via an 8088 IN instruction) to see if the *transmitter holding register* is empty. If it is, we can output a byte of data to the UART, and this byte is placed in the transmitter holding register. When the UART has completed transmitting the previous character or is currently not transmitting any data (the output line is at logical 1), the contents of the transmitter holding register are placed in the *transmitter shift register*. The transmitter hold-

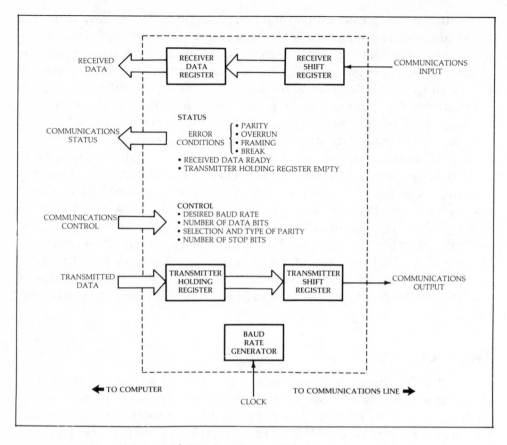

Fig. 7-3.   The UART.

ing register is then available for another output character from the computer. Only the low-order bits of the byte in the transmitter holding register are used if the protocol calls for fewer than eight data bits. The UART adds the appropriate start, parity, and stop bits to the character in the transmitter shift register, and then sends the entire string of bits out on the serial communications line.

Therefore, once the UART is initialized, all we have to do is output a byte of data to the UART, and the character is automatically transmitted serially with all the appropriate characteristics. While the transmission is taking place, the computer can be doing something else, periodically checking to see if the transmitter holding register is ready to accept another output byte.

The UART places any serial input it receives into the *receiver shift register*. After the appropriate number of stop bits are received and error checking is performed, the character is placed in the *receiver data register*. If fewer than eight bits of data are used, then only the low-order bits of the receiver data register are now valid. The UART then updates its status to show that receiver data is ready. The computer knows that it can read another byte of data from the UART when the receiver-data-ready status is correct. After the data is read by the computer, the UART does not show receiver data ready again until it has placed another character into the receiver data register.

The UART has made the reception of serial data very simple for us. All we have to do is monitor a single bit of status and input a byte of data whenever that status bit says the time is right. The UART also tells us whether any errors occurred in the input character. When the UART status is checked for receiver data ready, if data is ready, the status will reflect any of the possible input-error conditions.

If the UART must place a second character into the receiver data register before the first character is read by the computer, then an *overrun error* results. This error can occur if the computer does not monitor the receiver-ready status often enough. If the protocol being used requires seven data bits, parity, and one stop bit, then by dividing the baud rate by 10 (don't forget the start bit) we can calculate the maximum number of characters per second that the UART will want to place in the receiver data register. If a program we use does not monitor the UART status at least that many times a second, then an overrun error can result.

Sometimes transmission-line problems can cause some bits in the transmitted data to change before the receiver gets them. A noisy phone line can cause this problem. The data character that the UART reassembles will be incorrect if any of the data bits are changed. Because the parity bit should show the number of logical 1s in the data bits, the UART can use the parity bit to detect this problem. If a parity error is detected for a character we receive, then we must ask for a new transmission of at least a portion of the data that we are receiving.

If the UART does not receive a stop bit when it is expecting one, then a *framing error* results. This error can have many causes. The way the receiving UART is initialized may not match the way the transmitting UART is initialized. The clocks of the receiver and transmitter may be off just enough to cause loss of synchronization before an entire character is assembled. Transmission-line noise can garble the reception of the stop bits. In any case, the action taken should be the same for parity errors and framing errors.

Some asynchronous serial communications protocols allow for a special condition on the transmission line. This is called the *break condition*. To send a break condition, the line must be held in a spacing condition for at least as long as it takes to transmit one character with all its associated control bits. The UART will reflect the reception of a break condition in its status output.

It would be difficult to write many communications programs if we had to be concerned about constantly checking the UART status to see if a character is ready for input or if the UART is ready to accept another character for output. To help us get around this problem, the UART provides us with a programmed interrupt. The UART can be programmed to provide us with an interrupt if there is a character ready for reception, if there is an input error, or if the transmitter holding register is empty. Therefore, instead of constantly monitoring the UART status, our program can be doing something else, and when the time is right the program will be forced to interact with the UART.

We should now have a complete theoretical background concerning the way a UART works and the way it might be used with a software program. Later in this chapter, we will examine the 8250 Asynchronous Communications Element in detail. A simple 8088 program that performs serial communications will be presented.

THE MODEM

The RS232 interface (discussed in the next section) electronically connects the UART to the outside world. It can be directly connected to another RS232 interface only over short distances. If we want two computers to be able to talk to each other over long distances or over the phone lines, then the electronic output of the serial RS232 interface cannot be used without additional interfacing equipment. Shown in Fig. 7-4, this additional equipment is called a *modem*.

The output of the RS232 interface is an electrical voltage that cannot be placed directly on the phone lines. The modem converts the voltages that represent the logical ones and zeros to different tones that can be transmit-

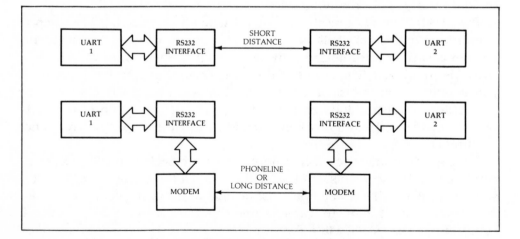

Fig. 7-4. Use of modem.

ted over the phone lines. The modem on the other end of the phone line converts the tones back to electrical ones and zeros that the RS232 interface can understand. With this method, logical ones and zeros can be transmitted over long distances without any problems.

The most popular inexpensive modems can transmit binary data over an ordinary phone line at either 300 baud or 1200 baud. Modems that allow both computers to transmit and receive data at the same time are called *full-duplex* modems. Most modems that the casual computer user can purchase are full-duplex. Some modems have the capability to dial a remote computer modem and establish a connection under program control. These are called *autodial* modems. *Autoanswer* modems have the capability to detect when the phone to which they are attached is ringing and can answer the phone to establish a computer connection.

All the control information necessary to transmit and receive a data character serially is contained in the bit stream that is sent over a single line. However, the RS232 interface contains many more control lines that are sometimes used to interact with a modem. These control signals are accessible under program control through the UART. The extra control lines do not represent a cabling problem because the modem is always physically close to the computer.

The modem control signals are described in Chart 7-1. When a communications program is written, the desire to use some or all of the modem control signals is situation-dependent. For instance, if a computer is always connected to a modem that is always in contact with another modem, then it is not necessary to check any of the modem control signals. If the connection breaks, it will be obvious to the operator by the way the program acts. However, through the monitoring of the modem control sig-

Chart 7-1. Modem Control Signals

Signals to Modem From Computer

DTR—DATA TERMINAL READY—Under program control. Used to tell the modem that the computer is powered up and ready.

RTS—REQUEST TO SEND—Under program control. Used to tell the modem that the computer wants to send data now.

Signals From Modem to Computer

DSR—DATA SET READY—Used to tell the computer that the modem is powered up and ready.

CTS—CLEAR TO SEND—Used to tell the computer that the modem is ready to accept data transmission.

DCD—DATA CARRIER DETECT—Used to tell the computer that the modem has established a connection with the modem on the other end of the phone line.

RI—RING INDICATOR—Used to tell the computer that the phone connected to the modem is ringing.

nals the program could detect the breaking of a connection and inform the operator. This could be desirable in many situations. For our purposes, we will set the "data terminal ready" and "request to send" outputs active on initialization and forget about them. To simplify matters, we will not monitor any modem-control-signal inputs in our sample program.

THE PHYSICAL INTERFACE

The communications adapter for the IBM PC provides a standard RS232 interface to the outside world. The connector that comes out of the adapter is a standard male 25-pin "D" shell. Fig. 7-5 shows the connector with the pins numbered.

The RS232 interface converts the electrical signals from the UART to standard EIA voltage levels, which are present on the physical connector. A logical 0, which is a spacing condition, is represented by +3 to +15 volts. A logical 1, which is a marking condition, is represented by −3 to −15 volts. The interface will also convert the input voltages back to the correct binary electrical signals for the UART.

The physical pinout for the RS232 connector is shown in Table 7-1. With the communications adapter powered up and initialized, we should be able to measure a negative voltage between pins 2 and 7. This corresponds to the marking condition that the line should be in when no data is being transmitted. This interface can be plugged directly into a modem with no changes to the correlation of the pins.

However, if we wish to connect a PC to another PC, we cannot simply connect pin 2 to pin 2, and so on. If we did this, then the two transmit-data pins would be connected to each other, which wouldn't work very well. The correct way to connect two machines with the interface shown in Table 7-1 is shown in Fig. 7-6. This connection scheme is sometimes called a *null modem*. Notice the way the modem control signals correlate. This is necessary because even though a modem is not in use, some programs require the appropriate modem control inputs, which can be provided by the corresponding modem control outputs. It should be noted that if none of the modem control signals are used, then only pins 2, 3, and 7 must be

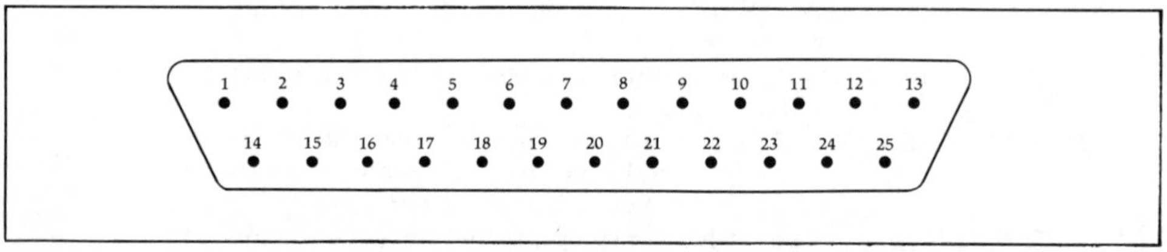

Fig. 7-5.   Standard 25-pin male "D" connector.

Table 7-1. Standard RS232 Pinout

Pin Number	Direction	Function
2	Output	Transmitted Data
3	Input	Received Data
4	Output	Request To Send
5	Input	Clear To Send
6	Input	Data Set Ready
7		Signal Ground
8	Input	Data Carrier Detect
20	Output	Data Terminal Ready
22	Input	Ring Indicator

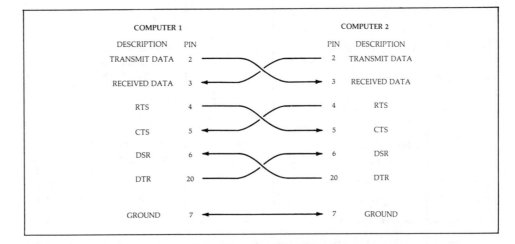

Fig. 7-6. Connecting two RS-232 interfaces.

connected between the two computers. This is why we will ignore the modem control signals when we write our communications program.

SERIAL I/O BIOS CALLS

As we have seen, the BIOS provides us with a convenient way to perform i/o without having to understand the details of the hardware. This is also true for serial i/o. Table 7-2 and Fig. 7-7 contain the information needed to implement a simple serial-communications program.

All the serial-i/o BIOS calls use an INT 14H. On entry, AH is used to differentiate among the function calls. If more than one communications adapter is installed, then BX can be 0 or 1 on entry. For our purposes it will be 0.

When we want to initialize the communications port with all the necessary information that the UART requires to function properly, we use an

Table 7-2. Serial I/O BIOS Calls

Invoke via	Input Requirements	Registers Altered	Output/Results
INT 14H	AH=0, BX=0, AL=init parms (see Fig. 7-7A).	AX	Initialize serial port as per parameters specified in AL. Return serial status in AX as per Figs. 7-7B and 7-7C.
	AH=1, BX=0, AL=character.	AH	Transmit data character specified in AL register. Return status in AH as per Fig. 7-7B, except bit 7 of AH is set if the character could not be transmitted.
	AH=2, BX=0.	AX	Wait for character to be received, and return it in the AL register. Return status in AH as per Fig. 7-7B, except bits 5 and 6 of AH are always zero.
	AH=3, BX=0.	AX	Return serial status in AX. AH will contain the communications line status as per Fig. 7-7B, and AL will contain the modem status as per Fig. 7-7C.

INT 14H with AH=0. This function call does not allow us to perform serial communications with interrupts.

When we want to transmit a character, we use an INT 14H with AH=1. This call sets the ''data terminal ready'' and ''request to send'' modem control signals and will not transmit a character if it does not receive correct modem control signals for ''data set ready'' and ''clear to send.'' The character will be sent to the UART when the transmitter holding register is empty. If the above conditions are not met within a preset period of time, then a *time out* condition will be set as part of the returned status in AH.

When we want to receive a character, we use an INT 14H with AH=2. This call sets the ''data terminal ready'' modem control signal and will not look for a received character until it gets a correct modem control signal for ''data set ready.'' If the signal is not received within a preset period of time, then BIOS returns to the caller with a time-out error in AH. Otherwise, control is not returned until a character is received by the UART and placed in AL.

The status of the communications line and the modem can be obtained by using an INT 14H with AH=3. The delta status bits are used to show

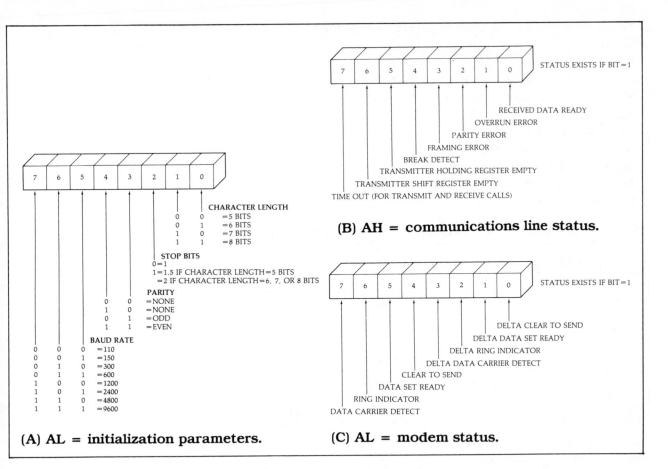

(B) AH = communications line status.

(A) AL = initialization parameters.   (C) AL = modem status.

Fig. 7-7.   Serial-i/o BIOS calls.

that a change occurred in the corresponding modem status bit. In order to prevent a call to receive a character from never returning, this call should be used first to make sure that there is a character in the UART to receive.

It should be quite simple to write a program using these BIOS calls. However, when we examine the hardware details of the 8250, we will discover many features that cannot be used unless we control the 8250 directly from an 8088 program. In many instances, the necessary degree of control over the UART is not available unless it is programmed directly.

PROGRAMMING THE 8250

Fortunately, the 8250 is not as complex as it appears at first glance. Even though the 8250 has ten registers that can be accessed by the 8088, most of them can be ignored once the 8250 has been initialized. A list of the 8250 registers and their associated i/o addresses appears in Table 7-3. Note that the high-order bit of the line-control register must be set to 1 in order to access the baud-rate-divisor registers. This bit should be 0 at all other times.

Five of the registers must be programmed by the 8088 with an OUT instruction to initialize the 8250. Once these registers have been initialized, they can be ignored for the rest of the time that the 8250 is used. These registers are:

Baud-rate divisor (LSB)
Baud-rate divisor (MSB)
Line-control register
Modem-control register
Interrupt-enable register

Table 7-3. Accessing the 8250 Registers

I/O Port Address	Input or Output	Register Selected
3F8H*	Output	Transmitter Holding Register
3F8H*	Input	Receiver Data Register
3F8H†	Output	Baud-Rate Divisor (LSB)
3F9H†	Output	Baud-Rate Divisor (MSB)
3F9H*	Output	Interrupt-Enable Register
3FAH	Input	Interrupt-Identification Register
3FBH	Output	Line-Control Register
3FCH	Output	Modem-Control Register
3FDH	Input	Line-Status Register
3FEH	Input	Modem-Status Register

* Bit 7 of the line-control register = 0
†Bit 7 of the line-control register = 1

During the course of the communications program, the line-status register is used by the 8088 to determine when to transmit or receive a character. Characters to be transmitted are output to the transmitter holding register. Received characters are input from the receiver data register.

If the modem control signals are important, then the modem-status register can be used to monitor those signals or changes in those signals. If the modem control signals are not used, then this register can be ignored.

If the communications program uses interrupts with the 8250, then the interrupt-identification register is used to identify the cause of the interrupt. The appropriate action can then be taken. If interrupts are not being used, then this register can be ignored.

INITIALIZING THE 8250

Before we can use the 8250 for serial communications, it must be properly initialized. As we have seen, there are many parameters that must be set up to match the parameters of the system with which we are communicating.

The first parameter that should be initialized is the baud-rate divisor. This value is used to divide a high-frequency clock output into a clock signal that represents the baud rate that we wish to use for the transmission and reception of serial data. Table 7-4 contains the MSB and LSB values of the baud-rate divisor needed to obtain a given baud rate.

Table 7-4. Baud-Rate-Divisor Values

Desired Baud Rate	Value for Baud-Rate-Divisor Registers	
	MSB	LSB
50	09H	00H
75	06H	00H
110	04H	17H
134.5	03H	59H
150	03H	00H
300	01H	80H
600	00H	C0H
1200	00H	60H
1800	00H	40H
2000	00H	3AH
2400	00H	30H
3600	00H	20H
4800	00H	18H
7200	00H	10H
9600	00H	0CH

To initialize the baud-rate divisor, we must first set the high-order bit of the line-control register to 1 with an OUT to i/o address 3FBH. We can then output the correct LSB and MSB values for the baud-rate divisor to i/o addresses 3F8H and 3F9H, respectively. For example, if we wanted a transmission to take place at 1200 baud, we would first output an 80H to i/o address 3FBH. Then we would output a 60H to i/o address 3F8H and a 00H to i/o address 3F9H.

After the baud-rate divisor is initialized, the line-control register should be initialized. This register determines the character length, number of stop bits, and type of parity to be used in the serial transmission. Fig. 7-8 shows how to initialize this register for the desired transmission parameters. Note that the low-order five bits of this register are the same as the input parameter for the BIOS call used to initialize the communications port.

Normally, the high-order three bits of this register should be set to 0 at this time. The high-order bit should be set to 0 so that we do not access the baud-rate-divisor registers any more. The set-break bit should be set to 1

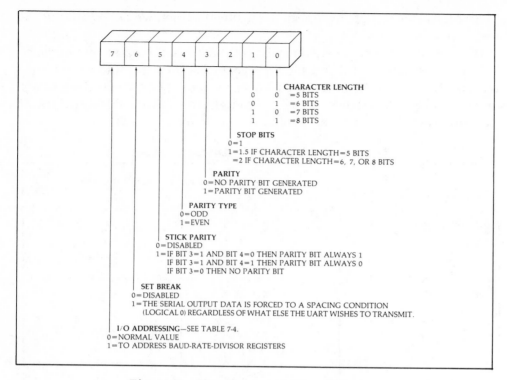

Fig. 7-8. The line-control register.

only if we wish to cause a break condition to be output on the line. The stick-parity bit should be set to 1 only if we wish the parity bit to be a constant value.

As an example, suppose we want the transmission to have characters with seven bits of data, one stop bit, and even parity. We would output a 1AH to i/o address 3FBH.

The next register to be initialized should be the modem-control register. Fig. 7-9 shows how to initialize this register. Normally, we would set this

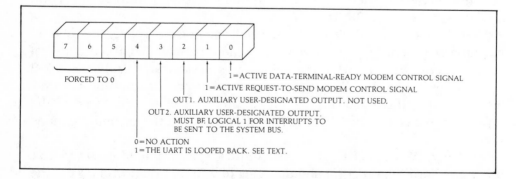

Fig. 7-9. The modem-control register.

register to 03H and forget about it. This value gives the correct output for the ''data-terminal-ready'' and ''request-to-send'' modem control signals. If there is no modem present in the system, it still can't hurt to do this.

If we intend to use interrupts, then the OUT2 bit must also be set to 1. This allows the interrupt that the 8250 generates to be passed along to the PC system bus where it will eventually reach the 8259 Interrupt Controller chip.

Normally, bit 4 of this register should be set to 0. If it is set to 1, then the serial output of the 8250 is looped back to the serial input within the 8250 itself. This feature allows a program to test whether or not the 8250 is working properly. We will use this feature to allow us to write and test a serial-communications program on our PC without having to make any physical connections to the PC. This feature is not available if the BIOS calls are used.

The last register that needs to be initialized is the interrupt-enable register. If interrupts are not being used, then this register should be set to 0. Programming serial communications with interrupts can be very complex. Fortunately, the use of interrupts is not necessary for our purposes.

The interrupt-enable register allows us selectively to enable or disable four different classes of communications interrupts, as shown in Fig. 7-10. This feature allows us to design our program around the specific events that we would like to be interrupt driven.

COMMUNICATING WITH THE 8250

Once the 8250 has been initialized, it can be used to perform serial communications. Whenever we desire to transmit a character of data, we can output that character to the transmitter holding register if the transmitter holding register is empty. All characters received by the 8250 can be input from the receiver data register. But how do we know when the transmitter holding register is empty or when the receiver data register has a valid data character?

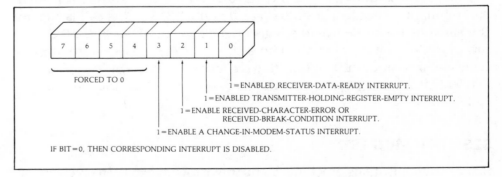

Fig. 7-10. The interrupt-enable register.

The line-status register can be used to tell us when to input or output a character of data. This register is the same as the returned communications status of the BIOS status call (Fig. 7-7B). The only difference is that the high-order bit of this register is always 0. We can input this register from i/o address 3FDH.

If we want to transmit a character, we must read this register and check bit 5. A character cannot be output to the transmitter holding register until bit 5 is 1. If the bit is 0, we must keep on inputting the register into the 8088 and testing bit 5 until it turns to 1. Once it is 1, the next data character to be transmitted can be output to the transmitter holding register. After the character is output, bit 5 of the line-status register will become 0 until the transmitter holding register is ready to accept another character.

Normally, bit 0 of the line-status register is 0. If it becomes 1, then a character of data has been received by the 8250 and has been placed in the receiver data register. When a program detects this condition, it must input the received data character from the receiver data register before another character is completely received by the 8250. If the character is not input by this time, an overrun error will result. When the character is input, bit 0 of the line-status register becomes 0 until the next character is received by the 8250.

As shown in Fig. 7-7B, the line-status register is also used to detect any received data-error conditions or a received break condition. If any of the appropriate bits is 1, then the receiver data register does not contain a valid data character. Many communications programs must know that a data-transmission error has occurred. Once the line-status register has been input, all the error bits are automatically reset to 0 in the 8250. Therefore, the next time the register is input, the bits will be 0 even if the input error has not been processed by the program. We must be aware of this because we also check this register when we want to transmit a character. If we just check bit 5 of the register, an input error might go by unnoticed.

The modem-status register allows us to determine the state of the modem control inputs. The modem-status return of the BIOS status call is exactly the same as the modem-status register. This is shown in Fig. 7-7C. The low-order four bits allow us to check if any of the modem-status inputs have changed since the last time this register was read. This can be a very convenient feature for programs that are concerned with the modem control signals.

8250 INTERRUPTS

Some communications programs do not have the time to keep on checking the line-status register, waiting for certain events to happen. Instead, these programs must spend most of their time processing the input data or processing data for output. Instead of checking the line-status register, the program would rather be told of the event with an interrupt. When the interrupt occurs, the program will stop whatever it is doing and process the event. Such a program will maintain circular queues for serial input and output data. Data is transferred between the queues and the UART by a routine that is triggered by a UART interrupt. When the program needs an input character, it can read the input queue; when the program wishes to output a character, it can place it in the output queue. This type of queue was covered when we wrote a keyboard-scan routine and is shown in Fig. 5-8. A representation of this type of program design is shown in Fig. 7-11.

Assuming that the OUT2 bit of the modem-control register is set to 1, the interrupt output of the 8250 is sent to the IRQ4 input of the 8259 Interrupt Controller chip. For the 8088 to receive this interrupt, the 8259 interrupt-mask register must be properly initialized, the interrupt-service-routine address table (location 0CH*4) must be set up, and the 8088 must be enabled for interrupts. These procedures were covered in Chapter 5.

The interrupt-enable register allows us to program the 8250 to generate interrupts for some or all of the four event classes described in Fig. 7-10. When an interrupt is generated, the interrupt-identification register is used to tell us which condition caused the interrupt. This register is described in Fig. 7-12. Only those event classes that are enabled will appear in this register.

Because more than one interrupt condition can occur at the same time, the conditions are presented in the interrupt-identification register in priority order. Table 7-5 lists the four different conditions in priority order and shows what action is needed to reset the interrupt. Once an interrupt is serviced, the interrupt-identification register should be checked again for

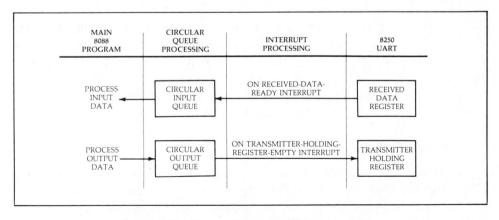

Fig. 7-11.   Processing 8250 interrupts.

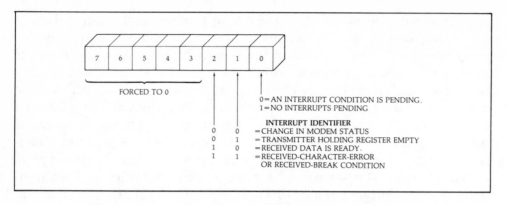

Fig. 7-12.   The interrupt-identification register.

any other pending interrupt conditions. This is necessary because another 8250 interrupt will not be generated in the system if it becomes pending when an 8250 interrupt is currently being serviced. This is due to the way the 8259 Interrupt Controller chip is initialized.

Table 7-5.   8250 Interrupts

Interrupt Type	Interrupt ID (See Note)	Priority	Action to Reset Interrupt
Received character error or "break condition"	1 1	First	Read the line-status register
Received data is ready	1 0	Second	Read the receiver data register
Transmitter ready	0 1	Third	Output a character to the transmitter holding register
Modem status changed	0 0	Fourth	Read the modem-status register

Note: The "Interrupt ID" above is obtained from bits 2 and 1 (in that order) of the interrupt-identification register.

If we enabled only interrupts on a receiver-data-ready condition, then when the interrupt occurred we would not have to check to see which class it is because only one class is enabled. Instead, the interrupt-service routine would input the character from the receiver data register and would check the line-status register to see if there was an error in the received character. This is a much simpler way to put 8250 interrupts to good use.

A SIMPLE TERMINAL PROGRAM

A classic use for serial communications on a personal computer is to turn that computer into a terminal. On a terminal, everything that is typed is transmitted, and everything that is received is displayed. A program that performs these basic functions is shown in Fig. 7-13.

```
00020 ; EXAMPLE OF SIMPLE 1200 BAUD TERMINAL PROGRAM
00030 ;
00040 ;
00050 STACK     SEGMENT PARA STACK 'STACK'
00060           DB      256     DUP(0)  ;256 BYTES OF STACK SPACE
00070 STACK     ENDS
00080 ;
00090 CODE      SEGMENT PARA PUBLIC 'CODE'
00100 START     PROC    FAR
00110 ;
00120 ;STANDARD PROGRAM PROLOGUE
00130 ;
00140           ASSUME  CS:CODE
00150           PUSH    DS      ;SAVE PSP SEG ADDR
00160           MOV     AX,0
00170           PUSH    AX      ;SAVE RET ADDR OFFSET (PSP+0)
00180 ;
00190 ;PART1: INITIALIZE THE 8250 UART FOR:
00200 ;       7 DATA BITS, 1 STOP BIT, ODD PARITY, AND 1200 BAUD
00210 ;       SET UP FOR LOOPBACK FEATURE
00220 ;
00230           MOV     DX,3FBH ;ADDRESS OF LINE CONTROL REGISTER
00240           MOV     AL,80H
00250           OUT     DX,AL   ;TO ADDRESS BAUD RATE DIVISOR REGISTERS
00260           MOV     DX,3F8H ;ADDRESS OF BAUD RATE DIVISOR LSB
00270           MOV     AL,60H  ;LSB VALUE FOR 1200 BAUD
00280           OUT     DX,AL
00290           MOV     DX,3F9H ;ADDRESS OF BAUD RATE DIVISOR MSB
00300           MOV     AL,0    ;MSB VALUE FOR 1200 BAUD
00310           OUT     DX,AL
00320 ;THE BAUD RATE HAS NOW BEEN INITIALIZED
00330 ;NOW INITIALIZE THE LINE CONTROL REGISTER
00340           MOV     DX,3FBH ;ADDRESS OF THE LINE CONTROL REGISTER
00350           MOV     AL,0AH  ;ODD PARITY, 1 STOP BIT, 7 DATA BITS
00360           OUT     DX,AL
00370 ;NOW INITIALIZE THE MODEM CONTROL REGISTER FOR:
00380 ;       REQUEST TO SEND AND DATA TERMINAL READY SIGNALS
00390 ;       AND SET THE LOOPBACK FEATURE
00400 ;
00410           MOV     DX,3FCH ;ADDRESS OF MODEM CONTROL REGISTER
00420           MOV     AL,13H  ;SET LOOPBACK AND MODEM CNTL SIGNALS
00430           OUT     DX,AL
00440 ;NOW DISABLE ALL FOUR CLASSES OF INTERRUPTS
00450           MOV     DX,3F9H ;ADDRESS OF INTERRUPT ENABLE REGISTER
00460           MOV     AL,0
00470           OUT     DX,AL
00480 ;THE INITIALIZATION OF THE 8250 IS NOW COMPLETE
00490 ;
00500 ;
00510 ;PART2:  DISPLAY WHAT IS RECEIVED FROM THE 8250
00520 ;        TRANSMIT WHAT IS INPUT FROM THE KEYBOARD
```

Fig. 7-13. Terminal-program listing.

Continued on next page.

```
00530 ;
00540 FOREVER: MOV      DX,3FDH ;ADDRESS OF LINE STATUS REGISTER
00550          IN       AL,DX   ;LINE STATUS REGISTER IN AL
00560          TEST     AL,1EH  ;TEST FOR A RECEPTION ERROR
00570          JNZ      ERROR   ;RECEIVE ERROR HANDLING
00580          TEST     AL,01H  ;TEST FOR RECEIVED DATA READY
00590          JNZ      RECEIVE ;RECEIVED CHARACTER HANDLING
00600          TEST     AL,20H  ;TEST FOR TRANSMITTER HOLDING
00610 ;                                 REGISTER EMPTY
00620          JZ       FOREVER ;IF THE 8250 IS NOT READY FOR ANOTHER
00630 ;                          CHARACTER TO TRANSMIT THEN LOOP
00640 ;
00650 ;IF FALL THROUGH TO HERE THEN THE 8250 IS READY FOR ANOTHER
00660 ;CHARACTER TO TRANSMIT
00670 ;IF THE KEYBOARD BUFFER HAS A CHARACTER THEN GET IT AND
00680 ;OUTPUT IT TO THE 8250.
00690 ;
00700          MOV      AH,1    ;CHECK KEYBOARD BUFFER CODE
00710          INT      16H     ;BIOS CALL
00720          JZ       FOREVER ;IF NO KEYBOARD CHARACTER THEN
00730 ;                                 NOTHING TO TRANSMIT
00740 ;IF FALL THROUGH TO HERE THEN THERE IS A KEYBOARD
00750 ;CHARACTER TO TRANSMIT
00760          MOV      AH,0    ;GET KEYBOARD INPUT CODE
00770          INT      16H     ;BIOS CALL
00780 ;AL HAS THE KEYBOARD CHARACTER FOR TRANSMISSION
00790          MOV      DX,3F8H ;ADDRESS OF TRANSMITTER HOLDING REGISTER
00800          OUT      DX,AL   ;TRANSMIT THE CHARACTER
00810          JMP      FOREVER
00820 ;
00830 ;
00840 ;THIS POINT IS REACHED IF A CHARACTER WAS RECEIVED BY THE
00850 ;8250 WITH NO ERRORS
00860 ;
00870 RECEIVE: MOV      DX,3F8H ;ADDRESS OF THE RECEIVER DATA REGISTER
00880          IN       AL,DX   ;AL HAS THE RECEIVED CHARACTER
00890          AND      AL,7FH  ;BECAUSE THERE ARE ONLY 7 BITS OF
00900 ;                          DATA, THE HIGH ORDER BIT IS NOT VALID
00910          PUSH     AX      ;SAVE THE RECEIVED CHARACTER
00920 ;PREPARE TO DISPLAY THE CHARACTER
00930          MOV      BX,0
00940          MOV      AH,14   ;DISPLAY FUNCTION CODE
00950          INT      10H     ;BIOS CALL
00960          POP      AX      ;RESTORE THE CHARACTER
00970          CMP      AL,0DH  ;WAS IT A CARRIAGE RETURN?
00980          JNZ      FOREVER ;NO, SO START OVER AGAIN
00990 ;IF IT WAS A CARRIAGE RETURN, THEN A LINE FEED MUST
01000 ;ALSO BE DISPLAYED
01010          MOV      AL,0AH  ;LINE FEED
01020          MOV      BX,0
01030          MOV      AH,14
```

Fig. 7-13 (cont).   Terminal-program listing.

Continued on next page.

```
01040              INT      10H       ;BIOS CALL
01050              JMP      FOREVER
01060 ;
01070 ;IF THIS POINT IS REACHED THEN THERE WAS AN ERROR IN THE
01080 ;RECEIVED CHARACTER. CLEAR THE RECEIVER DATA REGISTER
01090 ;AND DISPLAY A ?
01100 ;
01110 ERROR:      MOV      DX,3F8H   ;ADDRESS OF THE RECEIVER DATA REGISTER
01120              IN       AL,DX     ;AL HAS THE INCORRECT CHARACTER
01130              MOV      AL,'?'    ;DISPLAY A ? INSTEAD
01140              MOV      BX,0
01150              MOV      AH,14
01160              INT      10H       ;BIOS CALL
01170              JMP      FOREVER
01180 ;
01190 START      ENDP
01200 CODE       ENDS
01210              END      START
```

Fig. 7-13 (cont).   Terminal-program listing.

Type in the program as shown, and then assemble and link it. No physical connections must be made to the back of the PC for this program to work, because we use the loopback feature of the 8250 to cause whatever is transmitted to be received. Run the program. Whatever is typed should be displayed on the screen.

Statements 190–480 initialize the 8250 to the desired transmission parameters. An interesting enhancement to the program would be to input the desired transmission parameters when the program is invoked. The desired parameters would then have to be transformed to the correct control data for the 8250.

Statements 540–630 check the line-status register of the 8250 for any conditions that must be handled. Notice that the first condition that is checked for is a received-data error. If there is a received-data error, then the received data register is cleared and a ? is displayed. The ? on the display will tell us that we are getting transmission errors. If there are no errors and a data character has been received, then we get it and display it. If it is a carriage return, then a line feed must also be displayed.

If the transmitter holding register is empty, then we get the next character from the keyboard buffer that the BIOS maintains for us. If no characters are ready for transmission, it is not a problem because the 8250 will just bring the transmission line to a marking condition. Notice that the program gives priority to a receiver-ready condition.

Now let us try removing the loopback feature from the program. This can be done by changing the constant in line 420 to 03H. In order for the program to work, pins 2 and 3 of the connector on the back of the communications adapter must now be shorted together. This allows the transmitted data to be received by the 8250.

The program can now be put to good use. If there is another PC in the same room, they can communicate with each other by using this program. Just hook pin 7 to pin 7, pin 2 to pin 3, and pin 3 to pin 2. Now, whatever is typed on one PC will be displayed on the other PC.

There is only one problem with the program in its present state. At 1200 baud, a character of data can be received every 8.3 milliseconds. Unfortunately, it takes longer than that amount of time to scroll the display. Therefore, if characters are being received at the maximum data rate of 1200 baud, then whenever the display scrolls, an overrun error will result. This will happen because the 8088 is busy scrolling the display instead of checking for receiver data ready.

There are many different ways to solve this problem. First of all, if someone is typing the message, then the characters will probably be arriving too slowly to cause a problem. Even though it takes only 8.3 milliseconds to transmit the character, there will be a great deal of time when no data is being transmitted on the line. However, if a computer is transmitting the message from a memory buffer, then the characters could be arriving with no pauses in between.

The correct way to get around this problem is to create a received-data-character circular queue. The 8250 should be programmed to generate interrupts when a character has been received. The interrupt-processing routine should place the received character in the circular input queue. The main program will get all of its input characters from this queue. Now, when the display is being scrolled by the 8088, if a character is ready in the 8250, then the 8088 will be interrupted. The 8088 will place the character into the input queue and then return to finish scrolling the display. This design will work for very high baud rates. Those readers who are interested in a very challenging project should try to modify the terminal program to support interrupts and queues.

CHAPTER 8

Disk I/O

The Diskette Drive Adapter provides the Personal Computer with an interface to up to four diskette drives. Each of these drives can accommodate a standard 5¼-inch floppy diskette. Floppy diskettes, which we will simply call *disks*, are invaluable when we need to store large amounts of data for indefinite periods of time. In this chapter, we will discuss the various resources available to the assembler-language programmer for reading and writing disks.

ANATOMY OF A DISKETTE

Two different views of a disk are presented in Fig. 8-1. In Fig. 8-1A, we see the disk as it appears physically. Inside the square jacket is a thin, flexible sheet of oxide-coated plastic, depicted in Fig. 8-1B. When this assembly is loaded into a disk drive, the inner sheet is clamped to a hub that is attached to the spindle of a drive motor. When the drive motor is activated, the inner sheet rotates at a speed of 300 rpm. At the same time, the *magnetic head* of the drive contacts the oxide surface through the access slot. As the disk rotates, the head traces out a circle, which is referred to as a *track*. A stream of data can thus be magnetically recorded along the track by the head. This same mechanism can then be used to read back the recorded information.

Independent of the circular motion of the disk itself, the drive head can be moved *in* (toward the center of the disk) or *out* (away from the center of the disk). It can thus be positioned to access any one of the 40 concentric tracks on the disk (Fig. 8-2). The disk drive has been designed so that the same amount of data can be reliably recorded on and retrieved from each track.

The tracks are numbered sequentially, starting with track 0, the outermost track, and increasing as we go toward the center of the disk. The

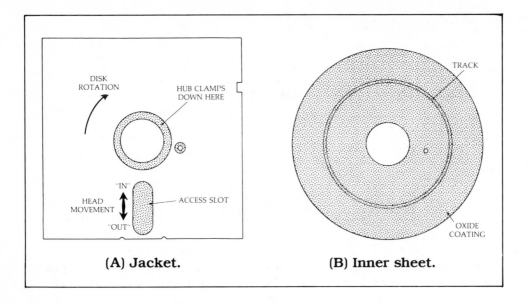

Fig. 8-1.   A floppy diskette.

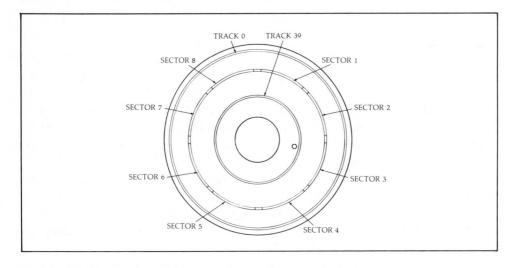

Fig. 8-2.   Disk tracks and sectors.

innermost track is thus track 39. Data is stored on each track in equal-sized blocks known as *sectors*. The Personal Computer disks store eight sectors on each track. Each sector holds 512 bytes of data. On each track, the sectors are numbered 1 through 8. On a single disk, we can thus store 40 tracks * 8 sectors/track * 512 bytes/sector = 163,840 bytes.

DISK ACCESS MECHANISMS

If we view the disk as shown in Fig. 8-2, it is evident that to access a specific byte of data stored on the disk we must know three numbers: its track (0–39), its sector (1–8), and its offset within the sector (0–1FFH). The BIOS provides us with a set of routines to read and write the disk in this fashion. Before we look at them in more detail, however, we will investigate a more sophisticated access mechanism.

Most of the time, data stored on a disk will be in a specific order and format defined by the program that will process the data. For example, a payroll program might maintain a list of data records containing employees' names and the amounts they are to be paid. The list may be kept in alphabetical order by last name. In this situation, we are more concerned with the order, format, and quantity of the data than with its physical storage location on the disk. We therefore view our data as being in a *file*, stored on the disk under a unique and symbolically meaningful *filename*. When we wish to access the data, we *open* the file. We can then read from or write to the data within it.

The Disk Operating System (DOS) provides the support necessary for this kind of disk access. It manages the allocation of physical disk space to files and lets us know when we have run out of room on the disk. It maintains a list of all files on the disk in the *directory*. The directory itself is stored on the disk at a dedicated location. Using the information in the directory, DOS can translate user requests for access to data within files

Fig. 8-3. Levels of disk i/o.

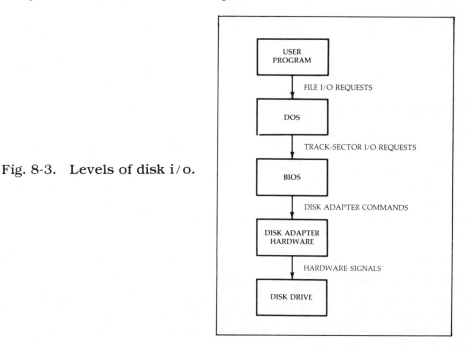

into requests for access to specific disk locations. The latter can be handled by the BIOS. This scheme is illustrated in Fig. 8-3. Notice that the user program, at the highest level, can manipulate the file data without regard

Table 8-1. DOS Disk I/O Functions

Invoke all DOS functions via INT 21H.		
Function	**Input Requirements**	**Output/Results**
SET DTA	AH = 1AH, DX = address of DTA.	DTA is set to specified address.
OPEN	AH = 0FH, DX = address of FCB	Specified file is opened and AL=0. If file not found on disk, then AL=0FFH.
CREATE	AH = 16H, DX = address of FCB	Same as OPEN, except if file is not found, then it is created on the disk.
CLOSE	AH = 10H, DX = address of FCB	Specified file is closed.
SEQUENTIAL READ	AH = 14H, DX = address of FCB	The record addressed by the current block and current record fields in the FCB is read into the DTA. These fields are then updated to point to the next record. AL= *.
SEQUENTIAL WRITE	AH = 15H, DX = address of FCB	Same as SEQUENTIAL READ, except data is written from the DTA to the file. AL= *.
RANDOM READ	AH = 21H, DX = address of FCB	The current block and current record fields are calculated from the relative record field in the FCB. The operation then proceeds as in SEQUENTIAL READ. AL= *.
RANDOM WRITE	AH = 22H, DX = address of FCB	Same as RANDOM READ, except data is written from the DTA to the file. AL= *.
RANDOM BLOCK READ	AH = 27H, DX = address of FCB, CX = record count	Same as RANDOM READ, except the operation is repeated until the count in CX is exhausted. AL= * and CX = number of records read.
RANDOM BLOCK WRITE	AH = 28H, DX = address of FCB, CX = record count	Same as RANDOM BLOCK READ except data is written from the DTA to the file. AL= * and CX = number of records written.

* A code is returned in AL to indicate the success or failure of the operation. AL=0 means the function was performed without error. AL=1 means the end of the file was encountered. AL=2 means there was not enough room at the DTA to read/write all of the data.

for the physical manner in which it is stored. As each i/o request is passed down to the lower levels, it becomes more specific and more closely related to the actual disk hardware.

DISK I/O UNDER DOS

The Disk Operating System provides the assembler-language programmer with a set of functions for manipulating disk files. The most commonly used functions are summarized in Table 8-1. Note that the interrupt used, INT 21H, does not pass control to the BIOS but rather to the DOS itself. In addition to accessing data on the disk, these functions will reference two data areas in memory. These areas are known as the *file control block* (FCB) and the *disk transfer area* (DTA).

The DTA is the memory location to or from which all disk i/o will take place. If we request a read of a disk file, the data read will be placed into the DTA. Similarly, when we write to a disk file, the data to be written is assumed to be in the DTA. When our program is initially given control by DOS, the DTA has been set to location 80H within the PSP (you may recall that this is also where DOS places the program parameter). We can redefine the DTA to be within our own data segment by using the SET DTA function listed in Table 8-1. We must ensure that there is enough room at the DTA to hold the largest block of data that will be read or written at any time.

For each file that we wish to process, we must set up an FCB. The FCB contains information used by DOS to manipulate the file. Its format is shown in Table 8-2. The processing of a file is always initiated by placing

Table 8-2. The File Control Block (FCB)

Field at FCB +	Field Length (in Bytes)	Field Description
00H	1	Drive (1—4 to correspond to drives A–D)
01H	8	Primary filename
09H	3	Filename extension
0CH	2	Current block
0EH	2	Record size (in bytes)
10H	4	Total file size in bytes (least significant word precedes most significant word)
14H	2	Date of last update
16H	10	Reserved for use by DOS
20H	1	Current record (0—127)
21H	4	Relative record (least significant word precedes most significant word)

the filename into an FCB (i.e., we fill in fields FCB+0 through FCB+0BH). The OPEN function is then called with the DX register pointing to the FCB. This will cause DOS to locate the file on the disk and place information about its location and size into the FCB (DOS fills in fields FCB+10H through FCB+1FH). At this point the file is said to be *opened.* We can read data from and write data into an open file by using the various READ and WRITE functions listed in Table 8-1. Examining this table, we see that there are three different kinds of READ/WRITE function calls; they are SEQUENTIAL, RANDOM, and RANDOM BLOCK. They differ in the manner in which the location and quantity of disk data to be transferred are specified. To understand these different access methods, we must understand how DOS stores our file data.

The smallest unit of data stored in a disk file is known as a *record.* A record can contain one or more bytes. The number of bytes held in a record is called the *record size* and is constant for any given file. The record size is specified by a field in the FCB; we shall see how to set this field in a moment. The important consideration now is that data is always transferred to and from files one record at a time. The records are stored on the disk in *blocks.* Each block can hold up to 128 records. The records within a block are numbered 0–127. The blocks are numbered starting with 0 and increasing by one for each subsequent block in the file. To locate a specific record within a file, DOS must know two numbers: the block number and the record number within the block. This scheme is illustrated in Fig. 8-4. Note that the last block in a file may not be full (i.e., it may have fewer than 128 records in it).

The simplest kind of READ/WRITE function is SEQUENTIAL. This method assumes that we wish to access the records of a file *in order* from beginning to end. When we perform a READ SEQUENTIAL or WRITE SEQUENTIAL function, DOS accesses the record specified by the current block and current record fields (FCB+0CH and FCB+20H, respectively). It then automatically updates these fields to point to the next record location in the file. If a series of records are written to a file using WRITE SEQUENTIAL, then they can be subsequently retrieved in the same order by using READ SEQUENTIAL.

Suppose we need to access the various records of a file in some order other than sequential (e.g., we may wish to read the 5th, 9th, and 23rd records of a file, in that order). In this case, we could use one of the RANDOM disk-access functions. These functions allow us to request any specific record in a file. By using them, we can access records in any order desired. We specify the record to be accessed by giving a *relative record number.* The relative record number for the first record in any file is zero; it goes up by one for each subsequent record. Relative record numbers are shown in Fig. 8-4. It is important to realize that the *relative record number*

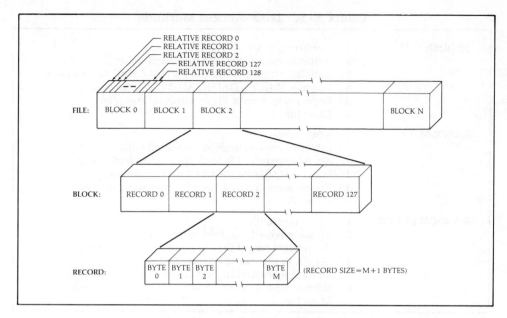

Fig. 8-4. DOS file structure.

is not the same as the *current block* and *current record* numbers mentioned earlier. We can perform RANDOM file accesses by specifying a relative record number (at FCB+21H), but it will be converted by DOS into the equivalent current block and current record numbers before the disk access actually takes place. The RANDOM BLOCK functions are similar to the RANDOM functions, except that they allow us to transfer more than one record at a time. In these cases, we specify a relative record number *and* a count in the CX register. The relative record number is used to locate the first record to be transferred. The rest of the records to be transferred are then taken sequentially from that location onward toward the end of the file, until the count in CX is exhausted.

These different disk-access methods are summarized in Chart 8-1. In general, we initialize an FCB and open it in the manner already described. After the file has been opened, we must specify its record size by filling in the field at FCB+0EH. If we are going to use sequential access, we also initialize the current-block and current-record fields at FCB+0CH and FCB+20H to zero. This ensures that we will begin processing at the beginning of the file. From this point on, these fields will be maintained by DOS automatically. All we have to do is issue SEQUENTIAL READ and/or SEQUENTIAL WRITE function calls to access the records of the disk file in order. If we wish to use RANDOM access, then we must fill in the relative-record-number field at FCB+21H prior to each RANDOM function call. When we have finished processing a file, it should always be *closed*. This

Chart 8-1. Disk-Access Methods

SEQUENTIAL	1. Open/create file.
	2. Initialize record-size field to desired value.
	3. Initialize current-block and current-record fields to zero.
	4. Perform SEQUENTIAL READ/WRITE function.
	5. Repeat step 4 until file operation is complete.
	6. Close file.
RANDOM	1. Open/create file.
	2. Initialize record-size field to desired value.
	3. Set relative-record field to point to desired record.
	4. Perform RANDOM READ/WRITE function.
	5. Repeat steps 3 and 4 until file operation is complete.
	6. Close file.
RANDOM BLOCK	1. Open/create file.
	2. Initialize record-size field to desired value.
	3. Set relative-record field to point to first desired record.
	4. Set CX to number of records desired.
	5. Perform RANDOM BLOCK READ/WRITE function.
	6. Repeat steps 3, 4, and 5 until file operation is complete.
	7. Close file.

is accomplished by using the CLOSE function call with DX pointing to the FCB for the file.

SEQUENTIAL-ACCESS EXAMPLE

A program illustrating the use of the sequential file access method is listed in Fig. 8-5. This program will open a disk file, read in its contents, and list them on the display screen. It is more useful than the built-in DOS command "TYPE" because it automatically pauses whenever the last line on the screen is reached. By striking any key, the operator can then cause the program to proceed. In this fashion, a long source file can be viewed, one screen at a time.

Our program assumes that the file it is to process is in a specific format. This is the standard *text file* format that is used by the EDLIN, ASM, and LINK programs. The source files that we create with the EDLIN program are in text file format. The optional listing files that can be produced by either ASM or LINK are also in this format. As you can imagine, the program we are about to write will be very handy.

The records that make up a text file are each one byte long. Each line of text is placed in the file as a series of these one-byte records. Each record obviously contains one ASCII character. The end of each line of text is denoted by two successive records containing 0DH and 0AH, respectively. These are the ASCII codes for "carriage return" and "line feed." This scheme allows lines of text with varying lengths to be placed in the file. The last text line in the file is followed by a record containing the value

```
00030 ; PROGRAM TO LIST TEXT FILES ON THE DISPLAY.
00040 ; ILLUSTRATES USE OF SEQUENTIAL DISK I/O UNDER DOS.
00050 ;
00060 STACK     SEGMENT PARA STACK 'STACK'
00070           DB      256 DUP (0)      ;256 BYTES OF STACK SPACE
00080 STACK     ENDS
00090 ;
00100 DATA      SEGMENT PARA PUBLIC 'DATA'
00110 FCB       DB      36 DUP (0)       ;FILE CONTROL BLOCK
00120 LINECOUNT DB      0                ;COUNT OF LINES ON SCREEN
00130 CHARPOS   DB      0                ;CHARACTER POSITION ON LINE
00140 DTA       DB      0                ;DISK TRANFER AREA
00150 ; ERROR MESSAGE:
00160 ERRMSG    DB      'FILE ACCESS ERROR !!!
00170 DATA      ENDS
00180 ;
00190 CODE      SEGMENT PARA PUBLIC 'CODE'
00200 START     PROC    FAR
00210 ;
00220 ; STANDARD PROGRAM PROLOGUE EXCEPT RETAIN DS AS PTR TO PSP
00230 ;
00240           ASSUME  CS:CODE
00250           PUSH    DS       ;SAVE PSP SEG ADDR
00260           MOV     AX,0
00270           PUSH    AX       ;SAVE RET ADDR OFFSET (PSP+0)
00280           MOV     AX,DATA
00290           MOV     ES,AX    ;ESTABLISH EXTRA SEG ADDRESSABILITY
00300           ASSUME  ES:DATA
00310 ;
00320 ; MOVE FCB PARAMETER FROM PSP TO OUR DATA SEGMENT:
00330 ;
00340           MOV     SI,5CH   ;SOURCE STRING OFFSET (WITHIN PSP)
00350           MOV     DI,OFFSET FCB  ;DEST. STRING OFFSET
00360           MOV     CX,12    ;STRING LENGTH TO MOVE
00370           CLD              ;SET 'FORWARD' STRING OPERATIONS
00380           REP     MOVSB    ;MOVE PARM INTO OUR DATA AREA
00390 ;
00400 ; ESTABLISH NORMAL DATA SEGMENT ADDRESSABILITY
00410 ;
00420           MOV     DS,AX
00430           ASSUME  DS:DATA
00440 ;
00450 ; SET DTA AND OPEN FILE:
00460 ;
00470           MOV     DX,OFFSET DTA    ;ADDRESS OF DTA
00480           MOV     AH,1AH   ;DOS FUNCTION = 'SET DTA'
00490           INT     21H      ;INVOKE DOS FUNCTION
00500           MOV     DX,OFFSET FCB    ;ADDRESS OF FCB
00510           MOV     AH,0FH   ;DOS FUNCTION = 'OPEN FILE'
00520           INT     21H      ;INVOKE DOS FUNCTION
```

Fig. 8-5. Program to list text files.

Continued on next page.

```
00530          CMP      AL,O     ;DID THE 'OPEN' WORK?
00540          JNZ      ERROR    ;BRANCH IF NOT
00550 ;
00560 ; INITIALIZE THE 'RECORD SIZE', 'CURRENT BLOCK', AND
00570 ;   'CURRENT RECORD' FIELDS WITHIN THE FCB:
00580 ;
00590          MOV      WORD PTR FCB+OCH,O      ;'CURRENT BLOCK' = O
00600          MOV      WORD PTR FCB+OEH,1      ;'RECORD SIZE' = 1
00610          MOV      FCB+2OH,O               ;'CURRENT RECORD' = O
00620 ;
00630 ; READ A CHARACTER FROM THE FILE AND DISPLAY IT ON
00640 ;   THE SCREEN, CHECK FOR SPECIAL CONTROL CHARACTERS
00650 ;   'TAB' (09H), 'END OF FILE' (1AH), AND 'LINE FEED' (OAH)
00660 ;   AND HANDLE THEM ACCORDINGLY:
00670 ;
00680 AGAIN:   MOV      DX,OFFSET FCB    ;ADDRESS OF FCB
00690          MOV      AH,14H   ;DOS FUNCTION = 'SEQUENTIAL READ'
00700          INT      21H      ;INVOKE DOS FUNCTION
00710          CMP      AL,O     ;DID THE 'READ' WORK?
00720          JNZ      ERROR    ;BRANCH IF NOT
00730          MOV      AL,DTA   ;GET THE CHARACTER JUST READ
00740          CMP      AL,1AH   ;IS IT 'CONTROL Z'?
00750          JZ       EOF      ;BRANCH IF IT IS (INDICATES END OF FILE)
00760          CMP      AL,09H   ;IS IT 'TAB'?
00770          JZ       TAB      ;BRANCH IF IT IS (MUST EXPAND THE TAB)
00780          CALL     DISPCHAR ;DISPLAY THE CHAR ON THE SCREEN
00790          INC      CHARPOS  ;MAINTAIN CURRENT CHARACTER POSITION
00800          CMP      DTA,OAH  ;WAS THAT THE END OF A LINE?
00810          JNZ      AGAIN    ;BRANCH IF NOT (GO DO MORE)
00820 ;
00830 ; A COMPLETE LINE HAS BEEN READ AND DISPLAYED, COUNT UP
00840 ;   THE NUMBER OF LINES ON THE SCREEN AND WAIT IF THE
00850 ;   SCREEN HAS BEEN FILLED:
00860 ;
00870          MOV      CHARPOS,O       ;RESET THE CHAR POSITION COUNTER
00880          INC      LINECOUNT       ;COUNT UP # OF LINES ON SCREEN
00890          CMP      LINECOUNT,24 ;IS THE SCREEN FULL?
00900          JNZ      AGAIN           ;BRANCH IF NOT (OK TO CONTINUE)
00910 ; THE SCREEN IS FULL, WAIT FOR THE USER TO HIT A KEY:
00920          MOV      AH,O            ;FUNCTION = 'READ KEYBOARD'
00930          INT      16H             ;CALL BIOS KEYBOARD ROUTINE
00940 ; THE USER HIT A KEY: ITS OK TO PROCEED:
00950          MOV      LINECOUNT,O ;RESET COUNT OF LINES ON SCREEN
00960          JMP      AGAIN           ;RESUME MAIN LOOP
00970 ;
00980 ; A 'TAB' CHARACTER HAS BEEN ENCOUNTERED, DISPLAY BLANKS
00990 ;   UNTIL WE REACH THE NEXT TAB STOP:
01000 ;
01010 TAB:     MOV      AL,' '
01020          CALL     DISPCHAR        ;DISPLAY A BLANK
01030          INC      CHARPOS         ;MAINTAIN CHARACTER POSITION
01040          TEST     CHARPOS,7       ;ARE WE AT A TAB STOP?
```

Fig. 8-5 (cont).   Program to list text files.

Continued on next page.

```
01050              JZ        AGAIN             ;BRANCH IF WE ARE (TAB EXPANDED)
01060              JMP       TAB               ;CONTINUE UNTIL WE REACH TAB STOP
01070 ;
01080 ; END OF FILE HAS BEEN ENCOUNTERED, CLOSE THE FILE AND
01090 ;   RETURN TO DOS:
01100 ;
01110 EOF:       MOV       DX,OFFSET FCB     ;ADDRESS OF FCB
01120              MOV       AH,10H            ;DOS FUNCTION = 'CLOSE FILE'
01130              INT       21H               ;INVOKE DOS FUNCTION
01140              RET                         ;RETURN TO DOS
01150 ;
01160 ; A FILE ACCESS ERROR HAS OCCURRED, TELL USER AND QUIT:
01170 ;
01180 ERROR:     MOV       BX,OFFSET ERRMSG
01190              CALL      DISPLAY ;DISPLAY THE MESSAGE AT [BX]
01200              RET                         ;RETURN TO DOS
01210 ;
01220 ; SUBROUTINE TO DISPLAY A MESSAGE ON THE SCREEN.
01230 ; ENTER WITH BX -> MESSAGE TO BE DISPLAYED.
01240 ; MESSAGE IS ASSUMED TO BE 30 CHARACTERS LONG.
01250 ;
01260 DISPLAY PROC     NEAR
01270              MOV       CX,30   ;NUMBER OF CHARACTERS TO DISPLAY
01280 DISP1:     MOV       AL,[BX] ;GET NEXT CHARACTER TO DISPLAY
01290              CALL      DISPCHAR ;DISPLAY IT
01300              INC       BX      ;POINT TO NEXT CHARACTER
01310              LOOP      DISP1   ;DO IT 30 TIMES
01320              MOV       AL,0DH  ;CARRIAGE RETURN
01330              CALL      DISPCHAR
01340              MOV       AL,0AH  ;LINE FEED
01350              CALL      DISPCHAR
01360              RET                 ;RETURN TO CALLER OF 'DISPLAY'
01370 DISPLAY ENDP
01380 ;
01390 ; SUBROUTINE TO DISPLAY A CHARACTER ON THE SCREEN.
01400 ; ENTER WITH AL = CHARACTER TO BE DISPLAYED.
01410 ; USES VIDEO INTERFACE IN BIOS.
01420 ;
01430 DISPCHAR PROC     NEAR
01440              PUSH      BX      ;SAVE BX REGISTER
01450              MOV       BX,0    ;SELECT DISPLAY PAGE 0
01460              MOV       AH,14   ;FUNCTION CODE FOR 'WRITE'
01470              INT       10H     ;CALL VIDEO DRIVER IN BIOS
01480              POP       BX      ;RESTORE BX REGISTER
01490              RET                 ;RETURN TO CALLER OF 'DISPCHAR'
01500 DISPCHAR ENDP
01510 START      ENDP
01520 CODE       ENDS
01530              END       START
```

Fig. 8-5 (cont). Program to list text files.

Continued on next page.

1AH (ASCII "control Z" character). We can therefore use the SEQUENTIAL READ function to retrieve the contents of a text file, after setting the record-size field to 0001H. By checking for the 0AH control code, we will be able to tell when we have reached the end of each line. By checking for the 1AH control code, we will be able to tell when we have reached the end of the file. So far, it sounds simple, but there is one complication.

To minimize the amount of disk space used by text files, multiple blank characters are compressed. The compression scheme is illustrated in Fig. 8-6. Imaginary *tab stops* are placed at every eighth character on the text line. Whenever a series of blank characters reaches a tab-stop position on a text line, they can be replaced by the special ASCII control character "tab" (09H). When text files contain data that is organized in columns, such as assembly-language source programs and listings, this scheme is very effective. Whenever we wish to view these files, however, we must be sure to detect the presence of "tab" characters. When a "tab" character is encountered, it must be "expanded" by replacing it with blanks until the next tab-stop position is reached.

Now that we have a good understanding of the task it must accomplish, let us look at the program in detail (Fig. 8-5). The name of the file to be listed will be supplied to the program via the now familiar DOS program parameter scheme. The DOS makes our job easier by placing the program parameter in the PSP at offset 5CH *in FCB format.* Our program begins by moving the filename from this area into the FCB we have set up in our own data segment (statements 340–380). We then set the address of the disk transfer area to label DTA within our data segment (statements 470–490). The file is then opened (statements 500–520). Most file operations return a

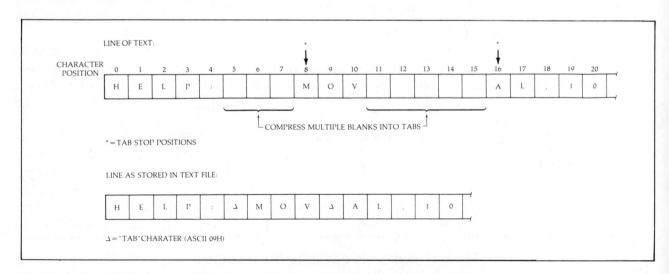

Fig. 8-6. Blank compression in text files.

code in the AL register to indicate their success or failure. In general, AL is returned as zero if there was no error. Any program that performs disk i/o must check for error conditions. Our program, which provides a minimum of error handling, simply branches to an error routine (ERROR) when a nonzero value is returned in AL (statements 530–540 and 710–720).

Since we intend to use the SEQUENTIAL READ function to access the file, we now initialize the "current block" and "current record" fields in the FCB to zero. The "record size" field is set to 1 at this time as well. The main body of the program, starting with label AGAIN, is now entered. Here we read characters (records) from the file and display them on the screen. If the "control Z" character is encountered, we branch to label EOF (end of file), close the file, and return to DOS. If the "tab" character is encountered, we branch to the special routine at label TAB to expand it into the appropriate number of blanks. To provide support for the TAB routine, we maintain the current character position on the present text line at all times. This value is held in variable CHARPOS. It is initialized to 0 and then incremented by 1 for every character printed (statement 790).

The end of a text line is detected when we display the "line feed" character (statements 800–810). When we reach the end of a line, the program falls through to statement 870. Here we reset variable CHARPOS to 0 (starting character position for the next line to be processed). We then increment the count of the number of lines currently displayed. This count is maintained in variable LINECOUNT and is initially zero. When LINECOUNT reaches 24, the screen has been filled, and we fall through to statement 920. The program is suspended at this point by calling the BIOS keyboard routine. When a key is struck, the program will resume. It will reset LINECOUNT to zero, thus allowing another 24 lines to be displayed, and then resume the main program loop. In this fashion, one page of text will be displayed at a time.

As we mentioned earlier, the TAB routine (statements 1010–1060) is entered when a "tab" character is encountered in the text file. This routine must "expand" it by displaying the appropriate number of blanks. This is accomplished by displaying blanks, one at a time, and incrementing the character-position counter CHARPOS for each blank displayed. When CHARPOS indicates that we have reached a tab stop, the tab has been expanded, and we can resume the main program loop. Since tab stops are at every eighth character position, we can detect them by determining when CHARPOS is evenly divisible by 8. In binary, this means that the rightmost 3 bits (representing the decimal values 0–7) must be zero. Tab stops are thus detected by testing the low-order 3 bits of CHARPOS, as accomplished by statement 1040.

If you type in, assemble, and link this program, you will be able to run it by typing in the program name followed by the name of the file to be listed.

The file will be displayed one screen at a time. Note that if a text line in the file is longer than a line on the screen, then some lines will be scrolled off the top of the screen before the program pauses. This is because our program assumes that each text line will occupy only one screen line. Alleviating this problem is left as an exercise for the reader.

DISK I/O THROUGH THE BIOS

As we have seen, the DOS provides a convenient and reliable mechanism for storing and retrieving data on disks. It does, however, have certain limitations. When using DOS disk i/o functions, we can access only areas on the disk that have been allocated to files—and then only when we know the appropriate filename. When programming in assembler language, we have the ability to go beyond these limitations. We can read or write any sector on any track and thus access hidden files, system files, the directory area, and even the bootstrap program area. We will rely on the BIOS to provide us with these abilities.

Table 8-3 lists some of the functions that we can perform by invoking the BIOS disk i/o routine. The reset function allows us to initialize the disk interface hardware. Normally, this is not necessary because it has already been done by DOS. If however, in performing disk i/o we encounter an error condition, then the reset function must be used before disk i/o can be attempted again. The read-status function allows us to obtain the status of the last disk operation performed. The read and write functions actually transfer data to or from the disk. Data is transferred in sectors, with each sector containing 512 bytes. To use the read and write functions, we must specify which of the four disk drives we wish to access. This is accomplished by placing a value from 0 to 3 in the DL register to correspond to physical drives A through D. The DH register specifies which side of the diskette is to be accessed. For single-sided drives, DH should always be zero. The location of the data is specified by track and sector numbers, placed in the CH and CL registers, respectively. The AL register contains the number of sectors to be transferred. A single function call can transfer one to eight sectors.

The BX register contains the address of the memory location to or from which the data will be transferred. It is important to realize that this memory area is assumed to be in the *extra segment*, as defined by the contents of the ES register. For most applications, this can be handled by simply setting ES equal to DS and letting the extra segment overlap and be equal to the data segment. This will allow us to define our disk buffer areas within our data segment in the usual manner.

When these functions are used, a more sophisticated approach to error handling is required. Unlike DOS, which detects and handles all hard-

Table 8-3.   BIOS Disk I/O Routines

Invoke via	Input Requirements	Registers Altered	Output/Results
INT 13H	AH = 0	AX	Resest disk system. AH = disk status
	AH = 1	AX	Read disk status. AH = disk status
	AH = 2 DL = drive (0–3) DH = side (0–1) CH = track (0–39) CL = sector (1–8) AL = number of sectors (1–8) BX = address of area to be filled *within extra segment*	AX	Read the specified sector(s) into memory. AH = disk status CF = 0 if successful CF = 1 if error
	AH = 3 DL = drive (0–3) DH = side (0–1) CH = track (0–39) CL = sector (1–8) AL = number of sectors (1–8) BX = address of area containing data to be written, *within extra segment*	AX	Write the specified sector(s) from memory AH = disk status CF = 0 if successful CF = 1 if error

ware-related disk errors, the BIOS routine expects its calling program (that's us) to perform all error detection and recovery. Each of the functions listed in Table 8-3 returns a *status value* in the AH register. If the status value is zero, then the function was performed successfully. Otherwise, the status value indicates what kind of error occurred. The various error conditions and their probable causes are listed in Table 8-4. The first time that a read function is issued, it may return an error status even though there is nothing wrong with the hardware or the diskette. This condition arises because the disk-drive motor takes about a half second to reach full speed, and the BIOS does not wait between starting the motor and issuing the read command to the disk interface. Thus, the hardware may try to read from the disk before it is rotating at the proper speed. To allow for this, any read function should be repeated at least three times before it is decided that an error condition exists. Remember that whenever an error status is returned, the reset function must be issued before further disk i/o attempts can be made. This will be illustrated by the example program that follows. When performing write operations, the BIOS does wait after starting the

Table 8-4. Disk Status Value

AH Register	Description	Probable Cause
0	No error	
2	Address mark not found	Bad diskette
3	Can't write on disk due to write protection	Protected diskette
4	Sector not found	Bad diskette
8	DMA error	Bad disk adapter card
10H	CRC error	Bad diskette
20H	FDC error	Bad disk adapter card
40H	Seek error	Bad disk drive
80H	Time-out error	Bad disk drive or disk drive not ready

motor, and so no retry is necessary. An error returned from a write-function call is definitely an error.

BIOS DISK I/O EXAMPLE: READING THE DIRECTORY

As an example of how to perform disk i/o through the BIOS, a program to read the directory of a disk is presented. As we mentioned earlier, a predefined area of each disk is reserved by DOS. Part of this area (the directory) is used to store the names of all the files on the disk. Another part is used to keep track of the physical disk sectors allocated to each file. By directly accessing the sectors in the reserved area, we can determine the names of the files on the disk, as well as where DOS has placed these files. You are probably familiar with the built-in DOS command "DIR," which lists the names of the files on a disk. Although it provides important information about each file, this command can be frustrating to use because it lists only one filename per line on the screen. We can therefore only see 25 filenames at a time. Our program solves this problem by listing the filenames across the screen. With an 80-column display, we will be able to place four filenames on each line and thus view as many as 96 filenames (the maximum the directory can hold) at the same time.

The program is shown in Fig. 8-7. It consists of two main parts. Part one reads the directory information from the disk and places it in our data segment, starting at label DIRECTORY. Part two extracts the filenames from the directory and lists them on the display screen. The same program technique that was used in the previous program is used here to ensure that the program pauses whenever the screen fills (this can happen only if we

```
00030 ; PROGRAM TO LIST DISK DIRECTORY ON THE DISPLAY.
00040 ; ILLUSTRATES USE OF DISK I/O THROUGH BIOS.
00050 ;
00060 STACK    SEGMENT PARA STACK 'STACK'
00070          DB      256 DUP (0)      ;256 BYTES OF STACK SPACE
00080 STACK    ENDS
00090 ;
00100 DATA     SEGMENT PARA PUBLIC 'DATA'
00110 DIRECTORY DB     2048 DUP (0)     ;READ DISK DIRECTORY SECTORS
00120 ;                                  INTO THIS AREA.
00130 NAMECOUNT DB     0                ;COUNT OF NAMES ON SCREEN
00140 ; ERROR MESSAGE:
00150 ERRMSG   DB      'DISK ACCESS ERROR !!!           '
00160 DATA     ENDS
00170 ;
00180 CODE     SEGMENT PARA PUBLIC 'CODE'
00190 START    PROC    FAR
00200 ;
00210 ; STANDARD PROGRAM PROLOGUE:
00220 ;
00230          ASSUME  CS:CODE
00240          PUSH    DS        ;SAVE PSP SEG ADDR
00250          MOV     AX,0
00260          PUSH    AX        ;SAVE RET ADDR OFFSET (PSP+0)
00270          MOV     AX,DATA
00280          MOV     DS,AX     ;ESTABLISH DATA SEG ADDRESSABILITY
00290          ASSUME  DS:DATA
00300          MOV     ES,AX     ;ESTABLISH EXTRA SEG ADDRESSABILITY
00310          ASSUME  ES:DATA
00320 ;
00330 ; PART 1 - READ DIRECTORY SECTORS FROM DISK INTO MEMORY:
00340 ;
00350          MOV     CX,3      ;TRY TO DO THE 'READ' 3 TIMES
00360 RETRY:   PUSH    CX        ;SAVE RETRY COUNT
00370          MOV     BX,OFFSET DIRECTORY ;ADDRESS TO READ INTO
00380          MOV     DL,0      ;DRIVE A, CHANGE FOR OTHER DRIVES
00390          MOV     DH,0      ;SIDE 0 OF DISKETTE
00400          MOV     CH,0      ;TRACK 0
00410          MOV     CL,4      ;SECTOR 4
00420          MOV     AL,4      ;NUMBER OF SECTORS = 4
00430          MOV     AH,2      ;FUNCTION = 'READ'
00440          INT     13H       ;CALL BIOS DISK I/O ROUTINE
00450          POP     CX        ;RESTORE RETRY COUNT
00460          JNC     READOK    ;BRANCH IF READ WAS OK
00470          MOV     AH,0      ;FUNCTION = 'RESET'
00480          INT     13H
00490          LOOP    RETRY     ;TRY IT AGAIN, (MAX OF 3 TIMES)
00500 ;
00510 ; A DISK ACCESS ERROR HAS OCCURRED, TELL USER AND QUIT:
00520 ;
```

Fig. 8-7. Program to list the directory.

Continued on next page.

```
00530 ERROR:    MOV      BX,OFFSET ERRMSG
00540           CALL     DISPLAY ;DISPLAY THE MESSAGE AT [BX]
00550           RET                      ;RETURN TO DOS
00560 ;
00570 ; PART 2 - DISPLAY DIRECTORY DATA ON SCREEN, FORMAT
00580 ;   IT NICELY:
00590 ;
00600 READOK: MOV      CX,64    ;NUMBER OF ENTRIES IN DIRECTORY
00610 NEXT:    CMP      BYTE PTR [BX],0E5H ;IS THIS ENTRY EMPTY?
00620         JZ       EMPTY    ;BRANCH IF IT IS
00630 ; ENTRY NOT EMPTY: DISPLAY IT ON SCREEN:
00640         PUSH     BX       ;SAVE START OF THIS ENTRY
00650 ; DISPLAY PRIMARY PART OF FILENAME:
00660         MOV      DL,8     ;LENGTH OF PRIMARY FILENAME
00670 PNAME:   MOV      AL,[BX]  ;GET CHARACTER OF FILENAME
00680         CALL     DISPCHAR ;DISPLAY IT
00690         INC      BX       ;GO ON TO NEXT CHARACTER
00700         DEC      DL       ;ANY MORE CHARACTERS TO DISPLAY?
00710         JNZ      PNAME    ;BRANCH IF THERE ARE
00720         MOV      AL,'.'   ;DELIMITER BETWEEN PRI AND EXT NAMES
00730         CALL     DISPCHAR
00740 ; DISPLAY EXTENSION PART OF FILENAME:
00750         MOV      DL,3     ;LENGTH OF EXTENSION FILENAME
00760 ENAME:   MOV      AL,[BX]  ;GET CHARACTER OF FILENAME
00770         CALL     DISPCHAR ;DISPLAY IT
00780         INC      BX       ;GO ON TO NEXT CHARACTER
00790         DEC      DL       ;ANY MORE CHARACTERS TO DISPLAY?
00800         JNZ      ENAME    ;BRANCH IF THERE ARE
00810         POP      BX       ;RESTORE START OF THIS ENTRY
00820 ; DISPLAY BLANKS BETWEEN EACH NAME ON THE SCREEN:
00830         MOV      DL,8     ;NUMBER OF BLANKS TO DISPLAY
00840 BLANK:   MOV      AL,' '
00850         CALL     DISPCHAR ;SEPARATE NAMES WITH BLANKS
00860         DEC      DL       ;ANY MORE BLANKS TO DISPLAY?
00870         JNZ      BLANK    ;BRANCH IF THERE ARE
00880 ; REMOVE STATEMENTS 890 - 960 WHICH FOLLOW IF USING AN 80
00885 ;   COLUMN WIDE SCREEN AS THEY ARE NOT NEEDED IN THIS CASE.
00890         INC      NAMECOUNT ;# OF NAMES CURRENTLY ON SCREEN
00900         CMP      NAMECOUNT,48  ;IS 40 COLUMN SCREEN FULL?
00910         JNZ      EMPTY        ;BRANCH IF NOT
00920 ; THE SCREEN IS FULL, WAIT FOR THE USER TO HIT A KEY:
00930         MOV      AH,0         ;FUNCTION = 'READ KEYBOARD'
00940         INT      16H          ;CALL BIOS KEYBOARD ROUTINE
00950 ; THE USER HIT A KEY: ITS OK TO PROCEED:
00960         MOV      NAMECOUNT,0  ;RESET COUNT OF NAMES ON SCREEN
00970 ; GO ON TO NEXT ENTRY IN DIRECTORY:
00980 EMPTY:   ADD      BX,32        ;POINT TO NEXT DIRECTORY ENTRY
00990         LOOP     NEXT         ;REPEAT FOR ALL 64 ENTRIES
01000 ; DIRECTORY LIST COMPLETE:
01010         RET                   ;RETURN TO DOS
01020 ;
01030 ; SUBROUTINE TO DISPLAY A MESSAGE ON THE SCREEN.
```

Fig. 8-7 (cont).   Program to list the directory.

Continued on next page.

```
01040 ; ENTER WITH BX -> MESSAGE TO BE DISPLAYED.
01050 ; MESSAGE IS ASSUMED TO BE 30 CHARACTERS LONG.
01060 ;
01070 DISPLAY PROC     NEAR
01080         MOV      CX,30     ;NUMBER OF CHARACTERS TO DISPLAY
01090 DISP1:  MOV      AL,[BX]   ;GET NEXT CHARACTER TO DISPLAY
01100         CALL     DISPCHAR  ;DISPLAY IT
01110         INC      BX        ;POINT TO NEXT CHARACTER
01120         LOOP     DISP1     ;DO IT 30 TIMES
01130         MOV      AL,0DH    ;CARRIAGE RETURN
01140         CALL     DISPCHAR
01150         MOV      AL,0AH    ;LINE FEED
01160         CALL     DISPCHAR
01170         RET                ;RETURN TO CALLER OF 'DISPLAY'
01180 DISPLAY ENDP
01190 ;
01200 ; SUBROUTINE TO DISPLAY A CHARACTER ON THE SCREEN.
01210 ; ENTER WITH AL = CHARACTER TO BE DISPLAYED.
01220 ; USES VIDEO INTERFACE IN BIOS.
01230 ;
01240 DISPCHAR PROC    NEAR
01250         PUSH     BX        ;SAVE BX REGISTER
01260         MOV      BX,0      ;SELECT DISPLAY PAGE 0
01270         MOV      AH,14     ;FUNCTION CODE FOR 'WRITE'
01280         INT      10H       ;CALL VIDEO DRIVER IN BIOS
01290         POP      BX        ;RESTORE BX REGISTER
01300         RET                ;RETURN TO CALLER OF 'DISPCHAR'
01310 DISPCHAR ENDP
01320 START   ENDP
01330 CODE    ENDS
01340         END      START
```

Fig. 8-7 (cont).   **Program to list the directory.**

are using a 40-column-wide display). Let us look at the program in more detail.

The program begins with the standard prologue. In addition, the ES register is set equal to the DS register so that the extra segment will be equal to the data segment (statements 300–310). In part one, statements 350–490, we read in the directory sectors (sectors 4, 5, 6, and 7 of track 0) with a single function call. Notice that this call is placed within a loop so that it can be retried if it fails. The CX register, initialized to 3, counts the number of times the function call has been attempted. Since CX is also used by the function call itself, it is saved on the stack during this time (statements 350–360 and 450). Notice how the reset function is always executed when the read function fails (statements 460–480). After three unsuccessful read attempts, we fall through the loop to the ERROR routine at statement 530 and report the condition to the user.

Assuming we successfully read the directory sectors, the program proceeds to part two (statements 600–1010). Here, we extract and display the

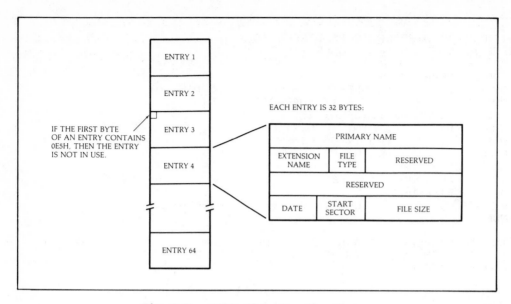

Fig. 8-8. DOS diskette directory.

filenames from the directory. The format of the directory is illustrated in Fig. 8-8. It consists of 64 entries. Each entry is 32 bytes long and can be used to hold information about one file. If the first byte of an entry contains 0E5H, then the entry is not being used. Otherwise, the first eight bytes of the entry contain the primary portion of the filename. The next three bytes contain the filename extension. The rest of the bytes in the entry contain information about the file. This latter information will not be used by our program. We simply loop through all 64 entries (statements 600 and 980–990), bypassing those that are not in use (statements 610–620). For all other entries, we list the primary name on the screen (statements 660–710), follow it with a "." as a delimiter, and then list the filename extension (statements 750–800). Each filename is followed by eight blanks (statements 830–870). Each 80-column screen line will therefore contain as many as four filenames. When the fourth name is displayed, the BIOS display routine will automatically move the cursor down to the next screen line, since the current line will have just been filled completely. We therefore do not need to display the "carriage return" and "line feed" characters at any time. By keeping track of how many names have been displayed, we can determine when the screen has filled so that we can wait for the operator (statements 890–960). This last operation is necessary only if we are using a 40-column display.

Type in this program, and assemble and link it. When run, it will read the directory of the disk in drive A and list it to the screen. You can improve the usefulness of the program by allowing it to accept an input parameter that specifies which drive is to be read. At present, drive A is "hard coded" into the program at statement 380. This is the last exercise of the book; your future assembler-language programs are limited only by your imagination!

APPENDIX A

The 8088 Instruction Set

The 8088 instruction set is summarized in the series of tables that makes up the bulk of this appendix. Examples of typical assembler-language statements are provided for each instruction listed. The time required to execute each instruction is indicated by the number of clocks specified. If "+EA" appears in this column, it indicates that time must be spent calculating the effective address of an operand that is located in main memory. This time depends on the addressing mode used to access the operand and can be obtained from Table A-1. The way each instruction affects the various 8088 flags is indicated in the box at the upper right corner of each table. The flag codes are explained in Table A-2.

The information provided here has been extracted from the *8086/8087/8088 Macro Assembly Language Reference Manual* and is reprinted with permission from Intel Corp.

Table A-1. Effective-Address Calculation Time

EA Components		Clocks*
Displacement Only		6
Base or Index Only	(BX, BP, SI, DI)	5
Displacement + Base or Index	(BX, BP, SI, DI)	9
Base + Index	BP + DI, BX + SI	7
	BP + SI, BX + DI	8
Displacement + Base	BP + DI + DISP BX + SI + DISP	11
Displacement + Base + Index	BP + SI + DISP BX + DI + DISP	12

*Add 2 clocks for segment override.

Table A-2.   Key to Flag Codes

Code	Meaning
1	unconditionally set
0	unconditionally cleared
X	altered to reflect operation result
U	undefined (mask it out)
R	replaced from memory (e.g., SAHF)
b	(blank) unaffected

INSTRUCTION-SET TABLES

AAA	**AAA** (no operands) ASCII adjust for addition	**Flags**	OD I TS Z AP C U UUXUX
Operands	**Clocks**	**Transfers***	**Bytes**	**Coding Example**
(no operands)	4	—	1	AAA

AAD	**AAD** (no operands) ASCII adjust for division	**Flags**	OD I TS Z AP C U XXUXU
Operands	**Clocks**	**Transfers***	**Bytes**	**Coding Example**
(no operands)	60	—	2	AAD

AAM	**AAM** (no operands) ASCII adjust for multiply	**Flags**	OD I TS Z AP C U XXUXU
Operands	**Clocks**	**Transfers***	**Bytes**	**Coding Example**
(no operands)	83	—	1	AAM

AAS	**AAS** (no operands) ASCII adjust for subtraction	**Flags**	OD I TS Z AP C U UUXUX
Operands	**Clocks**	**Transfers***	**Bytes**	**Coding Example**
(no operands)	4	—	1	AAS

* For the 8086, add four clocks for each 16-bit word transfer with an odd address. For the 8088, add four clocks for each 16-bit word transfer.

ADC	ADC destination,source Add with carry			Flags	OD I TS ZAP C X XXXXX
Operands	**Clocks**	**Transfers***	**Bytes**		**Coding Example**
register, register	3	—	2		ADC AX, SI
register, memory	9 + EA	1	2-4		ADC DX, BETA [SI]
memory, register	16 + EA	2	2-4		ADC ALPHA [BX] [SI], DI
register, immediate	4	—	3-4		ADC BX, 256
memory, immediate	17 + EA	2	3-6		ADC GAMMA, 30H
accumulator, immediate	4	—	2-3		ADC AL, 5

ADD	ADD destination,source Addition			Flags	OD I TS ZAP C X XXXXX
Operands	**Clocks**	**Transfers***	**Bytes**		**Coding Example**
register, register	3	—	2		ADD CX, DX
register, memory	9 + EA	1	2-4		ADD DI, [BX], ALPHA
memory, register	16 + EA	2	2-4		ADD TEMP, CL
register, immediate	4	—	3-4		ADD CL, 2
memory, immediate	17 + EA	2	3-6		ADD ALPHA, 2
accumulator, immediate	4	—	2-3		ADD AX, 200

AND	AND destination,source Logical AND			Flags	OD I TS ZAP C 0 XXUX0
Operands	**Clocks**	**Transfers***	**Bytes**		**Coding Example**
register, register	3	—	2		AND AL, BL
register, memory	9 + EA	1	2-4		AND CX, FLAG_WORD
memory, register	16 + EA	2	2-4		AND ASCII [DI],AL
register, immediate	4	—	3-4		AND CX0, F0H
memory, immediate	17 + EA	2	3-6		AND BETA, 01H
accumulator, immediate	4	—	2-3		AND AX, 01010000B

CALL	CALL target Call a procedure			Flags	OD I TS ZAP C
Operands	**Clocks**	**Transfers***	**Bytes**		**Coding Examples**
near-proc	19	1	3		CALL NEAR_PROC
far-proc	28	2	5		CALL FAR_PROC
memptr 16	21 + EA	2	2-4		CALL PROC_TABLE [SI]
regptr 16	16	1	2		CALL AX
memptr 32	37 + EA	4	2-4		CALL [BX], TASK [SI]

* For the 8086, add four clocks for each 16-bit word transfer with an odd address. For the 8088, add four clocks for each 16-bit word transfer.

CBW	CBW (no operands) Convert byte to word				Flags OD I T S Z A P C
Operands		**Clocks**	**Transfers***	**Bytes**	**Coding Example**
(no operands)		2	—	1	CBW

CLC	CLC (no operands) Clear carry flag				Flags OD I T S Z A P C 0
Operands		**Clocks**	**Transfers***	**Bytes**	**Coding Example**
(no operands)		2	—	1	CLC

CLD	CLD (no operands) Clear direction flag				Flags OD I T S Z A P C 0
Operands		**Clocks**	**Transfers***	**Bytes**	**Coding Example**
(no operands)		2	—	1	CLD

CLI	CLI (no operands) Clear interrupt flag				Flags OD I T S Z A P C 0
Operands		**Clocks**	**Transfers***	**Bytes**	**Coding Example**
(no operands)		2	—	1	CLI

CMC	CMC (no operands) Complement carry flag				Flags OD I T S Z A P C X
Operands		**Clocks**	**Transfers***	**Bytes**	**Coding Example**
(no operands)		2	—	1	CMC

CMP	CMP destination,source Compare destination to source				Flags OD I T S Z A P C X XXXXX
Operands		**Clocks**	**Transfers***	**Bytes**	**Coding Example**
register, register		3	—	2	CMP BX, CX
register, memory		9+EA	1	2-4	CMP DH, ALPHA
memory, register		9+EA	1	2-4	CMP [BP+2],SI
register, immediate		4	—	3-4	CMP BL, 02H
memory, immediate		10+EA	1	3-6	CMP [BX],RADAR [DI], 3420H
accumulator, immediate		4	—	2-3	CMP AL, 00010000B

* For the 8086, add four clocks for each 16-bit word transfer with an odd address. For the 8088, add four clocks for each 16-bit word transfer.

CMPS	CMPS dest-string,source-string Compare string			Flags OD I T S Z A P C X XXXXX	
Operands	**Clocks**	**Transfers***	**Bytes**	**Coding Example**	
dest-string, source-string	22	2	1	CMPS BUFF1, BUFF2	
(repeat) dest-string, source-string	9+22/rep	2/rep	1	REPE CMPS ID, KEY	

CWD	CWD (no operands) Convert word to doubleword			Flags OD I T S Z A P C	
Operands	**Clocks**	**Transfers***	**Bytes**	**Coding Example**	
(no operands)	5	—	1	CWD	

DAA	DAA (no operands) Decimal adjust for addition			Flags OD I T S Z A P C X XXXXX	
Operands	**Clocks**	**Transfers***	**Bytes**	**Coding Example**	
(no operands)	4	—	1	DAA	

DAS	DAS (no operands) Decimal adjust for subtraction			Flags OD I T S Z A P C U XXXXX	
Operands	**Clocks**	**Transfers***	**Bytes**	**Coding Example**	
(no operands)	4	—	1	DAS	

DEC	DEC destination Decrement by 1			Flags OD I T S Z A P C X XXXX	
Operands	**Clocks**	**Transfers***	**Bytes**	**Coding Example**	
reg16	2	—	1	DEC AX	
reg8	3	—	2	DEC AL	
memory	15+EA	2	2-4	DEC ARRAY [SI]	

DIV	DIV source Division, unsigned			Flags OD I T S Z A P C U UUUUU	
Operands	**Clocks**	**Transfers***	**Bytes**	**Coding Example**	
reg8	80-90	—	2	DIV CL	
reg16	144-162	—	2	DIV BX	
mem8	(86-96)+EA	1	2-4	DIV ALPHA	
mem16	(150-168)+EA	1	2-4	DIV TABLE [SI]	

* For the 8086, add four clocks for each 16-bit word transfer with an odd address. For the 8088, add four clocks for each 16-bit word transfer.

ESC	ESC external-opcode,source Escape			Flags OD I T S Z A P C
Operands	**Clocks**	**Transfers***	**Bytes**	**Coding Example**
immediate, memory	8+EA	1	2-4	ESC 6,ARRAY [SI]
immediate, register	2	—	2	ESC 20,AL

HLT	HLT (no operands) Halt			Flags OD I T S Z A P C
Operands	**Clocks**	**Transfers***	**Bytes**	**Coding Example**
(no operands)	2	—	1	HLT

IDIV	IDIV source Integer division			Flags OD I T S Z A P C U UUUUU
Operands	**Clocks**	**Transfers***	**Bytes**	**Coding Example**
reg8	101-112	—	2	IDIV BL
reg16	165-184	—	2	IDIV CX
mem8	(107-118) +EA	1	2-4	IDIV DIVISOR BYTE [SI]
mem16	(171-190) +EA	1	2-4	IDIV [BX] , DIVI- SOR__WORD

IMUL	IMUL source Integer multiplication			Flags OD I T S Z A P C X UUUUX
Operands	**Clocks**	**Transfers***	**Bytes**	**Coding Example**
reg8	80-98	—	2	IMUL CL
reg16	128-154	—	2	IMUL BX
mem8	(86-104) +EA	1	2-4	IMUL RATE__BYTE
mem16	(134-160) +EA	1	2-4	IMUL RATE__WORD [BP]| [DI]

IN	IN accumulator,port Input byte or word			Flags OD I T S Z A P C
Operands	**Clocks**	**Transfers***	**Bytes**	**Coding Example**
accumulator, immed8	10	1	2	IN AL, 0FFEAH
accumulator, DX	8	1	1	IN AX, DX

* For the 8086, add four clocks for each 16-bit word transfer with an odd address. For the 8088, add four clocks for each 16-bit word transfer.

INC	INC destination Increment by 1				Flags	OD I TS ZAP C X XXXX
Operands		**Clocks**	**Transfers***	**Bytes**	**Coding Example**	
reg16		2	—	1	INC CX	
reg8		3	—	2	INC BL	
memory		15+EA	2	2-4	INC ALPHA [DI] [BX]	

INT	INT interrupt-type interrupt				Flags	OD I TS ZAP C 0 0
Operands		**Clocks**	**Transfers***	**Bytes**	**Coding Example**	
immed8 (type=3)		52	5	1	INT 3	
immed8 (type=/3)		51	5	2	INT 67	

INTR	INTR (external maskable in- terrupt) Interrupt if INTR and IF=1				Flags	OD I TS ZAP C 0 0
Operands		**Clocks**	**Transfers***	**Bytes**	**Coding Example**	
(no operands)		61	7	N/A	N/A	

INTO	INTO (no operands) Interrupt if overflow				Flags	OD I TS ZAP C 0 0
Operands		**Clocks**	**Transfers***	**Bytes**	**Coding Example**	
(no operands)		53 or 4	5	1	INTO	

IRET	IRET (no operands) Interrupt Return				Flags	OD I TS ZAP C RRRRRRRR
Operands		**Clocks**	**Transfers***	**Bytes**	**Coding Example**	
(no operands)		24	3	1	IRET	

JA/JNBE	JA/JNBE short-label Jump if above/Jump if not below nor equal				Flags	OD I TS ZAP C
Operands		**Clocks**	**Transfers***	**Bytes**	**Coding Example**	
short-label		16 or 4	—	2	JA ABOVE	

* For the 8086, add four clocks for each 16-bit word transfer with an odd address. For the 8088, add four clocks for each 16-bit word transfer.

JAE/JNB	**JAE/JNB** short-label Jump if above or equal/Jump if not below				**Flags** OD I T S Z A P C
Operands		Clocks	Transfers*	Bytes	Coding Example
short-label		16 or 4	—	2	JAE ABOVE__EQUAL

JB/JNAE	**JB/JNAE** short-label Jump if below/Jump if not above nor equal				**Flags** OD I T S Z A P C
Operands		Clocks	Transfers*	Bytes	Coding Example
short-label		16 or 4	—	2	JB BELOW

JBE/JNA	**JBE/JNA** short-label Jump if below or equal/Jump if not above				**Flags** OD I T S Z A P C
Operands		Clocks	Transfers*	Bytes	Coding Example
short-label		16 or 4	—	2	JNA NOT ABOVE

JC	**JC** short-label Jump if carry				**Flags** OD I T S Z A P C
Operands		Clocks	Transfers*	Bytes	Coding Example
short-label		16 or 4	—	2	JC CARRY SET

JCXZ	**JCXZ** short-label Jump if CX is zero				**Flags** OD I T S Z A P C
Operands		Clocks	Transfers*	Bytes	Coding Example
short-label		18 or 6	—	2	JCXZ COUNT DONE

JE/JZ	**JE/JZ** short-label Jump if equal/Jump if zero				**Flags** OD I T S Z A P C
Operands		Clocks	Transfers*	Bytes	Coding Example
short-label		16 or 4	—	2	JZ ZERO

* For the 8086, add four clocks for each 16-bit word transfer with an odd address. For the 8088, add four clocks for each 16-bit word transfer.

JG/JNLE	JG/JNLE short-label Jump if greater/Jump if not less nor equal			Flags OD I T S Z A P C
Operands	Clocks	Transfers*	Bytes	**Coding Example**
short-label	16 or 4	—	2	JG GREATER

JGE/JNL	JGE/JNL short-label Jump if greater or equal/ Jump if not less			Flags OD I T S Z A P C
Operands	Clocks	Transfers*	Bytes	**Coding Example**
short-label	16 or 4	—	2	JGE GREATER EQUAL

JL/JNGE	JL/JNGE short-label Jump if less/Jump if not greater nor equal			Flags OD I T S Z A P C
Operands	Clocks	Transfers*	Bytes	**Coding Example**
short-label	16 or 4	—	2	JL LESS

JLE/JNG	JLE/JNG short-label Jump if less or equal/Jump if not greater			Flags OD I T S Z A P C
Operands	Clocks	Transfers*	Bytes	**Coding Example**
short-label	16 or 4	—	2	JNG NOT GREATER

JMP	JMP target Jump			Flags OD I T S Z A P C
Operands	Clocks	Transfers*	Bytes	**Coding Example**
short-label	15	—	2	JMP SHORT
near-label	15	—	3	JMP WITHIN SEGMENT
far-label	15	—	5	JMP FAR LABEL
memptr16	18+EA	1	2-4	JMP [BX],TARGET
regptr16	11	—	2	JMP CX
memptr32	24+EA	2	2-4	JMP OTHER,SEG [SI]

JNC	JNC short-label Jump if not carry			Flags OD I T S Z A P C
Operands	Clocks	Transfers*	Bytes	**Coding Example**
short-label	16 or 4	—	2	JNC NOT CARRY

* For the 8086, add four clocks for each 16-bit word transfer with an odd address. For the 8088, add four clocks for each 16-bit word transfer.

JNE / JNZ	JNE / JNZ short-label Jump if not equal / Jump if not zero			Flags OD I T S Z A P C	
Operands		Clocks	Transfers*	Bytes	Coding Example
short-label		16 or 4	—	2	JNE NOT EQUAL

JNO	JNO short-label Jump if not overflow			Flags OD I T S Z A P C	
Operands		Clocks	Transfers*	Bytes	Coding Example
short-label		16 or 4	—	2	JNO NO OVERFLOW

JNP / JPO	JNP / JPO short-label Jump if not parity / Jump if parity odd			Flags OD I T S Z A P C	
Operands		Clocks	Transfers*	Bytes	Coding Example
short-label		16 or 4	—	2	JPO ODD PARITY

JNS	JNS short-label Jump if not sign			Flags OD I T S Z A P C	
Operands		Clocks	Transfers*	Bytes	Coding Example
short-label		16 or 4	—	2	JNS POSITIVE

JO	JO short-label Jump if overflow			Flags OD I T S Z A P C	
Operands		Clocks	Transfers*	Bytes	Coding Example
short-label		16 or 4	—	2	JO SIGNED__OVRFLW

JP / JPE	JP / JPE short-label Jump if parity / Jump if parity even			Flags OD I T S Z A P C	
Operands		Clocks	Transfers*	Bytes	Coding Example
short-label		16 or 4	—	2	JPE EVEN__PARITY

* For the 8086, add four clocks for each 16-bit word transfer with an odd address. For the 8088, add four clocks for each 16-bit word transfer.

JS	JS short-label Jump if sign			Flags OD I TS Z AP C
Operands	Clocks	Transfers*	Bytes	Coding Example
short-label	16 or 4	—	2	JS NEGATIVE

LAHF	LAHF (no operands) Load AH from flags			Flags OD I TS Z AP C
Operands	Clocks	Transfers*	Bytes	Coding Example
(no operands)	4	—	1	LAHF

LDS	LDS destination,source Load pointer using DS			Flags OD I TS Z AP C
Operands	Clocks	Transfers*	Bytes	Coding Example
reg16, mem32	16+EA	2	2-4	LDS SI,DATA,SEG [DI]

LOCK	LOCK (no operands) Lock bus			Flags OD I TS Z AP C
Operands	Clocks	Transfers*	Bytes	Coding Example
(no operands)	2	—	1	LOCK XCHG FLAG,AL

LODS	LODS source-string Load string			Flags OD I TS Z AP C
Operands	Clocks	Transfers*	Bytes	Coding Example
source-string (repeat) source-string	12 9+13/ rep	1 1/rep	1 1	LODS CUSTOMER NAME REP LODS NAME

LOOP	LOOP short-label Loop			Flags OD I TS Z AP C
Operands	Clocks	Transfers*	Bytes	Coding Example
short-label	17/5	—	2	LOOP AGAIN

* For the 8086, add four clocks for each 16-bit word transfer with an odd address. For the 8088, add four clocks for each 16-bit word transfer.

LOOPE / LOOPZ	LOOPE/LOOPZ short-label Loop if equal/Loop if zero			Flags OD I T S Z A P C
Operands	Clocks	Transfers*	Bytes	Coding Example
short-label	18 or 6	—	2	LOOPE AGAIN

LOOPNE / LOOPNZ	LOOPNE/LOOPNZ short-label Loop if not equal/Loop if not zero			Flags OD I T S Z A P C
Operands	Clocks	Transfers*	Bytes	Coding Example
short-label	19 or 5	—	2	LOOPNE AGAIN

LEA	LEA destination,source Load effective address			Flags OD I T S Z A P C
Operands	Clocks	Transfers*	Bytes	Coding Example
reg16, mem16	2+EA	—	2-4	LEA BX, [BP] [DI]

LES	LES destination,source Load pointer using ES			Flags OD I T S Z A P C
Operands	Clocks	Transfers*	Bytes	Coding Example
reg16, mem32	16+EA	2	2-4	LES DI, [BX], TEXT__BUFF

NMI	NMI (external nonmaskable interrupt) Interrupt if NMI=1			Flags OD I T S Z A P C 0 0
Operands	Clocks	Transfers*	Bytes	Coding Example
(no operands)	50	5	N/A	N/A

* For the 8086, add four clocks for each 16-bit word transfer with an odd address. For the 8088, add four clocks for each 16-bit word transfer.

MOV	MOV destination,source Move				Flags OD I T S Z A P C
Operands	**Clocks**	**Transfers***	**Bytes**		**Coding Example**
memory, accumulator	10	1	3		MOV ARRAY [SI], AL
accumulator, memory	10	1	3		MOV AX, TEMP__RESULT
register, register	2	—	2		MOV AX,CX
register, memory	8+EA	1	2-4		MOV BP, STACK__TOP
memory, register	9+EA	1	2-4		MOV COUNT [DI], CX
register, immediate	4	—	2-3		MOV CL, 2
memory, immediate	10+EA	1	3-6		MOV MASK [BX] [SI], 2 CH
seg-reg, reg16	2	—	2		MOV ES, CX
seg-reg. mem16	8+EA	1	2-4		MOV DS, SEGMENT__BASE
reg16, seg-reg	2	—	2		MOV BP, SS
memory, seg-reg	9+EA	1	2-4		MOV [BX], SEG__SAVE, CS

MOVS	MOVS dest-string,source-string Move string				Flags OD I T S Z A P C
Operands	**Clocks**	**Transfers***	**Bytes**		**Coding Example**
dest-string, source-string	18	2	1		MOVS LINE,EDIT__DATA
(repeat) dest-string, source-string	9+17/rep	2/rep	1		REP MOVS SCREEN, BUF-FER

MOVSB/ MOVSW	MOVSB/MOVSW (no operands) Move string (byte/word)				Flags OD I T S Z A P C
Operands	**Clocks**	**Transfers***	**Bytes**		**Coding Example**
(no operands)	18	2	1		MOVSB
(repeat) (no operands)	9+17/rep	2/rep	1		REP MOVSW

MUL	MUL source Multiplication, unsigned				Flags OD I T S Z A P C X UUUUX
Operands	**Clocks**	**Transfers***	**Bytes**		**Coding Example**
reg8	70-77	—	2		MUL BL
reg16	118-133	—	2		MUL CX
mem8	(76-83)+EA	1	2-4		MUL MONTH [SI]
mem16	(124-139)+EA	1	2-4		MUL BAUD__RATE

* For the 8086, add four clocks for each 16-bit word transfer with an odd address. For the 8088, add four clocks for each 16-bit word transfer.

NEG	**NEG** destination Negate			**Flags** OD I TS ZAP C X XXXX1*
Operands	**Clocks**	**Transfers***	**Bytes**	**Coding Example**
register	3	—	2	NEG AL
memory	16+EA	2	2-4	NEG MULTIPLIER

*0 if destination = 0

NOP	**NOP** (no operands) No Operation			**Flags** OD I TS ZAP C
Operands	**Clocks**	**Transfers***	**Bytes**	**Coding Example**
(no operands)	3	—	1	NOP

NOT	**NOT** destination Logical NOT			**Flags** OD I TS ZAP C
Operands	**Clocks**	**Transfers***	**Bytes**	**Coding Example**
register	3	—	2	NOT AX
memory	16+EA	2	2-4	NOT CHARACTER

OR	**OR** destination,source Logical inclusive OR			**Flags** OD I TS ZAP C 0 XXUX0
Operands	**Clocks**	**Transfers***	**Bytes**	**Coding Example**
register, register	3	—	2	OR AL, BL
register, memory	9+EA	1	2-4	OR DX, PORT ID [DI]
memory, register	16+EA	2	2-4	OR FLAG BYTE, CL
accumulator, immediate	4	—	2-3	OR AL,0110110B
register, immediate	4	—	3-4	OR CX,01FH
memory, immediate	17+EA	2	3-6	OR [BX] CMD WORD,0CFH

OUT	**OUT** port,accumulator Output byte or word			**Flags** OD I TS ZAP C
Operands	**Clocks**	**Transfers***	**Bytes**	**Coding Example**
immed8, accumulator	10	1	2	OUT 44, AX
DX, accumulator	8	1	1	OUT DX, AL

* For the 8086, add four clocks for each 16-bit word transfer with an odd address. For the 8088, add four clocks for each 16-bit word transfer.

POP	POP destination Pop word off stack			Flags OD I T S Z A P C
Operands	**Clocks**	**Transfers***	**Bytes**	**Coding Example**
register	8	1	1	POP DX
seg-reg (CS illegal)	8	1	1	POP DS
memory	17+EA	2	2-4	POP PARAMETER

POPF	POPF (no operands) Pop flags off stack			Flags OD I T S Z A P C RRRRRRRR
Operands	**Clocks**	**Transfers***	**Bytes**	**Coding Example**
(no operands)	8	1	1	POPF

PUSH	PUSH source Push word onto stack			Flags OD I T S Z A P C
Operands	**Clocks**	**Transfers***	**Bytes**	**Coding Example**
register	11	1	1	PUSH SI
seg-reg (CS legal)	10	1	1	PUSH ES
memory	16+EA	2	2-4	PUSH RETURN CODE [SI]

PUSHF	PUSHF (no operands) Push flags onto stack			Flags OD I T S Z A P C
Operands	**Clocks**	**Transfers***	**Bytes**	**Coding Example**
(no operands)	10	1	1	PUSHF

RCL	RCL destination,count Rotate left through carry			Flags OD I T S Z A P C X X
Operands	**Clocks**	**Transfers***	**Bytes**	**Coding Example**
register, 1	2	—	2	RCL CX,1
register, CL	8+4/bit	—	2	RCL AL, CL
memory, 1	15+EA	2	2-4	RCL ALPHA, 1
memory, CL	20+EA+ 4/bit	2	2-4	RCL [BP], PARM, CL

* For the 8086, add four clocks for each 16-bit word transfer with an odd address. For the 8088, add four clocks for each 16-bit word transfer.

RCR	RCR destination,count Rotate right through carry			Flags	OD I T S Z A P C X X
Operands	**Clocks**	**Transfers***	**Bytes**	**Coding Example**	
register, 1	2	—	2	RCR BX, 1	
register, CL	8+4/bit	—	2	RCR BL, CL	
memory, 1	15+EA	2	2-4	RCR [BX], STATUS, 1	
memory, CL	20+EA+ 4/bit	2	2-4	RCR ARRAY [DI], CL	

REP	REP (no operands) Repeat string operation			Flags	OD I T S Z A P C
Operands	**Clocks**	**Transfers***	**Bytes**	**Coding Example**	
(no operands)	2	—	1	REP MOVS DEST, SRCE	

REPE / REPZ	REPE/REPZ (no operands) Repeat string operation while equal/while zero			Flags	OD I T S Z A P C
Operands	**Clocks**	**Transfers***	**Bytes**	**Coding Example**	
(no operands)	2	—	1	REPE CMPS DATA, KEY	

REPNE / REPNZ	REPNE/REPNZ (no operands) Repeat string operation while not equal/not zero			Flags	OD I T S Z A P C
Operands	**Clocks**	**Transfers***	**Bytes**	**Coding Example**	
(no operands)	2	—	1	REPNE SCAS INPUT LINE	

RET	RET optional-pop-value Return from procedure			Flags	OD I T S Z A P C
Operands	**Clocks**	**Transfers***	**Bytes**	**Coding Example**	
(intra-segment, no pop)	8	1	1	RET	
(intra-segment, pop)	12	1	3	RET 4	
(inter-segment, no pop)	18	2	1	RET	
(inter-segment, pop)	17	2	3	RET 2	

* For the 8086, add four clocks for each 16-bit word transfer with an odd address. For the 8088, add four clocks for each 16-bit word transfer.

ROL	ROL destination,count Rotate left			Flags	OD I T S Z A P C X X
Operands	**Clocks**	**Transfers***	**Bytes**	**Coding Example**	
register, 1	2	—	2	ROL BX, 1	
register, CL	8+4/bit	—	2	ROL DI, CL	
memory, 1	15+EA	2	2-4	ROL FLAG BYTE [DI], 1	
memory, CL	20+EA+ 4/bit	2	2-4	ROL ALPHA, CL	

ROR	ROR destination,count Rotate right			Flags	OD I T S Z A P C X X
Operands	**Clocks**	**Transfers***	**Bytes**	**Coding Example**	
register, 1	2	—	2	ROR AL, 1	
register, CL	8+4/bit	—	2	ROR BX, CL	
memory, 1	15+EA	2	2-4	ROR PORT STATUS, 1	
memory, CL	20+EA+ 4/bit	2	2-4	ROR CMD WORD, CL	

SAHF	SAHF (no operands) Store AH into flags			Flags	OD I T S Z A P C R R R R R
Operands	**Clocks**	**Transfers***	**Bytes**	**Coding Example**	
(no operands)	4	—	1	SAHF	

SAL/SHL	SAL/SHL destination,count Shift arithmetic left/Shift logical left			Flags	OD I T S Z A P C X X
Operands	**Clocks**	**Transfers***	**Bytes**	**Coding Example**	
register, 1	2	—	2	SAL AL, 1	
register, CL	8+4/bit	—	2	SHL DI, CL	
memory, 1	15+EA	2	2-4	SHL [BX], OVERDRAW, 1	
memory, CL	20+EA+ 4/bit	2	2-4	SAL STORE_COUNT, CL	

SAR	SAR destination,source Shift arithmetic right			Flags	OD I T S Z A P C X X X U X X
Operands	**Clocks**	**Transfers***	**Bytes**	**Coding Example**	
register, 1	2	—	2	SAR DX, 1	
register, CL	8+4/bit	—	2	SAR DI, CL	
memory, 1	15+EA	2	2-4	SAR N BLOCKS, 1	
memory, CL	20+EA+ 4/bit	2	2-4	SAR N BLOCKS, CL	

* For the 8086, add four clocks for each 16-bit word transfer with an odd address. For the 8088, add four clocks for each 16-bit word transfer.

SBB	SBB destination,source Subtract with borrow			Flags	OD I T S Z A P C X XXXXX
Operands	**Clocks**	**Transfers***	**Bytes**	**Coding Example**	
register, register	3	—	2	SBB BX, CX	
register, memory	9+EA	1	2-4	SBB DI, [BX], PAYMENT	
memory, register	16+EA	2	2-4	SBB BALANCE, AX	
accumulator, immediate	4	—	2-3	SBB AX, 2	
register, immediate	4	—	3-4	SBB CL, 1	
memory, immediate	17+EA	2	3-6	SBB COUNT [SI], 10	

SCAS	SCAS dest-string Scan string			Flags	OD I T S Z A P C X XXXXX
Operands	**Clocks**	**Transfers***	**Bytes**	**Coding Example**	
dest-string	15	1	1	SCAS INPUT__LINE	
(repeat) dest-string	9+15/ rep	1/rep	1	REPNE SCAS BUFFER	

SHR	SHR destination,count Shift logical right			Flags	OD I T S Z A P C X X
Operands	**Clocks**	**Transfers***	**Bytes**	**Coding Example**	
register, 1	2	—	2	SHR SI, 1	
register, CL	8+4/bit	—	2	SHR SI, CL	
memory, 1	15+EA	2	2-4	SHR ID BYTE [SI] [BX], 1	
memory, CL	20+EA+ 4/bit	2	2-4	SHR INPUT WORD, CL	

SINGLE STEP	SINGLE STEP (Trap flag interrupt) Interrupt if TF = 1			Flags	OD I T S Z A P C 0 0
Operands	**Clocks**	**Transfers***	**Bytes**	**Coding Example**	
(no operands)	50	5	N/A	N/A	

STC	STC (no operands) Set carry flag			Flags	OD I T S Z A P C 1
Operands	**Clocks**	**Transfers***	**Bytes**	**Coding Example**	
(no operands)	2	—	1	STC	

* For the 8086, add four clocks for each 16-bit word transfer with an odd address. For the 8088, add four clocks for each 16-bit word transfer.

STD	STD (no operands) Set direction flag			Flags	OD I T S Z A P C 1
Operands	**Clocks**	**Transfers***	**Bytes**	**Coding Example**	
(no operands)	2	—	1	STD	

STI	STI (no operands) Set interrupt enable flag			Flags	OD I T S Z A P C 1
Operands	**Clocks**	**Transfers***	**Bytes**	**Coding Example**	
(no operands)	2	—	1	STI	

STOS	STOS dest-string Store byte or word string			Flags	OD I T S Z A P C
Operands	**Clocks**	**Transfers***	**Bytes**	**Coding Example**	
dest-string	11	1	1	STOS PRINT LINE	
(repeat) dest-string	9+10/ rep	1/rep	1	REP STOS DISPLAY	

SUB	SUB destination,source Subtraction			Flags	OD I T S Z A P C X XXXXX
Operands	**Clocks**	**Transfers***	**Bytes**	**Coding Example**	
register, register	3	—	2	SUB CX, BX	
register, memory	9+EA	1	2-4	SUB DX, MATH TOTAL [SI]	
memory, register	16+EA	2	2-4	SUB [BP+2], CL	
accumulator, immediate	4	—	2-3	SUB AL, 10	
register, immediate	4	—	3-4	SUB SI, 5280	
memory, immediate	17+EA	2	3-6	SUB [BP], BALANCE, 1000	

TEST	TEST destination,source Test or nondestructive logical AND			Flags	OD I T S Z A P C 0 XXUX0
Operands	**Clocks**	**Transfers***	**Bytes**	**Coding Example**	
register, register	3	—	2	TEST SI, DI	
register, memory	9+EA	1	2-4	TEST SI, END COUNT	
accumulator, immediate	4	—	2-3	TEST AL, 00100000B	
register, immediate	5	—	3-4	TEST BX, 0CC4H	
memory, immediate	11+EA	—	3-6	TEST RETURN CODE, 01H	

* For the 8086, add four clocks for each 16-bit word transfer with an odd address. For the 8088, add four clocks for each 16-bit word transfer.

WAIT	**WAIT** (no operands) Wait while TEST pin not asserted			**Flags** OD I T S Z A P C
Operands	**Clocks**	**Transfers***	**Bytes**	**Coding Example**
(no operands)	3 + 5n	—	1	WAIT

XCHG	**XCHG** destination,source Exchange			**Flags** OD I T S Z A P C
Operands	**Clocks**	**Transfers***	**Bytes**	**Coding Example**
accumulator, reg16	3	—	1	XCHG AX, BX
memory, register	17 + EA	2	2-4	XCHG SEMAPHORE, AX
register, register	4	—	2	XCHG AL, BL

XLAT	**XLAT** source-table Translate			**Flags** OD I T S Z A P C
operands	**Clocks**	**Transfers***	**Bytes**	**Coding Example**
source-table	11	1	1	XLAT ASCII__TAB

XOR	**XOR** destination,source Logical exclusive OR			**Flags** OD I T S Z A P C 0 XXUX0
Operands	**Clocks**	**Transfers***	**Bytes**	**Coding Example**
register, register	3	—	2	XOR CX, BX
register, memory	9 + EA	1	2-4	XOR CL, MASK BYTE
memory, register	16 + EA	2	2-4	XOR ALPHA [SI],DX
accumulator, immediate	4	—	2-3	XOR AL, 01000010B
register, immediate	4	—	3-4	XOR SI, 00C2H
memory, immediate	17 + EA	2	3-6	XOR RETURN CODE, 0D2H

* For the 8086, add four clocks for each 16-bit word transfer with an odd address. For the 8088, add four clocks for each 16-bit word transfer.

References

1. The IBM Personal Computer Technical Reference Manual
2. The IBM Personal Computer Disk Operating System Manual
3. The IBM Personal Computer Macro Assembler Manual
4. *Intel iAPX 88 Book*
5. *Intel 8086 Family User's Manual*
6. *Intel 8086/8087/8088 Macro Assembly Language Reference Manual for 8086-Based Development Systems*
7. Intel product specifications for the following devices:
   A. 8255 Programmable Peripheral Interface
   B. 8259 Interrupt Controller
   C. 8237 DMA Controller
   D. 8253 Timer
8. Motorola product specification for the 6845 CRT Controller

Index

SAMS COMPUTER BOOKS

Many thanks for your interest in this Sams Book about IBM® PC microcomputing. Here are a few more products we think you'll like:

USING YOUR IBM® PERSONAL COMPUTER

Easily the most practical, most thorough guide on the market for computing with the IBM PC. Shows you how to use the PC's system unit, keyboard, display screen, disk drives, and printer. Also teaches you to program in PC BASIC, with scores of examples to help you learn quickly. Fully explains all commonly used PC BASIC commands, including those for graphics, music, sound effects, and more. Fully indexed and illustrated. By Lon Poole. 336 pages, 8 × 9¼, soft. ISBN 0-672-22000-8. © 1983.
Ask for No. 22000 . . . .$16.95

16-BIT MICROPROCESSORS

Carefully steps you through programming and designing with these state-of-the-art devices, discusses their advantages and disadvantages, and gives you numerous benchmarks to use in comparing different 16-bit chips. Takes an in-depth look at the 68000, the 8086, the Z8001/2, the 9900, and the NS16000. By Christopher A. Titus, Jonathan A. Titus, Alan Baldwin, W.N. Hubin, and Leo Scanlon. 352 pages, 5½ × 8½, soft. ISBN 0-672-21805-4. © 1981.
Ask for No. 21805 . . . .$15.95

THE 68000: PRINCIPLES AND PROGRAMMING

A complete introduction to one of the industry's fastest and most powerful 16-bit microprocessors. Guides you progressively through its complex architecture, instruction set, pinouts, and interfacing techniques. You'll need a basic knowledge of number systems, Boolean logic, and other computer fundamentals, plus a familiarity with some type of assembly language. By Leo J. Scanlon. 240 pages, 5½ × 8½ soft. ISBN 0-672-21853-4. © 1981.
Ask for No. 21853 . . . .$15.95

MICROCOMPUTER DESIGN AND TROUBLESHOOTING

If you're an advanced experimenter or practicing engineer, you can use these concepts to improve upon or modify an existing microcomputer design as you like it, or develop your OWN designs and carry them through. Not a cookbook. No expensive commercial development system needed—only your brain, this book, and some test equipment. By Eugene Zumchak. 368 pages, 5½ × 8½, soft. ISBN 0-672-21819-4. © 1982.
Ask for No. 21819 . . . .$17.95

SAMS FINANCIAL PLANNING MIND TOOLS™

Temporarily interlocks with the spreadsheet in your regular version of Multiplan©, VisiCalc©, or SuperCalc© so you can immediately perform 17 common financial planning calculations without wasting time manually setting up the sheet. All you do is enter the data—the proper formulas and column headings are there automatically!

Mind Tools allow you to instantly calculate present, net present, and future values, yields, internal and financial management rates of return, and basic statistics.

Also lets you do break-even analyses, depreciation schedules, and amortization tables, as well as compute variable- and graduated-rate mortgages, wraparound mortgages, and more!

Allows you to use your regular spreadsheet as you always have, at any time. Ideal for any businessman with financial planning responsibilities, as well as for business students and instructors.

Supplied with complete documentation, including 128-page text and 40-page quick-reference guide, all in a binder with the proper disk to match the brand of spreadsheet program and microcomputer you own.

Currently available for use with Multiplan©, VisiCalc©, or SuperCalc® as follows:

FINANCIAL PLANNING WITH MULTIPLAN™

Apple© II Version, ISBN 0-672-22058-X.
Ask for No. 22058 . . . . **$79.95**

IBM® PC Version, ISBN 0-672-22063-6.
Ask for No. 22063 . . . . **$89.95**

FINANCIAL PLANNING WITH VISICALC©

Apple® II Version, ISBN 0-672-22059-8.
Ask for No. 22059 . . . . **$79.95**

IBM® PC Version, ISBN 0-672-22060-1.
Ask for No. 22060 . . . . **$89.95**

TRS-80© Model II Version, ISBN 0-672-22062-8.
Ask for No. 22062 . . . . **$69.95**

FINANCIAL PLANNING WITH SUPERCALC©

IBM® PC Version, ISBN 0-672-22061-X.
Ask for No. 22061 . . . . **$89.95**

You can usually find these Sams products at better computer stores, bookstores, and electronic distributors nationwide.

If you can't find what you need, call Sams at 800-428-3696 toll-free or 317-298-5566, and charge it to your Master-Card or Visa account. Prices subject to change without notice. In Canada, contact Lenbrook Industries Ltd., Scarborough, Ontario.

For a free catalog of all Sams Books and Software available, write P.O. Box 7092, Indianapolis, IN 46206.

TO THE READER

Sams Computer books cover Fundamentals — Programming — Interfacing — Technology written to meet the needs of computer engineers, professionals, scientists, technicians, students, educators, business owners, personal computerists and home hobbyists.

Our Tradition is to meet your needs
and in so doing we invite you to tell us what
your needs and interests are by completing
the following:

1. I need books on the following topics:

_____

_____

_____

_____

_____

_____

2. I have the following Sams titles:

_____

_____

_____

_____

_____

_____

3. My occupation is:

_____ Scientist, Engineer   _____ D P Professional

_____ Personal computerist   _____ Business owner

_____ Technician, Serviceman   _____ Computer store owner

_____ Educator   _____ Home hobbyist

_____ Student   Other _____

_____

Name (print) _____

Address _____

City _____ State _____ Zip _____

Mail to: **Howard W. Sams & Co., Inc.**
Marketing Dept. #CBS1/80
4300 W. 62nd St., P.O. Box 7092
Indianapolis, Indiana 46206

22024